Translating Desire

in Medieval and
Early Modern Literature

Medieval and Renaissance Texts and Studies

Volume 294

Translating Desire

in Medieval and Early Modern Literature

Edited by

Craig A. Berry and Heather Richardson Hayton

Arizona Center for Medieval and Renaissance Studies
Tempe, Arizona
2005

© Copyright 2005
Arizona Board of Regents for Arizona State University

Library of Congress Cataloging-in-Publication Data

Translating desire in medieval and early modern literature / edited by Craig Berry and Heather Hayton.

    p. cm. — (Medieval and renaissance texts and studies ; v. 294)
Includes bibliographical references and index.
ISBN-13: 978-0-86698-338-9 (alk. paper)
    1. Literature, Medieval — History and criticism — Congresses. 2. Desire in literature — Congresses. I. Berry, Craig, 1961– II. Hayton, Heather, 1969– III. Series: Medieval & Renaissance Texts & Studies (Series) ; v.294.

PN663.T73 2005
809'.93353—dc22   2005020603

Cover image reprinted with permission of the J. Paul Getty Museum, Los Angeles. Attributed to Hans Holbein the Younger (German, 1497–1543), *An Allegory of Passion*, 1520s, 45.4 x 45.4 cm (17 ⅞ x 17 ⅞ in.).

∞
This book is made to last.
It is set in Adobe Brioso Pro,
smyth-sewn and printed on acid-free paper
to library specifications.
Printed in the United States of America

Table of Contents

Acknowledgements   *vi*

Translating Desire: An Introduction   *vii*

Translating Bodies: Materiality, Suffering, Concealment

Resisting the Father in *Pearl*
    Daniel T. Kline   1

Victim of Love: The Poetics and Politics of Violence in 'Le Printemps' of Theodore Agrippa D'Aubigné
    Kathleen Long   31

Body Politics in Ariosto's *Orlando furioso*
    Albert Russell Ascoli   49

Translating Form: Gender, Genre, Identity

Desire in Language and Form: Heloise's Challenge to Abelard
    Suzanne Wayne   89

Translating Petrarchan Desire in Vittoria Colonna and Gaspara Stampa
    V. Stanley Benfell   109

"Odious Ballads": Fallen Women's Laments and *All's Well That Ends Well*
    Mary Trull   133

Translating Power: City, Lineage, Ideology

Teaching How to Translate: Love and Citizenship in Brunetto Latini's *Tesoretto*
    Heather Richardson Hayton   157

What Silence Desires: Female Inheritance and the Romance of Property in the *Roman de Silence*
    Craig A. Berry   191

Resisting Translation: Britomart in Book 3 of Spenser's *Faerie Queene*
    Harry Berger Jr.   207

Index   251

ACKNOWLEDGEMENTS

Translating the scholarly fruits of a seminar on desire in the Middle Ages at the American Comparative Literature Association's annual conference into this book has been a labor of love, and the genesis of this collection resulted directly from the many wonderful conversations conceived and nurtured during that seminar. Further conversations of all sorts were essential to the growth of the project, and we are grateful for the many scholarly exchanges, formal and informal, that have helped us grow along with it. Of the many people who helped move the project along, we are especially grateful to Erin Maguire — Heather's research assistant extraordinaire, who cheerfully attended to some of the most onerous details. Michael Hunter also provided research assistance at a crucial time in the process. California State University San Marcos's Office of Research and Sponsored Projects, and Associate Vice President Pat Worden, were generous in providing Heather a professional development grant to keep the project going despite tightened funding and meager state budgets.

At ACMRS we are pleased to single out for thanks Director Robert Bjork and the Press's anonymous readers for their votes of confidence and useful suggestions, Managing Editor Roy Rukkila for gently shepherding us through the entire editorial and production process, and Leslie MacCoull for her thorough copy editing.

We owe a great debt to our authors, not only for their skill as soloists, but also for their patience and good nature through the many taxing labors of singing in chorus. Finally, it gives us particular pleasure to thank our students, whose insightful questions and close readings continued to shape and refine this collection throughout its development.

We dedicate this book to our families, who teach us how to translate desire each day.

CAB
HRH
September 2004

Translating Desire:
An Introduction

The noun *translatio* is — among other things — simply the Latin form of the word "metaphor," and thus an age-old figure for using one thing to talk about something else. The twelfth-century poetic theorist Geoffrey of Vinsauf tells the aspiring writer that the figure of *translatio* "serves you as a mirror, for you see yourself in it and recognize your own sheep in another's field."[1] Mirroring the self and recognizing the familiar in the foreign are also common ways of talking about desire. The essays in this volume take these two kindred principles of translation and desire and map out what happens when desire itself is translated from one realm of discourse to another. Our contributors address the translation of desire across the borders of nation, language, genre, and gender. They explore how medieval and early modern authors convert discourses of desire the conventions of which are primarily male, literary, and erotic into terms that serve the mixed social, religious, political, *and* literary aspirations of both male and female voices.

For writers in premodern Europe, using one form of desire to talk about another was a way to engage, comment upon, and cope with the particular risks and challenges of their cultural environments. The political changes, intellectual and religious crises, and social upheavals of the time often gave rise to multiple, competing allegiances, and the most obvious form of translated desire was a rhetorical method that accommodated conflict. Whether they were poets, clerics, or philosophers, the writers discussed here were all political subjects for whom the articulation of desire was a way to stake out the boundaries of the individual self in relation to the communal subject. In this context it is worth remembering that Aristotle's *Nicomachean Ethics* enjoyed a wide influence throughout the period. In Book 8 of the *Ethics*, Aristotle establishes analogies between individual governance of desire and

---

[1] *Poetria Nova of Geoffrey of Vinsauf*, trans. Margaret F. Nims (Toronto: Pontifical Institute of Mediæval Studies, 1967), 798–99.

political governance of a *polis*, and (like Freud) reminds us that since we are social creatures, it is our desire that leads to the creation of community (*koinonia*). But desire and its transformations also move inward from society to the individual and laterally across social and institutional boundaries, and the translation of desire, even (or perhaps especially) when it is not part of a conscious rhetorical strategy, provides a lens that brings into focus a wide range of human activity. Desire, like most phenomena, is easiest to observe and analyze when it is in flux. If the Freudian paradigm of uncovering sublimated desire occupies a deservedly important place in the way moderns and postmoderns analytically probe the articulation of the self, then for the premodern world — a world that characterized its own dislocations and transformations of empire and learning as translations — *translatio amoris*, or the translation of and through desire, offers an efficient yet flexible paradigm for examining the construction of the desiring subject and of the cultural authority invested in that subject.

In addition to pointing out its ancient association with metaphor and its resonances with the traditions of *translatio studii* and *translatio imperii*, we would also like to revive an older meaning of the English word *translation*. In the period under study, it sometimes preserves a stronger sense of simultaneous movement across social, psychological, and discursive space than it does in modern usage.[2] In Chaucer's *Clerk's Tale*, for example, when the peasant girl Griselda gets a new set of clothing in the process of her elevation to being the wife of the Marquis Walter, the change is described as a translation that makes her barely recognizable: "Unnethe the peple hire knewe for hire fairnesse / Whan she translated was in swich richesse" (384–85).[3] She has traversed an almost unthinkable social distance in an instant, and Chaucer chooses to call this radical alteration of identity a translation.[4] An equally unthinkable (but tonally quite different) identity transformation happens

---

[2] Judith Anderson helpfully surveys the many types of transformation and movement suggested by the word "translation" in premodern English, concluding, "in the early modern period *translation* is an implicitly metaphorical, multivocal pun just waiting to happen": "Translating Vestments: The Metaphoricity of Language, *2 Henry IV*, and *Hamlet*," *Texas Studies in Literature and Language* 40 (1998): 231–67, here 231–33.

[3] *The Riverside Chaucer*, ed. Larry D. Benson et al. (Boston: Houghton Mif-flin, 1987).

[4] David Wallace's perceptive comments on this passage emphasize the despotic power of Walter as translator: *Chaucerian Polity: Absolutist Lineages and Associational Forms in England and Italy* (Stanford: Stanford University Press, 1997), 284–86. For our purposes, the degree of change is most significant, regardless of its agency or ultimate direction.

Introduction

to Bottom the weaver in Shakespeare's *A Midsummer Night's Dream*. When it comes to being made an ass on stage, many are called but few are chosen in quite the literal, Ovidian sense that Bottom is. Bottom's associate Peter Quince, when he sees the ass's ears on his friend's head, cries out, "Bless thee, Bottom, bless thee! Thou art translated" (3.1.118–19).[5] In the examples of Griselda and Bottom, describing change as translation seems to imply that the transported person travels a great distance, a distance that must then be negotiated by the onlookers who struggle to recognize an individual who simultaneously remains the same and yet transformed. The principle of translation as we conceive it is therefore one that applies considerable torque to the engine of identity, both the identity of the affected individual and the identity of the community to which the individual belongs. If this is true of literary creations, it is also true of literary creators; translation as identity formation is something a writer does to the culture, but also something that the culture does to the writer. As Rita Copeland reminds us, the practice of translation "carries the ideological import of [cultural] systems, and it transfers their ideological tensions to another plane."[6] The cultural confrontation and adaptation inherent in the premodern practice of translation replicates or stands in for the very same processes that take place between the desiring subject and his or her social world.

If our use of translation as a defining paradigm has caused us to engage in a bit of etymological revivification, then presenting a book with "desire" in the title requires us to elbow our way into a rich and varied company. Our contributors take no unified stance on the proper role of psychoanalytic theory in the analysis of premodern literary texts, but collectively they do offer an antidote to a frequently mentioned problem with applying Freud and his successors to the documents of a pre-Freudian culture. Stephen Jaeger describes the problem succinctly when he notes, "The libido becomes the place of final appeal for arguments admitting of no contradiction, a Supreme Court of the psyche. Signs and signals on the surface of a text or of human actions that point to a hidden sexual motive answer all questions and place the inference

---

[5] *The Riverside Shakespeare*, ed. G. Blakemore Evans (Boston: Houghton Mifflin, 1974). On the literary and cultural significance of Bottom's trans-formation, see the section entitled "Ovid 'Translated'" in Leonard Barkan, *The Gods Made Flesh: Metamorphosis and the Pursuit of Paganism* (New Haven: Yale University Press, 1986), 251–70.

[6] Rita Copeland, *Rhetoric, Hermeneutics, and Translation in the Middle Ages: Academic Traditions and Vernacular Texts* (Cambridge: Cambridge University Press, 1991), 223.

of a libidinous source beyond refutation."[7] The essays here are not shy about addressing hidden sexual motives when they find them, but as a whole the collection kicks the libido out of the Supreme Court and onto the street, as it were, where it is jostled by and must interact with a range of other motivations. Indeed, many of the discourses of desire analyzed here inherit from their classical predecessors a tropological movement that is precisely the opposite of the Freudian one. As Duncan Kennedy reminds us with regard to Roman love elegy, "the conventional con-ceptual division between 'sexuality' and 'politics' has been challenged ... the tenor of signification is *from* sex *to* politics, reversing that familiar from Freud."[8] But we have no intention of replacing a psychoanalytic interpretive strategy with an equally totalizing historicist one; to do so would be to neglect the power of erotic attachment and the imaginative force of literary eroticism. It is our hope, rather, that the paradigm of translation provides a framework for explaining desire without explaining it away. Whatever its direction, our authors capture the movement of desire in premodern literature by tracing it through the historical, philosophical, political, linguistic, *and* erotic paths of their texts. Each of these essays, even when examining a form of desire the terms of which are primarily erotic and literary, also shows how desire gets mapped outward into social space and helps to construct social identity.

For the medieval as well as the postmodern, then, translating desire allows the writer to address and theorize social order, but this collection also seeks to expose the most basic relationship between readers and texts as an act of cultural translation. By paying attention to the way medieval and early modern authors read and translated poetic predecessors, and the expectations authors had for their own audiences, we can further speculate how social difference was articulated and subjectivity understood. The relationship

---

[7] C. Stephen Jaeger, *Ennobling Love: In Search of a Lost Sensibility* (Philadelphia: University of Pennsylvania Press, 1999), 16. For a strongly argued and copiously documented polemic against the misapplication of psychoanalysis to medieval literature, see Lee Patterson, "Chaucer's Pardoner on the Couch: Psyche and Clio in Medieval Literary Studies," *Speculum* 76 (2001): 638–80. L. O. Aranye Fradenberg's recent attempt to merge psychoanalytic methods and historicism in her reading of Chaucer's texts is a compromise that yields some fruitful results, especially regarding the cultural use and individual enjoyment of sacrifice: *Sacrifice Your Love: Psychoanalysis, Historicism, Chaucer* (Minneapolis: University of Minnesota Press, 2002).

[8] *The Arts of Love: Five Studies in the Discourse of Roman Love Elegy*, Roman Literature and Its Contexts Series (Cambridge: Cambridge University Press, 1993), 43 (emphasis in original).

between readers and texts in this period is neither uniform nor canonical, as many of the essays in this collection attest. Yet despite the seemingly individual act of interpreting or creating a text, the "reciprocal relationship between text and reader translates into a tangled correlation between reading material and the way the self and its relationship to the world is conceptualized."[9] Thus the diversity of this collection of essays exposes the always-in-flux, disparate attempts of premodern texts to contain gendered, social, and political — in addtion to poetic — anxieties particular to their own cultural moments. These attempts also reveal a tangible need by premodern authors to transform their social and temporal worlds while memorializing the past.

All of these essays trace the crossing of such boundaries as those between text and reader, past and present, imaginary desire and social engagement. Although the method, direction, and result of each boundary crossing is different, viewing it as a translation of desire helps to measure the distance traveled. The collection is organized into three categories that gauge the translation of desire on an expanding scale from private to public. The point of departure gradually shifts outward from such matters as the body and the lyric to such larger categories as, for example, citizenship and royal power, but the journey always includes an explication of desire as a means of negotiating the relations between individual and corporate subjects.

Whether or not selling one's body is the oldest profession, making figurative use of the body is surely the oldest metaphor. In the anguish of the courtly or Petrarchan lover, the significance of the eucharist, or the political persona of a monarch — to cite only three of the more famous premodern examples — bodily translation provides materiality and authenticity to otherwise intangible phenomena. The essays in our first section, "Translating Bodies: Materiality, Suffering, Concealment," explore literary situations where idealized discourses of corporality are translated back into the experiences of real bodies: the material existence of a child, the tortured lyrics of a poet threatened by the real tortures of religious repression, and the ambiguous status of a male poet using bodily metaphors to advocate a feminine poetics.

Daniel Kline's essay on the *Pearl* takes a fresh look at this Middle English dream-narrative by unearthing the text from a hundred years of allegorical readings. Maintaining that the child is neither courtly paramour nor theological abstraction, Kline argues that the poem translates the symbolic into

---

[9] Laurel Amtower, *Engaging Words: The Culture of Reading in the Later Middle Ages* (New York: Palgrave, 2001), 2–3.

the real, the fetishized female body into a material "faunt" (infant), and renders abstract loss into a present reality. By focusing on the marginalization of young female children in the period, Kline illustrates how *Pearl* translates biblical parables into subversive social discourses — and, in the process, how the poem covertly criticizes its own culture.

Charting French poet Theodore Agrippa d'Aubigné's often gruesome use of violence and sadomasochism in his Petrarchan and Catullan-inspired love lyrics, Kathleen Long's essay shows how d'Aubigné translates Petrarchan desire into a useful tool to comment on Catholic repression and religious violence in the period. Long argues that metaphors of love *as* death and suffering "function literally as well as figuratively" in d'Aubigné's sonnets, and shows how the "consistent pattern in d'Aubigné's work is the rendering of personal desire and personal relations on a larger political scale" even as it resists the diminishing role of love lyric in sixteenth-century French culture.

Albert Ascoli examines the construction of the female poetic voice during the Italian Renaissance in a meditation on the body and its secrets in Canto 37 of Ariosto's *Orlando furioso*. At this unusually digressive moment in the poem, the poet-narrator exhorts women to become poets and celebrate their own deeds, since male poets, riddled by envy, inevitably suppress the accomplishments of women. Female aspirations and actions should not be subjected to a denigrating translation into masculine discourse, this male narrator appears to say. Or does he? As Ascoli shows, the elaborately gendered discourse of the canto as a whole leaves open the question of whether Ariosto is perpetrating just the sort of translation he denounces, and the poem's internal debate is cast in terms of the disclosure of bodily secrets. In the end we are left to wonder whether the canto means to effect the same invidious subordination of female to male that it overtly condemns, or whether it means to expose, subversively, the discursive mechanisms by which such subordination repeatedly takes place.

If the body provides a relatively stable (if sometimes elusive) form upon which the changes of metaphor can be played, genre offers a framework for exploring more malleable aspects of human identity. In the essays belonging to our second category, "Translating Form: Gender, Genre, Identity," literary mode is the playground where delineations between form and function, style and content merge and combine. The negotiation of expectations that comprises a text's engagement with its genre works alongside the contest of expectations involved in the translation of identity. These essays consider how writers respond to and reshape generic expectations as a means of establishing new forms for their literary creations and for themselves.

For example, Suzanne Wayne's essay on the famous correspondence of Heloise and Abelard focuses on the way the epistle genre constrains and arranges desire — and how that form can be subverted linguistically. Wayne argues that Heloise "refuses to forget" her past with Abelard by overtly "fusing her previous role as wife and lover with her present role as abbess" throughout the epistles. Translating desire into epistolary struggle, Heloise attempts to continue an erotic exchange by destabilizing literary decorum and linguistic expectations. Wayne shows how Heloise uses language as a surrogate for the unreciprocated desire she seeks from Abelard — demanding he continue their relationship by disciplining her unruly *linguistic* body.

V. Stanley Benfell's essay considers the question of how authors translate themselves into poetic and lyric subjectivity by beginning with the premise that "the language of desire in lyric poetry must not be misunderstood as a simple translation of erotic longing into poetic form," but how it instead becomes a means of self-determination. Focusing on how two female poets in the Italian Renaissance translate Petrarch through a Catullan or Augustinian lens in their own sonnet sequences, Benfell argues that desire, and the act of desiring, remains a constant source of self-definition even when the object of desire is lost. This is especially true for how Gaspara Stampa constructs herself as a Petrarchan lover after her husband has passed away. For Vittoria Colonna, constructing herself as a desiring subject also allows her to remain embodied beyond her lover's rejection but, like Petrarch and Catullus, she finds that her identity does not "depend on his relationship to her," only on *her* relationship to love.

Mary Trull also examines how the language of a generic form can exert pressure on female identity. In her analysis of Shakespeare's *All's Well that Ends Well*, Trull shows how Helena, the play's heroine, struggles to free herself from the calumnious assertions of the fallen woman's ballad, a genre other characters in the play employ in their depictions of her. Helena responds to this social deflation by attempting to switch generic affiliations, characterizing herself instead as a female knight modeled on the heroines of romance and thus socially worthy of her beloved Bertram. The translation of desire in Helena's case is thus from desired (though morally suspect) object to desiring, ethically proactive subject. In the world of problem comedy no such translation can be complete or go unquestioned, but the generic movement reveals what is socially and erotically at stake for Helena.

While a social aspect informs nearly all the translations of desire we have described thus far, the essays in our final section, "Translating Power: City, Lineage, Ideology," explicate texts centrally concerned with social and political desire. Bodies, genres, and genders all undergo translation here, but they do so in the context of such macro-concerns as citizenship, feudal politics, and dynastic succession. These transformations may be eagerly sought, fruitlessly resisted, or some combination of both, but they all register the power of corporate forces on individual subjects.

Focusing on a powerless and exiled lover, Heather Richardson Hayton's essay examines poetic translation in the late thirteenth century. The *Tesoretto* transforms the journey of the seeking lover into an educational model for Florentine citizenship, as its exiled author, Brunetto Latini, translates *Aman*'s journey from the *Roman de la Rose* into a homosocial quest for entrance into a community of fellow lovers. The text, which "values desire as a conduit for citizenship rather than as an end in itself," offers a restorative to a city torn apart by the violence of uncorrected male desire. Identifying a process of "navigational reading" in the *Tesoretto,* Hayton shows that common to all "discourses of desire is the need for governance and measure — of the text, lover, citizen, and finally by analogy, of the city."

Craig Berry takes up a text in which the adventures of a feudal heiress record both the evasion and the propagation of royal power. In Heldris of Cornwall's thirteenth-century romance, the *Roman de Silence,* the heroine Silence is raised as a boy so that she can inherit the family estate despite a royal decree outlawing female inheritance. The gender translation on which she embarks gives unusually large scope to the trials and triumphs of a female protagonist, but the goal of preserving the patrimony is never far beneath the surface. Silence's quest addresses the anxieties of a moment when increasing royal control and widely varying female inheritance practices collided head-on, and her success in negotiating this feudal predicament gives voice to an aristocratic fantasy in which upward mobility extends even to the royal monopoly.

Harry Berger considers another cross-dressed knight who operates as both challenge to and conduit of monarchical power. Britomart, the female warrior whose task it is to uphold the virtue of chastity in Book 3 of Edmund Spenser's *Faerie Queene,* finds herself pulled from a protofeminist myth of female autonomy toward a more traditional destiny that makes her the vessel of an epic genealogy, and the narrative that puts her through this process of translation also criticizes itself for doing so. In other words, the narrative blows the whistle on its own ideological policing activity. What emerges is a libidinal economy in which for every translation there is an opposite — though not necessarily equal — counter-translation, and the poem offers many circuitous routes for the expression of desires that must inevitably succumb to the Tudor myth it promotes.

The variety of essays and the range of literary traditions covered in this collection attest to the multiplicity of registers for which desire can be translated: the self, the family, the polis, rhetoric, aesthetics, religion, and politics. Without diminishing or erasing desire, these essays insist upon the power of translation to render the familiar new and the foreign recognizable, and in doing so advance our goal of rendering medieval and early modern literature accessible and exciting, of transforming remote texts into fresh, inviting literary engagements. Each essay presented here affirms that desire's pleasure can be made profitable through the act of translation, and that our efforts to translate the past into something useful and modern have much in common with the narratives our contributors decode. We draw on a final meaning of translation — a practice that revises and supersedes its own model — to express our hope that these essays offer readers the opportunity to revisit their own readings of premodernity.

Craig A. Berry
Heather Richardson Hayton

Translating Bodies
Materiality, Suffering, Concealment

Resisting the Father in *Pearl*

Once fancifully elaborated by biographical critics and then all but eliminated by symbolic readings, the *Pearl*-child merits reexamination in terms of her particular status as a child in her social environment. In this essay I attempt both to resituate the *Pearl*-child squarely in the interpretive center of the poem and to locate the *Pearl*-child in the cultural context of late medieval childhood. While the poem's suggestive details summon a theological understanding of the state of the soul in the afterlife, many of the same particulars are equally grounded in the material culture of pregnancy, childbirth, baptism, and infant death and burial in late medieval England. However, in recent years, *Pearl* scholarship has focused upon the Dreamer, to the neglect of the child's deft and subtle critique of the adult's flawed understanding of the afterlife. My contention is a simple one: the depiction of the "*Pearl*-maiden" is the result of both the Dreamer's desire and his discourse, and in this failed mode of representation he is unable to assuage his grief or progress in understanding until this misrecognition of the child is corrected. In short, the Dreamer must again encounter the *Pearl*-child as the young child "who was nearer to him than aunt or niece" and not as a courtly paramour or theological construct.

By her resistance to the Dreamer's objectifying discourse, the *Pearl*-child's counterdiscourse articulates a "theology of childhood," which recognizes the anxieties of medieval parents over the fragility of their children's lives, mobilizes a series of biblical texts concerning children and their comparative status in the social hierarchy, and incorporates a variety of materials concerning the corporeal reality and lived experience of infants in the late medieval period, ultimately to criticize and eventually to subvert those cultural prejudices. By maintaining her contention that she is actually a child who "Ne neuer nawþer Pater ne Crede"[1]

---

[1] *Pearl*, line 485 in *Poems of the Pearl Manuscript*, ed. Malcolm Andrew and Ronald Waldron, York Medieval Texts, 2nd ser. (Berkeley: University of California Press, 1978). Unless otherwise noted, all subsequent references to *Pearl* will be from this edition and will be indicated parenthetically by line number in the body of the text.

(l. 485) and not a courtly paramour or theological abstraction, she effectively maintains her subjectivity *as a child* within the Dreamer's discourse and "dis-cerns" herself from within it, to use Paul Smith's term, leading the Dreamer into a renewed understanding of their earthly relationship and, as a result, a full awareness of his loss.[2] As opposed to many contemporary readings of *Pearl* that move from relation to symbol, I contend that the genius of the poem is its ability to move the Dreamer (and the reader) from symbol to relation.

Effacing the Child

Interest in the *Pearl*-child as a child has all but disappeared from the critical literature on the poem. This, however, was not always the case. Early criticism of *Pearl* took for granted the elegiac nature of the poem and the material reality of the *Pearl*-child. The poem's first editor, Richard Morris (1864), noted that "the author evidently gives expression to his own sorrow for the loss of his infant child, a girl of two years" and "represents himself as visiting the child's grave (or arbour) . . . and giving way to his grief."[3] This view, which gave rise to a number of wildly speculative elaborations of the *Pearl*-poet's "biography," found its way into the standard literary histories of the time and remained the critical consensus until 1904.[4] At

---

[2] Precisely because the "subject" is not coterminal with the "person," "individual," or "agent," the subject may be "discerned," according to Paul Smith in *Discerning the Subject* ([Minneapolis: University of Minnesota Press, 1990], xxxiii-xxxv). Drawing from two obscure English verbs — "to cern" ("to accept an inheritance or a patrimony") and "to cerne" ("to encircle or enclose") — Smith notes the tendency of academic discourse to circumscribe or "to cern" the subject rigidly by the types of questions it poses. Smith problematizes the tendency of theoretical inquiry to abstract the "subject/individual" from "the real conditions of its existence" and thereby to severely restrict "the definition of the human agent" to that of the "subject" alone (xxx).

[3] Richard Morris, *Early English Alliterative Poems*, EETS o.s. 1 (London: Trübner & Co., 1864), xi.

[4] John Conley reviews a number of these statements from early critics such as Baugh, Coulton, Gollancz, ten Brink, and a number of others in "*Pearl* and a Lost Tradition," *Journal of English and Germanic Philology* 54 (1955): 332–47; repr. in *The Middle English Pearl: Critical Essays*, ed. idem (Notre Dame: University of Notre Dame Press, 1969), 50–61. René Wellek, "*The Pearl*: An Interpretation of the Middle English Poem," in Blanch, *Sir Gawain and Pearl* (Bloomington: Indiana University Press, 1966), 3–36 provides a thorough survey of the critical opinion from the *Pearl*'s first editor (1864) to 1933.

that time William Henry Schofield essentially ended the biographical strain of criticism with his insistence that *Pearl* was an allegory of "pure maidenhood."[5]

Nonetheless, in making the case for a symbolic, and against an elegiac, reading of the poem, Schofield himself also posited a biographical basis to the poem, or at least a definite conception of the character of the *Pearl*-child specifically and of medieval childhood generally. He argued that *Pearl* could not be an elegy and the loss of a child could not motivate the poem because the relationship between the Dreamer and the child lacked, to his mind, the hallmarks of a caring father-daughter relationship. Precisely speaking, the *Pearl*-child's apparent lack of "filial tenderness at any time" precluded an elegiac reading.[6] In denying an experience of loss behind *Pearl*, Schofield still presupposed a thoroughly nostalgic view of the child-parent affinity, for an elegiac reading required, in his view, a sympathetic child figure, deferential and supportive of her elder. This sentimentalized view of childhood allowed Schofield to remove the *Pearl*-child from serious critical consideration and to discount those references in the poem to the materiality of medieval childhood. That the poem addresses virginity only peripherally and in an eschatological context posed no problem for Schofield. Instead, the *Pearl*-child, now representative of pure maidenhood, became a simultaneously gendered but disembodied symbol of conventional feminine ideals.

In addition to this convenient contradiction that allowed him to turn the dead child of *Pearl* into a symbol, what is striking about Schofield's article is how completely his symbolic-allegorical reading established both the method and the content of many subsequent studies. Removing the

---

[5] William Henry Schofield, "The Nature and Fabric of *The Pearl*," *PMLA* 19 (1904): 154–215, here 166.

[6] Schofield, "Nature and Fabric," 159. Schofield notes, in addition, that since it was commonly assumed that the poem was written by an ecclesiastic, *Pearl* could not be an elegy,

> for an English ecclesiastic in the fourteenth century could not possibly have had anything but an illegitimate child; [so] . . . it stands to reason that a priest would not deliberately go out of his way to call people's attention to his child of shame, and then without apology to exalt above all else purity of life. (157)

Schofield was answered in print by G. G. Coulton, whose chivalric advocacy of the autobiographical thesis he challenged: "In Defense of 'Pearl'," *Modern Language Review* 2 (1906): 39–43.

child figure and this child's relationship to the Dreamer from the center of the poem, Schofield substituted a host of literary texts, including suggestive parallels to Dante, Boccaccio, Boethius, and a host of lapidary, biblical, patristic, and courtly sources, that have held the attention of many later critics.[7] Following Schofield, succeeding studies also maintain specific assumptions about the figure of the child in *Pearl*, separating, as it were, the child from the text in order to sustain symbolic readings that further elevate the pearl of the text as a symbol and obfuscate the lost *Pearl*-child.

Charles Moorman's pivotal mid-century article on the Narrator shifted critical attention to the *Pearl*-Dreamer and his encounter with, as she was now called, the "*Pearl* Maiden." According to Moorman, the *Pearl*-Maiden "herself cannot be said to function except peripherally in the narrative movement of the poem."[8] What is important to Moorman and later critics emphasizing the Dreamer's development is not the child, who is now little more than a narrative effect, but the impact of the "Maiden's" instruction on the Narrator's progress toward enlightenment. According to this line of thought, keeping any such specific relationship between Dreamer and Maiden vague and undefined allows the poet to "write a poem not about one particular relationship but about human relationship in general,"[9] for *Pearl* succeeds "largely because it is a first-person narrative about feelings and about the universal theme of coming to terms with mortality."[10] Consequently, the poem argues that the "adult must be spiritually reborn and acquire the innocence and humility of a child if he would be admitted to the Kingdom of Heaven: the mourner's child is thus a 'type' or 'figure' of what he himself must become."[11] Such analyses commonly focus on the Narrator's own coming to terms with his situation, and the heavenly Maiden — no longer a dead child — provides only a provocation for the *Pearl*-Dreamer's development.

---

[7] Laurence Eldredge, "The State of *Pearl* Studies Since 1933," *Viator* 6 (1975): 171–94 surveys *Pearl* scholarship during the middle part of the last century, much of which often consists of elaborations of suggestions first raised by Schofield.

[8] Charles Moorman, "The Role of the Narrator in *Pearl*," *Modern Philology* 53 (1955): 73–81, here 74.

[9] A. C. Spearing, *The Gawain-Poet: A Critical Study* (Cambridge: Cambridge University Press, 1970), 147.

[10] W. A. Davenport, *The Art of the Gawain-Poet* (London: Athlone Press, 1970), 7.

[11] Ian Bishop, Pearl *in its Setting: A Critical Study of the Structure and Meaning of the Middle English Poem* (Oxford: Basil Blackwell, 1968), 61.

We might therefore chart the development of *Pearl* criticism in the twentieth century through the shift in critical attention from the *Pearl*-child, an historically particularized and culturally contextualized member of a medieval family with specific kinship to the Dreamer, to the *Pearl*-maiden, the symbolic construction of literary criticism and arbiter of timeless human and theological truths. Thus the cumulative effect of many studies since mid-century is to minimize the figure of the child by negating the *Pearl*-child's agency, diminishing her subjectivity, and making her a theological mouthpiece, all for the benefit of development of another, the adult narrator, whose relationship to the child is little more than incidental to illustrating a "universal" concept: the adult's growth toward enlightenment and salvation. In most current criticism, the *Pearl*-child is little more than a trace, empty except for what she signifies to the adult. Her worth is found more in what she represents as an idealized figure than in her particular relation to the Dreamer or her representative status as a child in late medieval culture. In these readings, the *Pearl*-child generally is reconfigured to serve the needs of the adult, whether critic or Dreamer. Hence conventional figurative and typological readings of the poem succeed in a triple effacement of the *Pearl*-child's subjectivity: her subject position is colonized by the Dreamer, who is figured as an adult, as a male, and as a representative of the universal human.

Although symbolic readings have subsumed the *Pearl*-child or marginalized her as a plot device, a persistent counter-criticism in *Pearl* studies has never completely disappeared. Against the prevailing critical opinion, René Wellek wrote in 1933 that "All purely allegorical interpretations break down completely" when the poem refers to the *Pearl*-child's existence,[12] for the materiality of the *Pearl*-child challenges any attempt to reify or to erase the figure of the child from the poem. A generation later Stanton Hoffman argued against the predominant view, saying, "I believe this is a poem about death, about the death of an infant child.... The poem is basically an elegy; its concern is actual death, its meaning, and its resolution."[13] Recently, Sarah Stanbury has noted that "One of the most remarkable features of this fourteenth-century text, in fact, and a feature that has not been sufficiently recognized, is its focus on the loss of a two-

---

[12] Wellek, "The *Pearl*: An Interpretation," 22.
[13] Stanton Hoffman "The *Pearl*: Notes for an Interpretation," *Modern Philology* 58 (1960): 73–80; repr. in *The Middle English Pearl*, ed. Conley, 82–102, here 101.

year-old girl."[14] Although scholars have attended to the gender dynamics of the poem, none has yet argued, as I will, that age is as important a variable as gender for understanding the complex interaction between Dreamer and *Pearl*-child. Taking seriously the *Pearl*-child's stage in life is essential to redefining her subjectivity in the historical and material context of the late medieval family.

Discourse and Desire

From its opening stanza, *Pearl* clearly is a poem concerning the experience of loss, a loss inextricably bound with desire. The narrator bemoans the lovely pearl he "leste ... in on erbere" (l. 9), a "pearl" which we later find to have been a young child. We may take as a starting point the Dreamer's highly overwrought expressions of grief, a profound anguish beyond the bounds of consolation:

> Syþen in þat spote hit fro me sprange,
> Ofte haf I wayted, wyschande þat wele
> þat wont watz whyle deuoyde my wrange
> And heuen my happe and al my hele —
> þat dotz bot þrych my hert þrange,
> My breste in bale bot bolne and bele. (ll. 13–18)

In his extravagant sorrow, the Dreamer languishes, "fordolked of luf-daungere," grievously wounded by the quality of distance ("daungere") separating him from his beloved (l. 11). His heart is "denned" by "deuely dele" (l. 51); he "playned" for his pearl that "watz penned" (l. 53); his "wreched wylle in wo ay wraȝte" (l. 56), until finally the Dreamer "slode vpon a slepyng-slaȝte" (l. 59) ("sleeping slaughter" or "sleep of death") that begins his dream-vision.

---

[14] Sarah Stanbury, "Feminist Masterplots: The Gaze on the Body of *Pearl*'s Dead Girl," in *Feminist Approaches to the Body in Medieval Literature*, ed. Linda Lomperis and eadem (Philadelphia: University of Pennsylvania Press, 1993), 96–115, here 108. Yet in her analysis, Stanbury vacillates in her identification of the *Pearl*-child's age and ultimately identifies her as a woman. Stanbury calls her "a girl" (99), "infant" (101), "maiden" (102), and provocatively "a starlet" (100–1). Interestingly, in defining the *Pearl*-child as "a graphically embodied woman, powerful, articulate, infinitely desirable, who dares to stare back" (111), she does question forcefully the problem that this vision is a product of the phallogocentric gaze of the Dreamer.

The Dreamer dances on the edge of melancholia, for his experience of grief threatens to turn inward toward silence and self-mortification.

Upon awakening to his dream-vision, the Dreamer becomes aware that he has set upon an "aventure" (l. 64), a term often associated with a romance quest, through a marvelous crystalline landscape, and as the poem moves through the second and into the third section, Section II's link word "adubbement," indicating the excessively jeweled geography of his vision, gives way to Section III's link term, "more and more," leading him directly to the focal point of the heavenly panorama, the *Pearl*-child. The immoderate language of grief leads to his description of "more and more" (cf. ll. 121–80), the depth of his mourning matched by his excessive description. He overlays the child wholly and completely in pearl: she "Rysez vp in hir araye ryalle, / A precios pyece in perlez pyȝt" (ll. 191–92); she is "Dubbed with double perle" (l. 202), adorned "Of marjorys and non oþer ston" (l. 206), and covered "Wyth whyte perle and non oþer gemme" (l. 219). The description is capped by a crown of pearl and the "wonder perle withouten wemme / Inmyddez hyr breste watz sette so sure" (ll. 221–22). The detailed description of the child's dress is at every turn bounded and laced "Wyth þe myryeste margarys, at my deuyse" (l. 199). The Dreamer's comment, "at my deuyse" (l. 199), is crucial, for through his description the *Pearl*-child is a product of his melancholic imagining; she is transformed into an object of his devising and of his discourse.

The link words of Section II ("adubbement") and III ("more and more") come into sharper focus in the term "pyȝte," the link word for Section IV, for in this section the language of embellishment overlaps into a discourse of subjectivity. "Pyȝte" appropriately denotes the literal "attaching" of the pearls to the fabric of the child's dress; it can likewise more generally mean to "fasten" or to "fix" in place. The Dreamer's description does both: it articulates the materiality of the *Pearl*-child's dress in its physical characteristics, but it also fixes her as an erotic object devoid of subjective standing. Pearls are "affixed" to her at the same time she is "fixed" as a pearl, reducing any sense of her status apart from his desire. It might be noted briefly that Freud's characterization of melancholy is an extension of his remarks on narcissism, and this observation is appropriate to the *Pearl*-Dreamer, particularly both his initial inability to see beyond himself and his situation and his need to fix the *Pearl*-child discursively in terms that satisfy his own erotic needs.[15]

---

[15] Cf. S. Freud, "Mourning and Melancholia," in *The Standard Edition of the Complete Psychological Works of Sigmund Freud*, gen. ed. and trans. James Strachey, 24 vols. (London: Hogarth and the Institute of Psycho-Analysis, 1953–1974), 14: 240.

As the Dreamer's language constructs the *Pearl*-child as a static commodity of desire, the "pyȝte" pearl, he also begins to transform the *Pearl*-child into the "*Pearl*-maiden" through highly erotically-charged language, a discourse which borders on the unsavory in its excessive desire for a young child. For the most part, the Dreamer's description of the *Pearl*-child echoes the erotic object of secular love lyrics and conventional romance. For example, the tactility of the *Pearl*'s opening description, "So rounde, so reken in vche araye, / So smal, so smoþe her sydez were" (ll. 4–5) blossoms into the conventional portrayal of the romance heroine, "þat gracios gay withouten galle / So smoþe, so smal, so seme slyȝt" (ll. 189–90), whose complexion is like a "flor-de-lys" (l. 195). In concert with his romantically tinged description, the Dreamer fashions himself a courtly figure pursuing an "aventure" in which he raises his complaint to the gray-eyed, ivory-skinned beauty through the language of courtly love.[16] This ritualized language of romance marks a compensatory move from the real subject of his loss (the child) to a figuration of that loss in the eroticized *Pearl*-maiden.

Despite the Dreamer's attempt to turn the *Pearl*-child into an eroticized love object, his fantasy betrays the very loss he attempts to deny and admits his true relationship to the *Pearl*-child. On the one hand, as Gordon details, the *Pearl*-child's pearl-encrusted dress is simply "a simple form of the aristocratic dress of the second half of the fourteenth century";[17] its adornment denotes the wearer's status and wealth. On the other

---

[16] This vein of criticism has produced a number of important and suggestive studies, including but not limited to C. A. Luttrell, "*Pearl*: Symbolism in a Garden Setting," *Neophilologus* 49 (1965): 160–76; Pamela Kean, *The Pearl: An Interpretation* (New York: Barnes and Noble, 1967), 38–45; Theodore Bogdanos, *Pearl: Image of the Ineffable* (University Park: Penn State University Press, 1983), 38–45; Anne Howland Schotter, "Vernacular Style and the Word of God: The Incarnational Art of *Pearl*," in *Ineffability*, ed. Peter S. Hawkins and eadem (New York: AMS Press, 1984), 23–34. For more recent examinations of the courtly dimension of *Pearl*, see John M. Bowers, *The Politics of Pearl: Court Poetry in the Age of Richard II* (Woodbridge: D. S. Brewer, 2001), 151–86; María Bullón-Fernández, "'Byȝonde þe water': Courtly and Religious Desire in *Pearl*," *Studies in Philology* 91 (1994): 35–49; Jane Gilbert, "Gender and Sexual Transgression," in *A Companion to the Gawain-Poet*, ed. Derek Brewer and Jonathon Gibson (Rochester, NY: D. S. Brewer, 1997), 53–69; and Jane Beal, "The *Pearl*-Maiden's Two Lovers," *Studies in Philology* 100 (2003): 1–21.

[17] E. V. Gordon, ed., *Pearl* (Oxford: Clarendon Press, 1953), 56, note to line 228.

hand, however, the pearl-bedecked attire appears equally to be the refraction of a child's christening garments, in which "the white vestments of the newly baptized signify the innocence which was lost through Adam and restored through the sacrament of baptism."[18] Pearls often figured in the baptismal ritual, particularly among the merchant and upper classes in England. As Barbara Hanawalt describes this important rite in late medieval London, the child, having been brought to the church, was anointed with oil or salt, immersed in the baptismal font, and given her Christian names. Then the "godparents raised the newly named Christian from the font and wrapped it in a christening robe. This gown or crysom was white and could be made elaborate with embroidery of pearls."[19] The Dreamer's description of the heavenly figure retains a trace of the child's naming as an individual and her entry into the Christian community at the same time it transforms the *Pearl*-infant's crysom into the dress of an aristocratic paramour.

Through his discourse, the child is thus constructed as the courtly "*Pearl*-maiden." Immediately upon "py3ting" the child in her place and in her garments, the Dreamer then abandons his grief-laden position as relative to the dead child and assumes the conventional, gender-determined position of courtly lover — a joyless, gentle, or "kynde jueler" (the link-word of Section V, l. 276) — and through his discursive construction of her, he inappropriately places her in the subject-position of the gray-eyed romance heroine (l. 254). In a very different reading of the poem, David Aers eloquently articulates the consequence of the Dreamer's language for his self-identity and for his relationship to the "*Pearl*-maiden." The Dreamer's turn to courtly discourse stabilizes his social and gender identity as an upper-class male, for "by invoking the received structure of gender relations [he seeks] to subvert her apparent superiority to him."[20] By adopting courtly, aristocratic discourse in his interaction with the *Pearl*-child, the Dreamer attempts to secure both his subjectivity and the child's and their relationship in readily recognizable and gender-specific patterns, thus militating against the interpersonal disorientation brought about by his grief.

---

[18] Bishop, Pearl *in its Setting*, 118.
[19] Barbara Hanawalt, *Growing Up in Medieval London: The Experience of Childhood in History* (London: Oxford University Press, 1993), 45.
[20] D. Aers, "The Self Mourning: Reflections on *Pearl*," *Speculum* 68 (1993): 61.

A Troubled Jeweler, an Active Pearl, a Dying Rose

A jeweler places a gem in its setting; he manipulates the stone and frames its beauty. In the argument I have been making, the *Pearl*-child as subject has become objectified in the *Pearl*-object through the obsessive nature of the Dreamer's desire and the eroticized character of his discourse. So, in contrast to the Dreamer's passive, fixated (and fixating) gaze, the *Pearl*-object's surprising agency in the opening stanza (ll. 9–10) begins to suggest the *Pearl*-child's subjective existence (her origin) and her relationship to the Dreamer (her history). This resistant discourse establishes the foundation from which the *Pearl*-child marshals her critique of the Dreamer's inappropriate language — but she must begin slowly, simply. In the proem, the pearl, when known only as a jewel, manifests surprising agency of its own apart from the Dreamer. In fact, the pearl operates with a willfulness the Dreamer in his grief lacks. He cries: "Allas! I leste hyr in on erbere; / þur3 gresse to grounde hit fro me yot" (ll. 9–10) and "Syþen in þat spote hit fro me sprange, / Ofte haf I wayted" (ll. 13–14). In these two key articulations of his loss, the Dreamer passively observes the pearl's purposeful activity: he does not simply lose the pearl; it moves away from him, and as he waits in his grief, it springs from his grasp.

Nonetheless, the Dreamer himself is continuously drawn to remember and to recognize, for he makes two early, provocative comments that he recognizes the child from some other context. Upon first seeing her, he remarks:

> At þe fote þerof þer sete a faunt,
> A mayden of menske, ful debonere;
> Blysnande whyt watz hyr bleaunt;
> I knew hyr well, I had sen hyr ere. (ll. 161–64)

His momentary glimpse of the "faunt," a term denoting a young child or infant prior to the acquisition of speech, recalls again the scene of baptism. The Dreamer instantly recognizes her as an infant he knows well and has seen before in gleaming white, though the connection is not immediately clear to him, and the longer he looks at her he knows her "more and more" (l. 168). His recognition grows during this encounter and is interrupted, but after fixing the *Pearl*-child as a pearl and turning her, in effect, into the pearl object, the Dreamer realizes "Ho watz me nerre þen aunte or nece" (l. 233). Framing his super-luminous description of the *Pearl*-child's baptismal garb, these two comments have together been taken as evidence that the *Pearl*-child, an infant nearer in relation to him than aunt or niece, is indeed a child of the Dreamer's close relation.

Moreover, in these cases of near-remembrance, the threat of awareness catapults the Dreamer into a panicked, hyper-illustration of the *Pearl*-child's physical features, and his continued description serves both to forestall his awareness and to stabilize the discursively mobile *Pearl*-symbol. The Dreamer's troubled, vague remembrances of the child and his stunned reaction to her appearance come to him as an experience of the uncanny (ll. 181–83), of the repressed returning to trouble his recollection. Speechless, he stands before her abjectly, wide-eyed and fearing "gostly watz þat porpose" (l. 185). In effect, each time the Dreamer approaches the full apperception of his loss and an awareness of the child's true identity, the mechanism of mourning distances him from that loss and displaces its effects onto a substitute — the descriptive symbolization of the fetishized *Pearl*-maiden — while he himself is dumbstruck and motionless.

If my argument is correct that through his discourse the Dreamer constructs the *Pearl*-child as an object and as a compensatory fetish for his grief, it is also true that the poem presents a subtle counter-movement against the Dreamer's mode of representation. The *Pearl*-child begins to educate the Dreamer in the following stanza:

> 'Bot, jueler gente, if þou shal lose
> þy joy for a gemme þat þe watz lef,
> Me þynk þe put in a mad porpose,
> And busyez þe about a raysoun bref;
> For that thou lestez watz bot a rose
> þat flowred and fayled as kynde hyt gef;
> Now þurȝ kynde of þe kyste þat hyt con close
> To a perle of prys hit is put in pref.' (ll. 265–72)

Traditional readings of this stanza find, in Gordon's words, "that the narrator's loss, like a rose, 'bloomed and faded as roses do, but through the nature of the casket which encloses it, has become a pearl of price.'"[21] Thus, through the process of death and burial, the mutable rose becomes

---

[21] E. V. Gordon, cited in *The Works of the Gawain-Poet*, ed. Charles Moorman (Jackson: University Press of Mississippi, 1977), 221.

the priceless, eternal Pearl. The crux of this stanza is "pref," which has been taken to mean "test of experience"[22] or "has proven in fact to be."[23] However, "put in pref" has also been interpreted by Marie Hamilton to mean "to put to the test" in a juridical, argumentative sense.[24] This interpretation is supported by the quasi-legal, debate-like stanzas that follow. Therefore, I would then render the *Pearl*-child's statement to the Dreamer as a proposition, a "raysoun bref" to be formally examined, rather than a foregone conclusion: "That your rose is now transformed into a pearl of price through the nature of the casket enclosing it must be put to the test of argument," one which God in "skyl may dem" (l. 312). Quite directly, she calls him "mad" to have forfeited his joy for a lost gem, a material object (ll. 265–67), when what he actually "lost was but a rose."

The Pearl-child's own formulation of her "symbolic" nature lays out in the most general terms her argument: she is (was) a living being, a rose, not simply an object. The shift in symbolism from pearl to rose is subtle but as important as the shift in perspective from the Dreamer's discourse to the Pearl-child's, for the symbolic associations of each image suggest quite different views of the subject-position of the Pearl-child. On the one hand, the pearl is a timeless gem, an object of beauty; on the other hand, the rose, though equally beautiful, is the time-bound product of growth, fruition, and, ultimately, decay. Whereas the pearl remains more or less static, the life cycle of the rose, as it were, more closely reflects the human developmental paradigm. Dying so young, the *Pearl*-child's own brief life minimizes the distinction between birth and death, for like a rose she faded as

---

[22] Andrew and Waldron, *Poems*, note to line 272.

[23] Gordon, *Pearl*, note to line 272.

[24] Cited in Moorman, ed., *Works*, 221. In the Towneley Cycle, for example, "bref" is used in the legal sense of a "writ" or "summons" by Nuncius, who addresses Herodes, "And lo, syrs, if ye trow not me, / Ye rede this brefe" ("Offering of the Magi," ll. 341–42); by 2 Demon, who informs the audience that he carries "A bag-full of brefes" ("Judgment," l. 210); and by Titiuillus, who, like 2 Demon, proffers the "breffes in my bag" ("Judgment," l. 328). In addition to the primary denotation of "proof," "pref" carries the sense of "put to the test" when used by Noah against the quarrelsome Uxor: "The thryd tyme will I prufe / What depnes we bere" ("Noah," ll. 664–65); Deus intends upon Abraham, "I will hym proue, / If he to me be trew of louf" ("Abraham," ll. 55–56); and Jesus responds to I Magister's query concerning the greatest commandment: "The seconde may men profe, / And clerly knaw therby: / Youre neghburs shall ye lofe / Right as yourself, truly" ("Christ and the Doctors," ll. 129–32). See *The Towneley Plays*, ed. Martin Stevens and A. C. Cawley, EETS s.s. 13–14. (Oxford: Oxford University Press, 1994).

quickly as she bloomed. Just as the pearl image suggests a material corollary in the infant's baptismal gown, it could equally suggest a burial shroud. In the same way the scent of the rose recalls the rose water in which newborn infants were bathed,[25] so rose derivatives were part of the medieval midwife's pharmacopoeia for the treatment of gynecological problems, difficult pregnancies, and traumatic deliveries.[26] One of the tragic realities was that birth and death were often inseparable in the Middle Ages.

Hence the development of the rose image corroborates the observation that the poem moves from lament and mortality to resurrection and renewal.[27] I would extend that argument to say, then, that not only is the Dreamer's perception brought from death to life, the *Pearl*-child herself also is (re)born: the objectified *Pearl*-object becomes a fully articulated and active subject, a redeemed child, in the *Pearl*-Dreamer's growing awareness. When the Dreamer initially calls the child a pearl, she names herself a rose (l. 269), and after the *Pearl*-child's instruction, the Dreamer realizes she is indeed a rose and names her by the child's own terms (l. 906). After her demonstration, rather than relying on his own inappropriate terminology, the Dreamer substantially accepts the *Pearl*-child's own title for herself. So the rose, simultaneously as a sign of childbirth, an emergent symbol of natural growth and fruition, and a portent of death and burial, contests the Dreamer's static formulation of the pearl as an object, and the suggestions of late medieval childbirth practices in the pearl and the rose further undercut the Dreamer's symbolic system and argue for a specific, material relationship between Dreamer and child.

In addition to the symbolic and material associations of the rose image, the rose functions as an important index in the *Pearl*-child's continuing challenge to the Dreamer's discourse. In the first cluster of references to the rose, upon the Dreamer's first encounter with the *Pearl*-child, he questions, "What Wyrde hatz hyder my juel vayned, / And don me in þys del and gret daunger?" (ll. 249–50). The *Pearl*-child's blunt reply, "Sir, ȝe haf your tale mysetente" (l. 257), is key. In my view, the "tale" the Dreamer mistakes is the one he has narrated thus far: the eroticized *Pearl*-maiden has been lost; he is a joyless jeweler and courtly lover wooing her again (l. 241–52). In response,

---

[25] Hanawalt, *Growing Up*, 43.
[26] *Medieval Woman's Guide to Health: The First English Gynecological Handbook*, ed. Beryl Rowland (Kent, OH: Kent State University Press, 1981), passim.
[27] Hoffman, "Notes," 99–100.

the *Pearl*-child specifies that the Dreamer's mistaken "tale" manifests a three fold error: first, he misrecognizes her place in that landscape; second, he believes that he may join her; and third, he thinks he may, in his present state, cross the river that separates them (ll. 289–300).

In a sense, these three points of contestation set the syllabus for the Dreamer's education in the rest of the poem. First, she must correct his objectifying gaze. She is not the pearl-object he describes, and she is not statically set in that crystalline landscape like a jewel in a setting. Second, the *Pearl*-child must correct the Dreamer's belief that he can erase distance between them — that is, collapse their differences — and conduct their relationship as he has constructed it. Third, she must demonstrate that he must change, as she is already changed, before he can cross the divide that separates them. In short, the *Pearl*-child's task is to interrupt the Dreamer's discourse with a corrective vision, and she does this by creating a subversive space for her childish subjectivity within his specular fantasy. The *Pearl*-child challenges his discursive construction of the pearl in this early stanza and throughout the rest of the poem, particularly in the parable of the vineyard.

The Parable of the Vineyard and the Dreamer's Complicity

In the well-known parable, based on Matthew 20:1–16 (ll. 500–76), a "lorde" (l. 502) goes out at different times during the day, starting in early morning and continuing until nearly sundown, to hire laborers to work in his vineyard. Significantly, the first group of workers agrees to work for "a pene on a day" (l. 510) and the following laborers for "What [is] resonabele" (l. 523). At the end of the day, the Lord's reeve "Set hem alle vpon a rawe / And gyf vchon a peny" (ll. 545–46) for their labor. All of the workers are paid equally, but those who have been working longer complain that "Vus þynk vus oȝe to take more" (l. 552) than those who have not worked as long. The lord replies that they received what they had agreed to by "couenaunt" (l. 562) and faults them for grumbling about his generosity to the others.

No longer simply characters in a biblical story, the lord's payment and the grumbling field hands of the parable were a fact of life in late fourteenth-century England, to judge by the fines imposed for noncompliance and by the criminal actions brought against uncooperative laborers.[28] The

---

[28] See L. R. Poos, "The Social Context of Statute of Labourers Enforcement," *Law and History Review* 1 (1983): 27–52.

Pearl-child's invocation of the parable of the vineyard textually reproduces the socio-economic hierarchies of the time (lord over laborer), only to undercut them. The lord goes out personally to hire for a day's work, a job more likely the responsibility of the reeve; he hires by the day, in direct opposition to the 1351 Statute; and he pays the laborers each the same wage, regardless of their time in the field.[29]

In effect, the parable sets a narrative trap that hinges on the illusory equality of the lord's agreement to pay the first group "a penny" and the later laborers "what is reasonable," for the distance between "a penny" and "what is reasonable" traps the unwary reader and the *Pearl*-Dreamer alike while it marks the graciousness of the lord's offer. Out of his generosity, the lord pays the other laborers an "unjust" wage, from the point of view of those first hired. Taken theologically, "the penny of heaven" is given not on the basis of an earthly system of work and reward, but by divine generosity. Yet, when the *Pearl*-child claims to have been paid the full penny of salvation for even her short time on earth as a child (l. 585), the Dreamer still finds the story "vnresounable" (l. 590), for labor, in his view, should be rewarded proportionately to its length and severity (ll. 595–600). With its emphasis on the payment of seemingly inequitable wages, the Parable of the Vineyard confronts the Dreamer with his own desire as it is embodied in an object, earlier in the pearl and now in the penny. The Dreamer's basic misrecognition — his creation of the *Pearl*-maiden out of the *Pearl*-child — permits him to complain, like the laborers, about unfair wages, for he envisions the operations of God to be organized in an economic rather than a relational model (ll. 597–600).

Hence the Dreamer continues to identify inappropriately with those who oppose God's grace and generosity, and his response to the *Pearl*-child focuses, again obsessively, on the economic, objective problem of the parable (the penny wage) and fails to see the social, relational solution offered in the

---

[29] The poem's explicit attention to a penny as a just wage for a day's work calls to mind the provisions of Edward III's Ordinance (1349) and Statute of Laborers (1351). Designed to stabilize wages and employment after the Black Death had decimated the labor pool in 1348–1349 and to prevent common workers from exploiting for higher pay the increased demand for their work, the 1351 Statute set wages equal to what had been paid five years earlier, penalized those who sought more money, restricted the movement of laborers who pursued work where labor was scarce, and specified that most field hands "be [allowed] to serve by the whole year, or by other usual Terms, and not by the Day." In addition, the Statute fixed a field worker's wage at "but a penny a day," although skilled laborers could earn a higher wage commensurate with their expertise. *Statutes of the Realm, 1225–1713.* 9 vols. London, 1810–1822.

lord's response to the laborers (seeking, finding, and rewarding). In answering the laborers' protests, the lord emphasizes not only his justice, having carried out the economic terms of their "couenaunt" (l. 562), but also his generosity, initiative, and autonomy:

> "'More, weþer louyly is me my gifte —
> To do wyth myn quatso me lykez?
> Oþer ellez þyn y3e to lyþer is lyfte
> For I am goude and non byswykez?'
> þus schal I," quoþ Kryste, "his skyfte:
> þe laste schal be þe fyrst þat strykez,
> And þe fyrst þe laste, be he neuer so swyft,
> For mony ben called, þa3 fewe be mykez." (ll. 565–72)

Bernard Brandon Scott, in a recent commentary on the parables, notes that the agreement in the parable of the vineyard to pay a penny for the day's work creates the expectation in the reader, and obviously in the *Pearl*-Dreamer, of a hierarchy of labor based on the time of day the laborers were hired. Scott contends, however, that in "the parable, value or worth (i.e., a place in the kingdom) is determined not by what is right but by acceptance.... It is not wages or hierarchy that counts but the call to go into the vineyard."[30]

Although the householder invites all available workers into his vineyard and pays them equally, it is particularly noteworthy here that the lord faults the laborers for exactly the same error the *Pearl*-child brings to the Dreamer. Like the Dreamer, they are fixated on the physical, their point of view is fully determined by economic cause and effect, and they render social relations into things, like a pearl or a penny. The call to the kingdom and its token, the penny of heaven, is determined not by what is "reasonable" in any earthly sense; the penny expresses equality and association rather than hierarchical domination or economic calculation, and in the same way that the reeve pays first those laborers who have worked least, so in the kingdom of God, in the familiar phrase from the gospel, the last shall be first and the first last. The Parable of the Vineyard thus challenges the Dreamer not so much in how to reconcile an equal wage for unequal work but in how to dispense with

---

[30] Bernard Brandon Scott, *Hear Then the Parable: A Commentary on the Parables of Jesus* (Minneapolis: Fortress Press, 1989), 297.

his mercantile fixation on the pearl as an object of erotic value and to arrive at a manner of personal relation and social acceptance not burdened by the violence of objectification.

After confronting the Dreamer with the economic paradox of the vineyard parable, in effect entering his objectifying discourse to challenge it from within, the *Pearl*-child interprets the parable by emphasizing her identity as an infant child, not a theological symbol or material object. Beginning with Origen, traditional medieval interpretation allegorized the parable generally in two ways: "The first interprets the day of the laborers as the history of the world, with the specified hours marking the principle divisions of mankind's spiritual history, and the second likens the day to the life of an individual, its phases of growth and decline designated by the intervals."[31] In a variation of the second reading, the *Pearl*-child, by virtue of her youth, is a figure of those workers who have worked the least for the same pay:

> 'Wheþer welnygh now I con bygynne —
> In euentyde into þe vyne I come —
> Fyrst of my huyre my Lorde con mynne:
> I watz payed anon of al and sum.
> 3et oþer þer werne þat toke mor tom,
> þat swange and swat for long 3ore,
> þat 3et of hyr noþynk þay nom,
> Paraunter no3t schal to-3ere more.' (ll. 581–88)

Andrew and Waldron take the view that "entry into the vineyard at the eleventh hour is taken to represent the death of a baptized Christian in childhood" or "any, including children, converted shortly before death."[32] As a child who entered the vineyard in the evening, she was not able to "swange and swat" ("hurry and labor") like the others; in fact, as a child she is dependent upon others to see to her spiritual disposition.

---

[31] Stephen L. Wailes, *Medieval Allegories of Jesus' Parables* (Berkeley: University of California Press, 1987), 138–39. For a more complete treatment of medieval exegesis of the Parable of the Vineyard, particularly in the vernacular homiletic tradition, see Ann Douglas Wood, "The *Pearl*-Dreamer and the 'Hyne' in the Vineyard Parable," *Philological Quarterly* 52 (1973): 9–19.

[32] Andrew and Waldron, *Poems*, 81, note to lines 581–88.

The *Pearl*-child's interpretation of the Parable of the Vineyard leads directly to another reference to her earthly subjectivity, for the abundant water symbolizing God's generosity (l. 607) becomes the waters of infant baptism and an *apologia* for the righteous innocents. Answering the Dreamer's accusation that "I my peny haf wrang tan here, / þou sayz þat I þat com to late" (ll. 614–15), the *Pearl*-child replies: "Bot innoghe of grace hatz innocent; / As sone as þay arn borne, by lyne / In þe water of babtem þay dyssente" (ll. 625–27). The *Pearl*-child's extensive teaching on infant baptism not only instructs the Dreamer theologically, it returns the Dreamer's attention to the material conditions of her brief life and death. The seriousness of infant baptism for the salvation of the young in the Middle Ages can be gauged by the allowances the Church made to provide for this sacrament. Suspending conventional patriarchal authority for the time being, Myrc's *Instructions for Parish Priests* gives midwives the authority to administer baptism at birth in cases of emergency, for example if "þe chylde bote half be bore / Hed and necke and no more" (ll. 91–92). Midwives were instructed both to carry consecrated water with them and to repeat the baptismal formula in either Latin or English when necessary (ll. 108–30), though the intent was as important as the exact recitation. In effect, no child was to die unbaptized, and even parents could christen the child if no one else were available (ll. 136–40);[33] if the child survived, she could be then taken to a nearby church where the rite could be (conditionally) administered after the priest inquired as to the circumstances of birth and the formula of the rite.[34] In fact, since deceased unbaptized infants technically were held to be separated from God in limbo and were to be buried outside hallowed ground, parental concern for their child's spiritual welfare led to sometimes immoderate measures. According to Ronald Finucane, "it was not unusual for very ill, dying, or even dead neonates to be brought into a church and placed near or on the altar or upon the tomb of a purported saint, into whose care the fearful parents commended them .... Any subsequent movement that was detected in the infant's body was taken as a sign of life that allowed baptism to follow."[35]

---

[33] John Myrc, *Instructions for Parish Priests*, ed. Edward Peacock, EETS o.s. 31 (London: Kegan Paul, 1902).

[34] Ronald C. Finucane, *Rescue of the Innocents: Endangered Children in Medieval Miracles* (New York: St. Martin's Press, 1997), 44.

[35] Finucane, *Rescue of the Innocents*, 44.

The miraculous though temporary "revival" of an infant would then allow for proper baptism and the welfare of the child's soul as well as for the parents' peace of mind.

Thus the *Pearl*-child's examination of the theology of infant baptism underscores the medieval recognition of the necessity of communal investment in the social and spiritual development of children. The Dreamer's fetishization of the *Pearl*-object has masked the underlying adult-child relationship, and he has questioned the *Pearl*-child's right to be crowned queen in heaven, particularly because she "watz so ȝonge" (l. 474):

'þou lyfed not two ȝer in oure þede;
þou cowþez neuer God nauþer plese ne pray,
Ne neuer nawþer Pater ne Crede —
And quen mad on þe fyrst day!' (ll. 483–86)

The radical equality of God's grace toward the *Pearl*-child confounds not only the Dreamer's conventional notions of economics (the penny of heaven) and of social class and status (a child made queen), but also of temporality (her less than two years on earth result in immediate reward in heaven). These lines ring with a specificity particular to the theology and social structure of late medieval England. After baptism initiated a child into the church, youngsters then had to master elementary Christian teaching before their first communion. The Pater Noster, Creed, and Ave Maria formed the rudiments of the faith and were the first things young Christians were expected to learn,[36] but a very young child like the *Pearl*-child, as the Dreamer himself points out, is the least able to respond to either the conventional requirements of institutionalized religion ("nauþer plese ne pray") or to the demands of spirituality in a theologically coherent way. Thus in the same way as young children depended completely upon parents and immediate family to care for their physical needs, so baptized infants relied upon the extended family, especially the godparents, to raise them in the faith.

In contrast to the portrait of young children brought happily into the social and spiritual kinship of their community, the *Pearl*-child, a young girl unschooled in the basic tenets of Christianity, also invokes an unfortunate and less felicitous tendency in late medieval society. By virtue of

---

[36] Hanawalt, *Growing Up*, 45.

their tender age and absolute dependence on others for their physical and spiritual needs, children as a group constitute the "least" in the earthly hierarchy. Although, contra Ariès, there is no longer any question that medieval families loved their children, there is evidence that male and female children were valued differently. Childrearing practices could apparently devalue female infants, and although there is no evidence supporting the view that medieval families practiced systematic abuse or infanticide deliberately,[37] Barbara Hanawalt accounts for higher death rates among infant females in the late medieval period by noting that "male children were apparently given better care because they had a higher social value. Londoners could not have been immune to thinking that a female child meant an outlay of wealth for dowry at the time of marriage, whereas a male child brought in wealth when he married."[38] Being the less-desired in the economic hierarchy, young girls were generally considered to be an economic drain rather than a financial benefit. Likewise, Finucane's analysis of miracles involving children from both Northern and Southern Europe indicates that "little boys were cured more quickly than girls" and that "girls languished in their illnesses longer than boys." Essentially agreeing with Hanawalt, Finucane concludes that in cases of childhood illness "medieval parents seem to have invested more care and more effort into their sons; in addition, they seem to have done so more quickly than for their daughters."[39]

It is in the cultural context of masculine privilege that the *Pearl*-child, as an infant girl, gains a particularly authoritative stature in her presentation of biblical texts like the Parable of the Vineyard, for her elevated status in heaven personalizes the hierarchical displacement summoned in the formula, "the last shall be first, and the first shall be last" (ll. 570–71). In the vineyard parable, the "last" are the "mykez" (l. 572), or friends of God, and those "wyth lyttel atslykez" (l. 575). Literally rendered, these lines refer to the little, lowly, or unworthy,[40] which Andrew and Waldron suggest the lines may allude "to the Maiden as a child on earth."[41] While

---

[37] See Hanawalt, *Growing Up*, 44, n.13.
[38] Hanawalt, *Growing Up*, 58.
[39] Finucane, *Rescue of the Innocents*, 160. See also Daniel T. Kline, "Female Childhoods," in *The Cambridge Companion to Medieval Women's Writing*, ed. Carolyn Dinshaw and David Wallace (Cambridge: Cambridge University Press, 2003), 13–20.
[40] Moorman, *Works*, 251.
[41] Andrew, *Poems*, 80, note to ll. 73–5.

the *Pearl*-child incarnates both the promise that comes with birth and the social ties that come with baptism, she occupies the most highly marginalized position in her culture: she is an infant girl. Her earthly disempowerment authorizes her heavenly discourse, and her preeminent position in the poem itself is an implicit criticism of a culture that marginalizes its female young, for the "poet's choice of an infant girl as elegiac subject thus would seem to centralize a normally marginal familial and gender category to evoke poignantly a female-centered family drama."[42] As opposed to those who view Dante's Beatrice and Boethius' Lady Philosophy as analogues to the *Pearl*-child, I would argue again that by virtue of her age and her social marginalization the *Pearl*-child is unique as a challenge to the social and cultural hierarchies of her day. So in the same way as "the least" are elevated in the vineyard parable's interpretation, the *Pearl*-child, "sauf" now in heaven, speaks with authority about the "ry3t" of children before God (ll. 661-720). The Parable of the Vineyard — like the poem itself — subverts the stereotypical hierarchies that place male over female and adult over child. This parable, however, is only the first in a calibrated series of biblical episodes carefully to challenge and ultimately subvert the Dreamer's discursive world view, and this deconstruction continues in the *Pearl*-child's story of Jesus and the Children.

Jesus and the Children and the *Pearl*-child's Spiritual Authority

In the vineyard parable, the *Pearl*-child filters contemporary economic unrest and social marginalization through the biblical text to confront the Dreamer with his own work-reward value system and to demonstrate a culturally subversive theology of equality and grace. Contrasting the lord-laborer relationship of the vineyard parable, which raises troubling questions of labor, wages, and justice in the public sphere, the story of Jesus and the Children confronts the Dreamer with more personal questions of love, parental involvement, and grace in a domestic context. Phrased differently, whereas the relationship of lord to laborer is less immediately pertinent to his grief and loss, Jesus and the Children confronts the Dreamer more directly with his personal relationship to the *Pearl*-child. In the first story, the relationships are formal and contractual; in the second, the relationships are

---

[42] Stanbury, "Feminist Masterplots," 109.

intimate and domestic. In the Gospel of Matthew, Jesus and the Children (19:13–15) precedes the vineyard parable (20:1–16), but rather than following the Matthean sequence, the *Pearl*-poet opens the Parable of the Vineyard with a statement concerning the actual youth of the *Pearl*-child (ll. 483–86) and then uses the story of Jesus' blessing the young to complete the parabolic instruction that "the last shall be first." Thus the poet's deliberate reordering of the biblical sequence indicates a clear, logical line of thinking, and the *Pearl*-child's narration of Jesus and the Children explores the broader social currents of the vineyard parable in a familiar, familial context. I would argue from the *Pearl*-poet's deliberate rearrangement of the biblical sequence that the interpretation of the Parable of the Vineyard is completed only with the *Pearl*-child's recounting of the story of Jesus and the Children (from Matthew 19:13–15, cf. Luke 18:15–17 and Mark 10:13–16):

> 'Ry3twysly quo con rede,
> He loke on bok and be awayed
> How Jesus Hym welke in areþede,
> And burnez her barnez vnto Hym brayde.
> For happe and hele þat fro Hym 3ede
> To touch her chylder þay fayr Hym prayed.
> His dessyplelz with blame "Let be!" hym bede
> And wyth her resounez ful fele restayed.
> Jesus then hem swetely sayde:
> "Do way, let chylder vnto Me ty3t;
> To such is heuenryche arayed":
> þe innocent is ay saf by ry3t.' (ll. 709–20)[43]

---

[43] Contrasting the *Pearl*-poet's deliberate reshaping of these gospel narratives, the *Pepysian Gospel Harmony* provides a different reading of Jesus and the Children:

> þo com a man to Jesu and offrede hym children, þat he schule touchen hem and blissen hem. And Jesus deciples rec[s]eden [sic] hem þat hem offreden. And whan Jesus sei3 þat, he remoeued hym, and cleped hem to hym & badde hem þat hij schulden leten þe children comen to hym; 'for to swich,' he seide, 'is þe blis of heuene. And who so nys nou3th swich as child is, he ne schalnou3th come þere jnne.' And þan biclept Jesus þe children and blissed hem, and 3ede hym forþ. (67–8)

Following the Matthean ordering of events, unlike *Pearl* which reverses the sequence of Jesus and the Children and the Parable of the Vineyard, the *Pepysian Gospel Harmony* follows this story with the Rich Young Ruler and then the briefest reference

Following on the heels of the vineyard parable, this anecdote echoes and corrects a constellation of concerns that have thus far shaped the Dreamer's misrecognition of the child. The passage depicts a bustling mass of children, brought by their parents, surrounding Jesus, asking for his blessing, and seeking his soothing touch. The disciples, however, equally intent on maintaining their own positions closest to Jesus and their monopoly over Jesus' attention, try to keep the throbbing rabble away. Responding forcefully to the disciples, Jesus insists on the children having direct passage to him, overturning the hierarchical boundary the disciples impose. In other words, the disciples attempt to keep "the least of these" away from Jesus, and against the disciples' disparaging "Let be!" ("Hands off!" or "Go away!"), Jesus responds, "Do way, let chylder vnto Me ty3t." Jesus answers the disciples' rebuke of the children with blessing and invitation. In the same way as the Dreamer occupied the position of the grumbling laborers in the vineyard parable, here he takes on the role of the supercilious disciples who prevent the innocent children from having contact with Jesus.

The *Pearl*-child's narration of Jesus and the Children again places the Dreamer in the position of identifying with and reproducing the dominant social structures of the age while overturning those hierarchies with the insistence that children are the model for theological perfection and reward. From the Dreamer's work-reward point of view, the efforts of children could not possibly result in salvation, yet the story of Jesus' blessing the children places the young squarely in a position of favor, for, being the least able to care for themselves on earth, they hold primacy of place in the kingdom of God. Only innocent children receive the penny of salvation in the *Pearl*-child's corrective narrative, and in the economics of heaven, only those who imitate them will receive like reward. As Jesus tells the disciples at the end of this narrative, "Hys ryche no wy3 my3t wynne / Bot he com þyder ry3t as a chylde" (ll. 722–23; see Matthew 18:1–3). The poem distinguishes the salvific dimensions of both "innocence" and "the innocent," the former denoting the condition of the penitent Christian and the latter little children under baptism. The poem's

---

to the vineyard parable, "And þanne tolde Jesus hem an ensaumple of a man þat brou3t werk men in to his vyner. And he paied hem þat comen late raþer, & als mykel 3af hem as hem þat comen first" (69). Unlike *Pearl*'s offering of an extensive interpretation of the vineyard parable, the *Pepysian Harmony* simply notes the householder's seemingly unfair pay arrangement. See *The Pepysian Gospel Harmony*, ed. Margery Coates (London: Oxford University Press, 1922).

use of "the innocent" denotes "infants and their salvation, and the *Pearl*, identified with total innocence, is most likely the symbol for infants or a specific infant."[44] This argument from innocence continually directs the Dreamer's attention to his own need for redemption and to the material reality of the dead "faunt" he has known so well.

Consequently, within the Dreamer's fantasy of the "*Pearl*-maiden," the story of Jesus and the Children allows the *Pearl*-child to add another facet to the potential space within which she negotiates her subject position with the Dreamer. Jesus completes the blessing story with the remark, "To suche is heuenryche arayed," a line that carries a double sense. First, in the immediate context, it indicates those who will be in heaven; heaven is full of innocents like these. Second, "heuenryche arayed" recalls the narrator's initial description of the *Pearl*-child in "araye ryalle" (l. 191). Here the story of Jesus' blessing the children provides a further corrective to the Dreamer's unseemly desire and objectifying discourse. The kingdom of heaven is not to be found in abstract symbolic qualities or material goods; rather, the kingdom consists in a specific quality of relationship, an affinity the Dreamer has misrecognized in the *Pearl*-child. Jesus' touch displaces the Dreamer's fetishizing gaze, and the intersubjective immediacy of Jesus' cradling a child in blessing amends the Dreamer's over-investment in the *Pearl*-object. The brief narrative of Jesus and the Children enjoins the Dreamer to recognize again the basic adult-child relationship he had enjoyed with the *Pearl*-child, has denied in his grief, has warped in his desire, and has distorted through his language.

The Pearl of Great Price and the Dreamer's Challenge

The third and final episode in this series of subversive narratives from the gospels, which began with the vineyard parable and continued through Jesus and the Children, now finds its completion in the parable of the Pearl of Great Price (Matthew 13: 44–5). In this well-known parable, a merchant looking for fine pearls sells all that he owns to purchase an unmatched pearl of great value, and his action is likened to the "the kingdom of heaven." If the episode of Jesus and the Children accents the place of children in the heavenly hierarchy, then the Pearl of Great Price stresses the means by which others — specifically adults like the *Pearl*-Dreamer — must enter a child-like subject

---

[44] Hoffman, "Notes," 101.

position of absolute trust through deliberate action. One must "com þyder ry3t as a chylde" (l. 723) to see heaven, for it was this bliss "þat the jueler [of the parable] so3te thur3 perre pres, / And solde alle hys goud, boþe wolen and lynne" to buy the spotless pearl (ll. 730–32). The *Pearl*-child's three gospel texts, each in succession, build upon the previous lessons to form a coherent theological lesson. If the Parable of the Vineyard subverts the Dreamer's hierarchical socio-economic worldview, and the story of Jesus and the Children presents the favored position of "the least of these," then the parable of the Pearl of Great Price outlines the process by which the Dreamer may enter the child-like subject position of absolute faith and dependence.

Normally, medieval allegories of this parable emphasize the symbolic nature of the merchant (as the penitent soul) and priceless worth of the pearl (as eternal life, Christian virtue, the church, or the contemplative life).[45] However, the *Pearl*-poet's rendition shares the emphasis of the Matthean text: "The kingdom of heaven is like a merchant *in search of* fine pearls" (Matthew 13:45, emphasis added). The poem triply accentuates the merchant's *action* in the parable ("so3te . . . solde . . . bye") and again challenges the Dreamer's grief-stricken paralysis. This process is given as an example of the complete devotion that finds heavenly reward, for the *Pearl*-child asks the Dreamer to "forsake þe worlde wode / And porchace þy perle maskelles" (ll. 743–44). Continuing the *Pearl*-child's critique of earthly economics established in the Parable of the Vineyard, here she bids the Dreamer to dispense completely with a mode of thought that finds joy in the object itself or the normal economics of risk and monetary return, and she challenges the Dreamer's economic worldview by taking it to its *telos*, its absolute, even irrational, ending: risk, and risk losing, absolutely everything. Coming to the kingdom as a child involves both innocence and reckless trust, and the pearl parable insists on the risk and dispossession of all of one's goods, exactly the opposite of the Dreamer's tendency anxiously to accumulate and indeed fetishistically create a *Pearl*-object from his *Pearl*-child.

Not only is her interpretation of the parable a challenge, it is also directly and unambiguously targeted at the Dreamer. In this third story, the *Pearl*-child inserts the Dreamer by name and character into her counterdiscourse, entering the Dreamer's discursive register to undermine it. The "joylez juelere" (l. 252) of the poem's opening now must become the enterprising "jueler" of

---

[45] Wailes, *Medieval Allegories*, 122–23.

the parable (l. 730), and rather than "pyȝting" the pearl in its jewelled setting — or the *"Pearl*-maiden" in her crystalline landscape — as he did earlier, the Dreamer must relinquish his goods and his control over their disposition. The *Pearl*-child's teaching brings the Dreamer's attention to the merchant's process — searching and finding — rather than the product alone. Thus only after her complex theological demonstration does the *Pearl*-child finally answer the Dreamer's opening query: "'Schall I efte forgo hit er I fyne? / Why schal I hit boþe mysse and mete?'" (ll. 328–29). In the parable of the pearl, the *Pearl*-child has again offered the Dreamer a counteractive to his fetishistic grief and its consequences. Like the merchant of the parable, the *Pearl*-Dreamer must also lose and find. He must recognize the reality of his loss and must persevere through the loss to eventually find her again — in heaven.

Conclusion: The Theology of Childhood and the Heavenly Vision

Beyond the immediate narrative schema of the *Pearl*-child's confrontation with the Dreamer, we might regard the *Pearl*-child's discourse as the articulation of a "theology of childhood," which, on one hand, mobilizes a series of biblical texts concerning children and their comparative status in the social hierarchy, and on the other, incorporates a variety of materials concerning the corporeal reality and lived experience of children in the late medieval period. It is particularly significant that the first strand of this theology, the biblical object lessons in *Pearl*, incorporates a variety of parables. Rather than supporting a body of beliefs, in effect an ideological mythos, the parable, a particularly powerful type of metaphor, is a subversive — even deconstructive — genre that instead confounds the reader (or hearer's) expectations with often stunning turns of event or language.[46]

---

[46] In *The Dark Interval: Towards a Theology of Story* (Sonoma, CA: Polebridge, 1988), John Dominic Crossan situates parable as the polar opposite of myth:

> Myth has a double function: the reconciliation of an individual contradiction and, more importantly, the creation of belief in the permanent possibility of reconciliation. Parable also has a double function which opposes that double function of myth. The surface function of parable is to create contradiction within a given situation of complacent security but, even more unnervingly, to challenge the fundamental principle of reconciliation by making us aware of the fact that we made up the reconciliation. (40)

In John Dominic Crossan's phrase, the parable "creates the participation whereby its truth is experienced."[47] This is exactly the effect of the carefully chosen series of gospel texts mobilized by the *Pearl*-child. The Parable of the Vineyard confronts the Dreamer with the limitations of his own restricted monetary worldview; the parabolic actions of Jesus and the Children demonstrate his implicit opposition to "the least" in the kingdom of God; and the Pearl of Great Price encourages him to abandon his anxious tendency to accumulate. Instead, he should embark on the risky venture of trust in God and the full recognition of the child apart from an earthly system of work and reward. In essence, these parables are narrative traps into which the Dreamer falls, and by placing him in the position of being judged, the *Pearl*-child's "theology of childhood" renders the Dreamer's excuses untenable before the subversive logic of heaven.

In heaven, these gospel texts, particularly the story of Jesus blessing the children, find eschatological fulfillment when the *Pearl*-child joins the 144,000 virgins in heaven (Revelation 14:1–5); at the same time, the heavenly celebration of the virgins before the Lamb recalls another significant gospel precedent involving violated children. Late-medieval religious thought often associated the 144,000 virgins with the young victims of Herod's slaughter, the Holy Innocents, in Matthew 2. Like the *Pearl*-child, the children of Herod's slaughter were two years old, and "the Innocents are represented in the liturgy as dying in the same state as Pearl,"[48] but saved in post-baptismal grace. The poem here echoes the liturgy for Childermas, whose signal text is Matthew 18:3 ("Truly, truly, I say to you, unless you repent and become like little children, you will never enter the kingdom of heaven"), a text closely associated to the tale of Jesus and the Children. Hence the predecessor text directs the Dreamer's attention again to the physical death of the young, while the celestial cortege reveals the ultimate dispensation of the innocent children. The *Pearl*-child's "theology of childhood," bolstered by biblical texts from Matthew to Revelation, admonishes the Dreamer permanently to internalize the cultural inversion indicated in the gospel formula of the last being first. According to the *Pearl*-child, and from her privileged point of view, the "last" are truly and eternally the "first" in the eyes of God.

---

[47] John Dominic Crossan, *In Parables: The Challenge of the Historical Jesus* (San Francisco: Harper & Row, 1973), 18.

[48] Bishop, Pearl *in its Setting*, 109.

In accord with the *Pearl*-child's adoption of the Dreamer's discourse to disable his mode of symbolizing, the pearl set in the *Pearl*-child's breast is no longer seen as the construction ("pyȝt") of the Dreamer (l. 192), but was indeed set, "pyȝt," in heaven by Jesus (l. 742). Building upon the three previous gospel lessons, the *Pearl*-child now takes up the language of courtly love, not to echo the Dreamer's fetishizing tendencies, but to describe her eschatological relationship to Christ: "My Lombe, my Lorde, my dere Juelle, / My Joy, my Blys, my Lemman fre" (ll. 795–96). By adopting the Dreamer's own eroticized language, but directing that desire to the appropriate subject, the *Pearl*-child redirects the Dreamer's desire to that same subject, the salvific and eschatological Jesus, rather than to herself, and by virtue of her status as a child "sauf" in post-baptismal innocence, she embraces the doubleness of her redeemed nature: she is now indeed both the bride of Christ and the Dreamer's "faunt" and is no longer the Dreamer's paramour and eroticized love-object.

The second element in the *Pearl*-child's "theology of childhood" involves the unmistakable references to the materiality of the *Pearl*-child, the practices associated with young children and childhood, and the *Pearl*-child's specific relationship to the Dreamer. In the same way the parables subvert the Dreamer's own worldview by situating him in the place of narrative judgment, so they also create a discursive space in which the tantalizing references to the *Pearl*-child coalesce into a representation of her as a specific subject with a history of relationship to the Dreamer. In contrast to the recent contention that the poem enacts "a visual drama about the loss of a female body,"[49] I would argue that although the fetishized *Pearl*-maiden fades as the poem progresses, the infant female body of the *Pearl*-child is resurrected. The poem's references to the materiality of childhood are not opposed to, but are an integral part of, the poem's theology of childhood, for we find a coherent picture of the birth, brief life, and death of an infant girl who articulates this theology. The *Pearl*-child, swathed in the scent of roses, wears the *Pearl*-encrusted crysom of infant baptism; she is a "faunt," a young child who was nearer to the Dreamer than aunt or niece, whose relationships extended to godparents and even the wider parish community, and who died before she could learn the rudiments of Christian faith.

---

[49] Stanbury, "Feminist Masterplots," 99.

The poem's use of parables and parabolic actions thereby reverses the Dreamer's hierarchical conceptions while enlarging the potential space for the *Pearl*-child's self-articulation. By presenting children as exemplars of faith and subjects in their own right, the *Pearl*-child's theology of childhood forms, then, a discourse resistant to the socio-economic hierarchies of the late fourteenth century. In short, *Pearl* is critical of the social and discursive structures of dependence and powerlessness that render children, particularly young girls, as passive objects of parental and cultural desire. Instead, by placing this counterdiscourse in the mouth of the *Pearl*-child, the "least of these" in late medieval English culture, *Pearl* creates the possibility for a fully-fledged subjectivity of childhood by creating a valued and honored subject position for the *Pearl*-child outside the traditional roles usually occupied by children, whether in late medieval culture or in contemporary literary criticism.

Daniel T. Kline
University of Alaska, Anchorage

Victim of Love:
The Poetics and Politics of Violence in 'Le Printemps' of Théodore Agrippa d'Aubigné

The Latin term *translatio* means, among other things, a carrying or removing from one place to another; transplanting or grafting; shifting. French Petrarchism performs these operations throughout the sixteenth century, as poets engage in complex acts of imitation. Petrarch's *Rime* is translated and imitated innumerable times in French verse, carrying the Italian poetic tradition, itself an heir of the Provençal *troubadours*, into a French cultural context.[1] Catullan themes and forms are then grafted onto Petrarchan verse and the ground of Petrarchan verse shifts from courtly love and sexual politics to a consideration of aesthetics and poetics, as well as to theological and political controversy. Each of these transformations renews the body of Petrarchan verse, at least until the multitudinous possibilities of the tradition seem exhausted. All of these moves seem to be subsumed into the love poetry of Théodore Agrippa d'Aubigné, who reverses the usual French Petrarchan disengagement from the beloved and from worldly concerns to present an impassioned political and theological engagement against religious persecution. In the end, French Petrarchan verse, even while retaining the fundamental themes and images of the *Rime*, exists in a very different realm from that of the Italian Petrarchists.

The metaphor of love as death, and the associated images of battle, torment, and fire, have been integral to love-lyric sequences at the least since the works of Catullus. Different forms of suffering might vary in intensity

---

[1] For reception of Petrarch, see William Kennedy, *Authorizing Petrarch* (Ithaca: Cornell University Press, 1994), as well as Sara Sturm-Maddox, *Ronsard, Petrarch, and the Amours* (Gainesville: University Press of Florida, 1999).

and duration, but the suffering itself is a constant. Petrarch's *Rime*, the chief model for French Renaissance lyric, contains the typical metaphors of suffering: piercing arrows, a wounded heart, the flames of love, and martyrdom. As in Catullus's works, the love poems are placed in a larger political context which shades the poet alternately as disempowered and desiring of power. In Catullus, even more than in the *Rime*, sexuality and power are closely linked; and sexual violence, along with other forms of violence, is the guarantor of power.[2] Although Petrarch mutes this message to some degree, it returns with a vengeance in the Petrarchan poetry of late sixteenth-century France, at precisely the moment that Petrarchism is losing its force. What I would like to investigate is how the political or historical contextualization of the metaphor of love as death or suffering causes it to function literally as well as figuratively in the late sixteenth-century French lyric. I would also like to speculate on possible links between this literalization of a predominant metaphor of love-lyric, and the demise of the love-lyric in late sixteenth-century France (particularly the Petrarchan sonnet).

In the history of French Renaissance lyric, one cause for this shift is quite evident. Marc-Antoine de Muret's lectures on Catullus, held between 1551 and 1553 in Paris and eagerly welcomed by the Brigade (the pre-Pléiade group including Antoine de Baïf, Joachim du Bellay, and Pierre de Ronsard), granted these poets new insight into Latin poetics.[3] Catullus's poetry in particular tempered a Petrarchism that was already verging on *préciosité*. Nonetheless, Petrarchan conceits continued to dominate French Renaissance poetics, and in fact Catullus was largely used as a repository of new conceits or metaphors[4] until the period of massive bloodletting that began in 1562, with the

---

[2] For a more detailed and subtle discussion of these issues in Catullus, see Ellen Greene, "Gendered Domains: Public and Private in Catullus," in eadem, *The Erotics of Domination: Male Desire and the Mistress in Latin Love Poetry* (Baltimore: Johns Hopkins University Press, 1998), 18–36. William Fitzgerald touches upon these issues as well in *Catullan Provocations: Lyric Poetry and the Drama of Position* (Berkeley: University of California Press, 1995).

[3] For a comprehensive history of reception of Catullus in the Renaissance, and the Muret / Scaliger controversies in particular, see Julia Haig Gaisser, *Catullus and his Renaissance Readers* (Oxford: Clarendon Press, 1993), "*Commentarius*: Marc-Antoine de Muret, Achilles Statius, and Joseph Scaliger," 146–92.

[4] One example among many is sonnet 135 of Pierre de Ronsard's *Amours* of 1552: "Puis que je n'ay pour faire ma retraite / Du Labyrinthe, qui me va seduysant, / Comme Thesée, un filet conduysant / Mes pas doubteux dans les erreurs de Crete" ("Since I have nothing to make my retreat from the Labyrinth, which is seducing me, like Theseus,

massacre of Protestants at Vassy, and continued until the promulgation of the Edict of Nantes in 1598, which enforced a certain level of toleration of the practice of Protestantism in France. Particularly after the massacre on Saint Bartholomew's Day in 1572, images of the violence of love intensify in French lyric poetry, as is particularly evident in Philippe Desportes' *Les Amours d'Hippolyte*, published in 1573:[5]

> Comme quand il advient qu'une place est forcée
> Par un cruel assaut du soldat furieux,
> Tout est mis au pillage, on voit en mille lieux
> Feux sur feux allumez, mort sur mort amassée   (LXXIII)

> [When it happens that a town is taken / by the cruel assault of an enraged soldier, / Everything is laid to waste, and one sees in a thousand places / Fire lit upon fire, the dead piled up upon the dead....]

Virtually every poem in the collection contains images of the poetic persona being violently assaulted by his Lady, apparently because of his lack of due subservience. This violence is carried to an extreme in allusions to the Massacre of the Innocents (LXXIX), images of human sacrifice (again the separable heart, for example in sonnet VIII), and martyrdom (V and elsewhere). Although Desportes is pushing the limits of these Petrarchan conceits, it is interesting to note that virtually every violent image in his poetry is an imitation of a Petrarchan source (most often the more obscure Italian Petrarchists). And, although the images may be troubling, particularly in their insistent accumulation, their status as metaphors (or similes) is clear.

An even more extreme form of this violence, and the imagery used to depict it, occurs in Théodore Agrippa d'Aubigné's *Hécatombe à Diane*, the sonnet sequence that forms one part of his collection of love poetry, *Le Printemps*. D'Aubigné was a Huguenot (a militant Protestant) who wrote political pamphlets, a universal history of his time, and an epic about the Wars of Religion in France, *Les Tragiques*. *Le Printemps*, although heavily reworked and revised by d'Aubigné, was not published as a sequence in his lifetime, but was discovered and published in the nineteenth century. Nonetheless, some

---

who was guided by a thread"): ed. Paul Laumonier (Paris: Nizet, 1982), 131. This sonnet mixes allusions to Petrarch and Italian Petrarchan poets such as Pietro Bembo with an allusion to Catullus 64.

[5] Ed. Victor Graham (Geneva: Droz, 1960).

of the poems did circulate in manuscript form,[6] as well as in various collections published at the beginning of the seventeenth century.[7] D'Aubigné's *Tragiques* is cited in the epigraph of the first edition of *Les Fleurs du Mal*; it is intriguing to speculate on what part d'Aubigné's work might have had in Baudelaire's resuscitation and revision of the sonnet form. D'Aubigné's sonnets and *stances* can be seen as taking the violent metaphors of Petrarchan love to an extreme that might itself have defied imitation prior to Baudelaire. D'Aubigné's use of these images seems to call into question their status as metaphors, as they are initially presented as a sort of direct narration of events, more in the manner of a Catullan love-lyric than in the allegorical style refined by Petrarch's followers. The third *stance* is a fairly typical example of albinian poetics:

> A longs filetz de sang, ce lamentable cors
> Tire du lieu qu'il fuit le lien de son ame,
> Et séparé du cueur qu'il a laissé dehors
> Dedans les fors liens et aux mains de sa dame,
> Il s'enfuit de sa vie et cherche mille morts.
>
> Plus les rouges destins arrachent loin du cueur
> Mon estommac pillé, j'espanche mes entrailles
> Par le chemin qui est marqué de ma douleur:
> La beauté de Diane, ainsy que des tenailles,
> Tirent l'un d'un costé, l'autre suit le malheur.[8]

[With long streams of blood, this pitiable body brings its soul with it as it flees, and, separated from the heart that it has left behind, in strong bonds and in the hands of its Lady, flees from its life and seeks a thousand deaths.

The farther the bloody fates tear my pillaged stomach from my heart, the more I spill my entrails over the path that is marked with my

---

[6] As well as the manuscript of *Le Printemps* in the Tronchin collection at the University of Geneva, there is another at the Bibliothèque de la Société de l'Histoire du Protestantisme français in Paris, known as the *Manuscrit Monmerqué*.

[7] *Seconde partie des Muses Ralliées* (Paris: Guillemot, 1600), as well as others. See Henri Weber, ed., *Le Printemps* (Paris: Presses Universitaires de France, 1960), 32.

[8] The edition of *Le Printemps* I am using in this paper is that of Henri Weber, cited above. All translations are my own.

suffering. The beauty of Diane, like pincers [a large form of the tool, used for torture and for executions requiring a tearing apart of the body], pulls the heart one way, while the body pursues sorrow.]

The poet continues with a description of the various pieces of his body scattered over the forest, and the continuing hunt.

This poem does more than an emulatory take on the metaphor of love as a hunt; it complicates the picture a great deal by its use of a very specific reference to a current torture used on Protestants called the *tenailles*. Diane the huntress has become Diane the Catholic persecutor. This transformation is very much bound up in the particulars of d'Aubigné's poetics, and of his imitation. Diane de Salviati, the purported beloved of *Le Printemps*, was after all the niece of Pierre de Ronsard's Cassandre (the inspiration for the first book of the *Amours*), and this relationship complicates the expression of desire from the opening of the sequence:

> Ronsard, si tu as sceu par tout le monde espandre
> L'amitié, la douceur, les graces, la fierté,
> Les faveurs, les ennuys, l'aise et la cruauté,
> Et les chastes amours de toy et ta Cassandre,
>
> Je ne veux à l'envy, pour sa niepce entreprendre
> D'en rechanter autant comme tu as chanté,
> Mais je veux comparer à beauté la beauté,
> Et mes feux à tes feux, et ma cendre à ta cendre.
>
> Je scay que je ne puis dire si doctement,
> Je quitte de sçavoir, je brave d'argument
> Qui de l'escript augmente ou affoiblit la grace.
>
> Je sers l'aube qui naist, toy le soir mutiné,
> Lorsque de l'Océan l'adultère obstiné
> Jamais ne veult tourner à l'Orient sa face.
>   (Hécatombe, 5)

[Ronsard, as you knew how to disseminate throughout the world the friendship, sweetness, graces, pride, favors, annoyances, ease and cruelty, and the chaste loves of you and your Cassandre, I do not wish in addressing [accosting, assaulting] her niece, to sing again as you have sung, but I wish to compare beauty to beauty, my fires to your fires, my ashes to your ashes. I know that I cannot speak in so learned a manner, I leave the learning to you, I defy you with my argument, which augments or weakens the grace of the writing. I serve the dawn which is newly born, you the rebellious night, since the obstinate adulterer of the Ocean [Apollo, the sun] will never turn his face towards the East.]

D'Aubigné renders overt an emulation that most poets would submerge as a subtext, and thus introduces the sequence as a dialogue with his Catholic predecessor. He also posits this rivalry as one of substance over eloquence and of the current generation of writers over an outdated style of erudition. But this dialogue also echoes to some degree that discerned by Edwin Duval between Ronsard's *Discours de misères de ce temps*, which justifies Catholic persecution of the Protestants, and d'Aubigné's *Tragiques*, which calls into question this Ronsardian view of history.[9] D'Aubigné underscores the comparison ("Je veux comparer..."). He also seems to hint at a broader context in his reference to fire and ashes: given their relative religious perspectives, fire and ashes ("Et mes feux à tes feux, et ma cendre à ta cendre") mean something quite different for d'Aubigné compared to what they mean for Ronsard. The fire of love becomes the fire of Protestant martyrdom; it could be argued that d'Aubigné thus achieves the spiritual sublimation that Petrarch seeks at the end of the *Rime*. Yet this reading would efface the reinscription of the corporeal as a central image of *Le Printemps*. The tortured body, or the ashes left from the *acte de foi*, are crucial markers not only of devoted love, but also of personal salvation. This is the submerged challenge to Ronsard: d'Aubigné implies that his own salvation is assured by means of the torment he endures, while Ronsard may well be damned by his focus on a more earthly sort of love. While this distinction fits nicely with the Neoplatonic aspects of both Ronsard's and d'Aubigné's poetry, its theological importance is underscored by the words "je ne puis dire si doctement" (that is: "I cannot speak as a *docteur* would," when of course the only doctors in France allowed to speak of theological matters were Catholic, thus implying a deliberate silencing of the Protestant perspective). D'Aubigné continues to hint at a theological subtext in this sonnet when he rejects the notion that the quality

---

[9] Edwin M. Duval, "The Place of the Present: Ronsard, d'Aubigné, and the 'Misères de ce Temps,'" in *Baroque Typographies: Literature/History/Philosophy*, ed. Timothy Hampton (special number of *Yale French Studies* 80 [1991]), 13–29.

Victim of Love: The Poetics and Politics of Violence   37

of writing might increase or lessen "la grace," also a loaded term at the time. In fact, the term *grace* evolves from evoking a quality of feminine beauty in the opening lines of the sonnet, to a state marked in this world by suffering, forged in the fire of martyrdom.

If the Petrarchan images of fire have been translated into the context of the Wars of Religion in France, they become in this sonnet a fierce proclamation of the nascent sovereignty of Protestant poetics, and the image of d'Aubigné's dawn opposing Ronsard's *soir mutiné* (rebellious night) takes on the fervor of a struggle between good and evil. The concluding allusion to Scève's *Délie*[10] merely cements the rejection of Ronsard and all that he stands for. The intensity of the allusion to fire and ashes makes Ronsard's poetry seem like an innocent game, as it does if one compares a famous sonnet by Ronsard with the *stance* cited above:

> Comme un Chevreuil, quand le printemps destruit
> L'oyseux crystal de la morne gelée,
> Pour mieulx brouster l'herbette emmielée
> Hors de son boys avec l'Aube s'en fuit,
> Et seul, & seur, loing de chiens & de bruit,
> Or sur un mont, or dans une vallée,
> Or pres d'une onde à l'escart recelée,
> Libre follastre où son pied le conduit:
> De retz ne d'arc sa liberté n'a crainte,
> Sinon alors que sa vie est attainte,
> D'un trait meurtrier empourpré de son sang:
> Ainsi j'alloy sans espoyr de dommage,
> Le jour qu'un oeil sur l'avril de mon age
> Tira d'un coup mille traitz dans mon flanc.
>   (*Les Amours*, L., IV, 1552, XLIX)[11]

[Like a deer [roebuck], when spring destroys the lingering crystals of melancholy frost, that he might better browse in the honeyed grass, flees from his wood with the Dawn. Alone and secure, far from dogs and noise, now on a hill, now in a valley, now near the wave, hidden away, free and careless where his foot leads him. His liberty fears neither nets

---

[10] The opening lines of *Délie*, XI.
[11] Pierre de Ronsard, *Les Amours*, 52.

nor the bow, until his life is assaulted by a murderous arrow made purple with his blood. So I went along without thought of injury, that day in the April of my youth, when an eye shot a thousand arrows into my flank.]

Whereas Ronsard distances himself from this portrayal of the suffering of love by means of a simile ("Comme un Chevreuil..."), d'Aubigné paints a more immediate and stark description of a hunted man/animal from its own perspective. Ronsard's suffering seems more detached and distant, even aesthetic, as he focuses on the arrow made purple with blood, rather than the bleeding body itself. In other words, the focus is on the instrument of torment, rather than the victim of suffering.

Another striking difference between Ronsard's Petrarchism and d'Aubigné's is that of agency. In Ronsard's "hunting" poems, such as sonnet 89 of the 1552 *Amours*, an allegorical depiction of emotions as dogs distances the poetic persona/victim of love from responsibility for his self-destruction:

> Franc de raison, esclave de fureur,
> Je voys chassant une Fère sauvage,
> Or sur un mont, or le long d'un rivage,
> Or dans le boys de jeunesse & d'erreur.
>
> J'ay pour ma lesse un cordeau de malheur,
> J'ay pour limier un trop ardent courage,
> J'ay pour mes chiens, & le soing, & la rage,
> La cruaulté, la peine, & la douleur.
>
> Mais eulx voyant que plus elle est chassée,
> Loing loing devant plus s'enfuit eslancée,
> Tournant sur moy la dent de leur effort,
>
> Comme mastins affamez de repaistre,
> A longz morceaux se paissent de leur maistre,
> Et sans mercy me traisnent à la mort.   (L. IV, 89)

[Free from reason, a slave to madness, I go on the hunt for a savage beast, now on a mountain, now along the river bank, now in the woods of youth and error. I have for my leash a rope made of woe, I have for my trap too ardent a heart, I have as my dogs care and passion, cruelty, pains, and sorrow. But they, seeing that the more she is pursued, the farther ahead she flees in a rush, turning on me the tooth of their effort, like mastiffs starved and ready to devour, they feed on their master ripped into long pieces, and without mercy drag me to my death.]

The figure of the poetic persona as an active participant in the hunt of love dominates the two quatrains, but the situation reverses suddenly with the opening *mais* of the first tercet. From that moment, the violence is perpetrated by a depersonalized *eulx*, the *mastins* that were merely images of the persona's own compulsions are now detached from their point of origin.

D'Aubigné begins his third *stance* with the image that closes Ronsard's sonnet ("a longs filetz de sang," "a longz morceaux") and proceeds to reverse the movement away from personal agency. It is his own body that tears the soul from itself, and separates itself from its own heart. It is the poetic persona who spills his own intestines ("j'espanche mes entrailles"), leaving a trail of blood for the huntress Diane to track him. The hunted participates fully in his own victim-ization; whether this is an image of the destruction carnal love works on the soul, or the willing self-sacrifice the poetic persona incurs in order to save the soul from the predations of the body, is left unclear.

Although one could accuse d'Aubigné of mere baroque excess, both the disemboweling and the tearing out of the heart were current practices in torture and ritual execution during the Wars of Religion. This link between poetic expression of desire and current events becomes evident in other poems as well:

Je vis un jour un soldat terrassé,
Blessé à mort de la main ennemie,
Avecq' le sang, l'ame rouge ravie
Se debattoit dans le sein transpercé.

De mille mortz ce perissant pressé
Grinçoit les dentz en l'extrême agonie,
Nous prioit tous de luy haster la vie:
Mort et non mort, vif non vif fust laissé.

"Ha, di-je allors, pareille est ma blesseure,
Ainsi qu'à luy ma mort est toute seure,
Et la beauté qui me contraint mourir

> Voit bien comment je languy à sa veue,
> Ne voulant pas tuer ceux qu'elle tue,
> Ny par la mort un mourant secourir."
> <div align="right">(<i>Hécatombe</i>, XIV)</div>

> [One day I saw a soldier lying on the ground, fatally wounded by an enemy hand; his blood and his torn red soul fought in his pierced breast. This dying man, menaced with a thousand deaths, ground his teeth in the final agony, and prayed to us all to end his life. He was left dead, yet not dead, alive but not alive. "Ah," I said then, "such is my wound, and my death is as certain as his. And the Beauty who forces me to die sees quite well how I languish at the sight of her, and does not wish to kill those whom she kills, nor save a dying man by death."]

The most striking formal element of this sonnet, and the source of its effectiveness, is the delaying of the comparison until the first tercet. What we seem to have in the poem is an eyewitness account of the horrors of war. The Petrarchan allusions ("mille mortz," and the heart torn from the body, which recalls the 23rd canzone) compete on the field with the more realistic depictions of grinding teeth and the soldier begging for death. The image of the soldier becomes a sort of hinge linking the suffering of Petrarchan desire with the mass suffering of the Protestants. In this translation of Petrarchan desire, d'Aubigné seems to approach Catullus's sexual poetics: the disempowered lover is also a social outcast, and the economy of sexual power echoes and informs the power structures of society itself. Whereas Petrarchan desire, at least as translated into French Renaissance lyric, often seems isolated from its social context (note that this is not true of the *Rime*) — one thinks of Scève's almost hermetic *Délie* — d'Aubigné frequently punctuates his *Printemps* with allusions to the Wars of Religion.

The distance between d'Aubigné and Petrarchism can be more easily measured in a close examination of one recurrent image, that of the "separable" or "stolen" heart (itself taken from medieval lyrics and allegories):

> Questa che col mirar gli animi fura
> m'aperse il petto el' cor prese con mano,
> dicendo a me: "Di ciò non far parola."
> <div align="right">(<i>Rime</i>, 23, 72–4)</div>

[She, who with her glance steals souls, opened my breast and took my heart with her hand, saying to me: "Make no word of this."][12]

In this passage, the subjugation of the poetic persona is rendered more complete by the mysterious powers of his Lady. This linking of loss of voice and that of power is already evident in Catullus's 51st poem:

Ille mi par esse deo videtur,
ille si fas est, superare divos,
qui sedens adversus identidem te
spectat et audit
dulce ridentem, misero quod omnis
eripit sensus mihi: nam simul te,
Lesbia, aspexi, nihil est super mi

◊ ◊ ◊ ◊ ◊ ◊

lingua sed torpet, tenuis sub artus
flamma demanat, sonitu suopte
tintinant aures, gemina teguntur
lumina nocte.
otium, Catulle, tibi molestum est;
otio exsultas nimiumque gestis.
otium et reges prius et beatas
perdidit urbes.[13]

---

[12] *Petrarch's Lyric Poems: The* Rime Sparse *and other Lyrics*, trans. and ed. Robert M. Durling (Cambridge, MA: Harvard University Press, 1976), 62–63. All references to Petrarch in this essay are to Durling's edition.

[13] From *Catullus: The Poems*, ed. Kenneth Quinn (London: Macmillan, 1973), 29–30. All citations from and references to Catullus are to this edition. It should be noted that this poem is itself inspired by Sappho (fragment 31), of which it is arguably a translation with extensive modifications. D'Aubigné was aware of Sappho; he called Louise Labé "la Sapho de son temps" in his letter "A mes filles touchant les femmes doctes de nostre siecle," in *Oeuvres*, ed. H. Weber (Paris: Gallimard, 1969), 852. But it is unlikely that he had read her works. Still, this translation of female desire to the domain of male desire has interesting and complex implications. Cf. David Coray, *Catullus and the Poetics of Roman Manhood* (Cambridge: Cambridge University Press, 2001), 88–109.

[That man seems to me to be equal to a god; he, if it can be said, surpasses the gods, who always sitting facing [opposite or against — *adversus*] you watches and hears you sweetly laughing, which steals [pillages] all my sense from wretched me, for as soon as I behold you, Lesbia, I lose all my power [OR: when I am with you, Lesbia, nothing is superior to me] .... But my tongue is sluggish, the thin flame flows down through my limbs, my ears ring with their very own din, and double darkness covers my eyes. Idleness, Catullus, is irksome to you: you run riot in leisure and do too much. Idleness has ruined kings and wealthy cities before you.]

The comparison to the gods opens this poem with the notion of power and conquest in love. The words *superare* (to be superior to, to surpass, to conquer) and *adversus* (facing, opposite, against) suggest battle. And these words demonstrate a fairly typical aspect of Catullan poetics: by manipulating words with varying meanings, and by manipulating syntax, the poem calls for several different readings within what may seem to be a direct and simple (rather than obscure) form of writing. This coexistence of alternative readings becomes clear in lines six and seven of the poem, which suggest both that the lover is powerless when faced with Lesbia's infidelity, and that he is unconquerable when joined to her. This creation of alternative, even mutually contradictory, meanings offers a significant model for a Huguenot poet writing under Catholic rule. Catullus offers a way of using love poetry as a code, so that the Protestant message can be embedded in a widely accepted poetic form. This is, quite possibly, one way of reading d'Aubigné's sonnet to Ronsard.

It is particularly appropriate that this model of coding appear in a discussion of silence or of linguistic failure. Petrarch is told by his lady not to tell the truth of what he has experienced; he cannot remain silent, and so is punished:

> Poi la rividi in altro abito sola,
> tal ch' i' non la conobbi, o senso umano!
> anzi le dissi 'l ver pien di paura;
> ed ella ne l'usata sua figura
> tosto tornando fecemi, oimè lasso!
> d'un quasi vivo et sbigottito sasso.

[Later I saw her alone in another garment such that I did not know her, oh human sense! rather I told her the truth, full of fear, and she, to her accustomed form quickly returning, made me, alas, an almost living and terrified stone.] (ed. Durling, 62–3)

In Petrarch's case, although the threat of punishment does not silence the poetic persona, the punishment itself does, as he is turned into a rock. Or does it? The poem continues, as does the collection, in defiance of the tyranny of love and of the Lady. Nonetheless, the poetic persona's attitude seems, at least on the surface, to be more accepting of his disempowerment than that of Catullus or of d'Aubigné.

In the context of the Wars of Religion in France, and of the heresy and witchcraft trials of late sixteenth-century France, the issue of silence turns in a slightly different direction. Most obviously in the trials, individuals are forced by torture to speak the words of their inquisitors/tormentors: quite often a formulaic confession, tantamount to suppressing the accused's own voice, is imposed.[14] Elaine Scarry has examined the mechanics and ethics of torture and confession con-vincingly and in detail in the first chapter of her book *The Body in Pain*:

> World, self, and voice are lost, or nearly lost, through the intense pain of torture and not through the confession as is wrongly suggested by its connotations of betrayal. The prisoner's confession merely objectifies the fact of their being almost lost, makes their invisible absence, or nearby absence, visible to the torturers. To assent to words that through the thick agony of the body can be only dimly heard, or to reach aimlessly for the name of a person or a place that has barely enough cohesion to hold its shape as a word and none to bond it to its worldly referent, is a way of saying, yes, all is almost gone now, there is almost nothing left

---

[14] William Monter points out this dynamic in *European Witchcraft* (New York: Wiley, 1969), 75. Walter Stephens analyzed this procedure in some detail in a paper given at the colloquium on *Religious Differences in France: Past and Present* (Cornell University, April 1998), entitled "Witchcraft Theory and the Problem of Belief: Some Early Modern Continuities." Aspects of this mechanism are discussed in idem, *Demon Lovers: Witchcraft, Sex, and the Crisis of Belief* (Chicago: University of Chicago Press, 2002).

now, even this voice, the sounds I am making, no longer form my words but the words of another.[15]

To Scarry, interrogation is an integral part of the act of torture: it is contained within the act, and this interrogation operates on the false assumptions that the torturer is seeking information rather than imposing his own world view, and that the answer is an act of betrayal.

Later in this first chapter Scarry traces how, by positioning of the body, the victim of torture is often made into the agent of his own pain. This enforced agency can also operate at a larger social level, as the structure of some of the Nazi concentration camps and as the operations at Tuol Sleng demonstrate. This participation is also apparent in the literary domain in the confession that elicits punishment in Petrarch's 23rd canzone, cited above. In his third *stance*, d'Aubigné's persona takes this agency to an extreme, tearing his own body apart. Elsewhere, I have examined how d'Aubigné transfers this agency to the reader,[16] who, merely by reading the text, is eliciting the events that are described in it.

But it is d'Aubigné's appropriation of the images of torture and confession, of the instruments and words used by his Catholic per-secutors, which points to a way of subverting this mechanism.[17] He uses the technique of *imitatio*, which to some extent involves the ap-propriation of another's voice

---

[15] Elaine Scarry, *The Body in Pain: The Making and Unmaking of the World* (Oxford: Oxford University Press, 1985), 35. This mechanism has been seen yet again in the recently rediscovered tapes and documents of S-21, or Tuol Sleng, the site of thousands of confessions extracted by torture, many of which included accounts of joining the CIA, even though it is evident from the confessions themselves that the accused did not even know what the CIA was. See David Chandler, *Voices from S-21: Terror and History in Pol Pot's Secret Prison* (Berkeley: University of California Press, 1999), particularly chap. 4, "Framing the Questions."

[16] See Kathleen Long, "Improper Perspective: Anamorphosis in d'Aubigné's Les Tragiques," in *Figuring Protest and Lament: Perspectives on Sixteenth-Century France*, ed. D.E. Polachek (special number of *Mediævalia* 22 [1999], 103–26.

[17] For two analyses of d'Aubigné's appropriation of Catholic doctrine, forms, and objects, see Catharine Randall (Coats), "Text, Torture and Truth in Agrippa d'Aubigné's Les Tragiques," in eadem, *(Em)bodying the Word: Textual Resurrections in the Martyrological Narratives of Foxe, Crespin, de Bèze and d'Aubigné* (New York: Peter Lang, 1992), 117–44, and Ullrich Langer, "Tasso, d'Aubigné: Return to Absolute Necessity," in idem, *Divine and Poetic Freedom in the Renaissance* (Princeton: Princeton University Press, 1990), 42–50.

and thus suppression of one's own, as the means of liberating himself from the silence or ventriloquism enforced by Catholic domination of France and repression of the Huguenots. By taking Petrarchan conceits to an extreme, he can condemn Catholic practices of torture, but under the cover of writing mere love poetry. By playing with Petrarchan commonplaces such as "grace," he can even raise the specter of theological controversy in his work.

One example of such an appropriation occurs in the fiftieth sonnet of the *Hécatombe à Diane*. D'Aubigné's version of the image of the separable heart, in contrast to Petrarch's, is revolting in every way:

> Quand du sort inhumain les tenailles flambantes
> Du milieu de mon corps tirent cruellement
> Mon coeur qui bat encor' et pousse obstinement,
> Abandonnant le corps, ses pleintes impuissantes,
>
> Que je sen de douleurs, de peines violentes!
> Mon corps demeure sec, abbatu de torment
> Et le coeur qu'on m'arrache est de mon sentiment,
> Ces partz meurent en moy, l'une de l'autre absentes.
>
> Tous mes sens esperduz souffrent de ses rigueurs,
> Et tous esgalement portent de ses malheurs
> L'infiny qu'on ne peut pour departir esteindre,
>
> Car l'amour est un feu et le feu divisé
> En mille et mille corps ne peut estre espuisé,
> Et pour estre party, chasque part n'en est moindre.   (L)

[When the flaming pincers of inhuman fate cruelly tear my heart, which still beats and pulses obstinately, from my body, abandoning it to its powerless laments, how I feel the suffering, the violent pains! My body remains dry, beaten down by torment, and the heart which has been torn from me still shares in my feeling. These two [body and heart], taken from one another, die in me. All of my crazed senses suffer from her harsh-ness, and all bear her cruelty equally, since one cannot diminish that which is infinite by dividing it. For love is a fire, and fire cannot be extinguished, even when divided into a thousand and a thousand bodies, and even though divided, each part is not less than was the whole.]

The first act of rebellion is to describe in excruciating detail the very thing the Petrarchan lady silenced in *Rime* 23 — the sight of the heart torn, still beating, from a living body by an executioner; in this, again, d'Aubigné is merely taking Petrarch's transgression a step further. And again, love is not mentioned until the second tercet, which seems to reverse the effect of the typical Petrarchan sonnet. In most Petrarchan love-lyrics, as one might expect, love is established as the focus, the primary topic, of the poem, the ground on which the metaphors of war, hunting, and torment are based. Even when a comparison is delayed, the fact that the image offered is a comparison rather than having some independent force or meaning, is underscored, as in "Comme un chevreuil." The reader is supposed to transfer his sympathy to the desir-ing and thus suffering poetic persona, rather than focus it on the hunted animal. In still other examples, the metaphor is clearly marked by mythological allusions, allegorical descriptions, or other devices that dis-tance the poetic persona from his own suffering, and turn the situation into a sort of intellectual game.

D'Aubigné's use of direct language (even though the intertextual references are numerous) and his suppression of the metaphoric qualities of the images he is offering until late in the sonnets (and it is a fairly common technique of his even in the *Stances*) changes completely the register in which Petrarchan desire plays out. The torment itself is the focus of his poetry, a torment that is presented as itself rather than (or as well as) a metaphor for love, and that is historically contextualized by references to the Wars of Religion and to the persecution of French Protestants.

The effect of this reversal is to portray the revolt of the victim of love against his subjugation (at the hands of the Lady or of the Catholic authorities). His torn heart still beats and pulses obstinately, and retains a sympathetic connection with the body from which it was torn, rather than following the Lady's commands and obeying her demands without question. If there is any desire in d'Aubigné's *Printemps*, it is a desire to flee, to escape, to be free from torment. Rather than the Platonic notion of desire as a movement from lack to (at least the attempted) acquisition of that which is lacking, a pursuit of the other, d'Aubigné sees desire as creating the lack, the gap, and thus as something to avoid. In this, he is echoing some aspects of Petrarchan lyric (the fall from grace of the opening canzoni). But in the vehemence of his presentation of a sort of anti-desire (often akin to repulsion, as when he compares Diane's white skin to arsenic, *L'Hécatombe*, 42.5-8), he resembles more clearly the Catullan presentation of desire as disempowerment (as described by Greene and Fitzgerald). In this modification of Petrarchan desire, d'Aubigné creates a syntagmatic relationship between the suffering caused by desire and that caused by religious persecution, similar to the relationship Catullus portrays between sex and politics in ancient Rome. Whereas the paradigmatic, or metaphoric, relationship between desire and the images of suffering in Petrarch and Ronsard creates a safe zone of the imagination in which the poetic persona can control, and the reader enjoy (the game of love), d'Aubigné refuses repeatedly to send the signal that "this is just love poetry." Quite to the contrary, he is using the almost universal experience of the troubling effect of love to bring home to his readers the very real possibility of persecution, suffering, and torment. Just as everyone can fall in love, anyone could fall into the hands of the authorities. The very immediate expression of religious persecution as a personal experience accessible to all vividly re-minds the reader of his or her own vulnerability. The extreme, and extremely personal, nature of this representation of love and torment makes d'Aubigné a very tough act to follow indeed. In fact, in the early seventeenth century, French Petrarchism follows two very different paths: becoming either more and more *précieux*, loaded with contrived and already overused conceits, or highly satirical, as in the works of the *libertins* Théophile de Viau and Saint-Amant, later dissuaded from this work by the condemnation of Théophile himself. Once these satirical versions are censored, French Petrarchism, having lost any force it might once have had, fades rapidly.

D'Aubigné's lyrics thus stand, as if in isolation, as the epitome of a certain form of Petrarchism, one informed and modified by Catullan poetics. They offer a more stark and immediate portrait of the pain of desire, and its disempowering qualities. They also reverse the operation of Petrarchan poetics, which use images of battle and torment to convey the pain of love. In *Le Printemps*, love becomes a means of personalizing the pain of suffering and loss caused by war, massacre, and martyrdom, and so individual desire becomes a means of eliciting sympathy, a call for the end of domination and persecution, a plea for life itself.

Kathleen Long
CORNELL UNIVERSITY

BODY POLITICS IN
ARIOSTO'S ORLANDO FURIOSO[1]

At the beginning of the thirty-seventh canto of the third and final edition of his *Orlando furioso*[2] — an episode marginal to the principal plots of the poem but central to its insistent thematics of sexuality and gender identity[3] —

---

[1] A very early draft of this essay was delivered as a conference paper in 1985, and some of the materials presented here are reworked from A. R. Ascoli, "Il segreto di Erittonio: poetica e politica sessuali nel canto 37 dell'*Orlando furioso*," *La rappresentazione dell'altro nei testi del Rinascimento*, ed. S. Zatti (Lucca: Paccini Fazzi, 1998), 53–76. I owe particular debts for suggestions to the late Joy Hambuechen Potter, to Constance Jordan, to Lauren Berlant, and to Barbara Spackman.

[2] On this canto see E. Carrara, "Marganorre," *Annali della Scuola Normale di Pisa: Lettere, storia, e filosofia* ser. 2, 9 (1940): fasc. 1–2, pp. 1–20, 155–82; John McLucas, "Ariosto and the Androgyne: Symmetries of Sex in the 'Orlando furioso'" (Ph.D. diss., Yale University, 1983), 233–46; C. P. Brand, "From the Second to the Third Edition of the *Orlando furioso*: The Marganorre Episode," in *Book Production and Letters in the Western European Renaissance*, ed. A. L. Lepschy, J. Took, and D. E. Rhodes (London: Modern Humanities Research Association, 1986), 32–46; Nuccio Ordine, "Vittoria Colonna nel *Orlando furioso*," *Studi e problemi di critica testuale* 42 (1991): 55–92; Pamela Benson, *The Invention of Renaissance Woman* (University Park, PA: The Pennsylvania State University Press, 1992), 131–48. Cf. also Deanna Shemek, "Of Women, Knights, Arms, and Love: The 'Querelle des Femmes' in Ariosto's Poem," *MLN* 104 (1989): 68–97, esp. 95–97; Valeria Finucci, *The Lady Vanishes: Subjectivity and Representation in Castiglione and Ariosto* (Stanford: Stanford University Press, 1992), 166–67 and passim; Cinzia Sartini-Blum, "Pillars of Virtue, Yokes of Oppression: The Ambivalent Foundation of Philogynist Discourse in Ariosto's *Orlando furioso*," *Forum Italicum* 28 (1994): 3–21.

[3] For Ariosto's representations of women and gender, see Robert M. Durling, *The Figure of the Poet in Renaissance Epic* (Cambridge, MA: Harvard University Press, 1965), 150–60; Mario Santoro, "'Rinaldo ebbe il consenso universale...' *Furioso* 4.51–67," in idem, *Letture ariostesche* (Naples: Liguori, 1973), 83–133; McLucas, "Ariosto and the Androgyne"; Maggie Günsberg, "'Donna liberata?': The Portrayal of Women in the Italian Renaissance Epic," *The Italianist* 7 (1987): 7–35; Shemek, "Of Women, Knights, Arms, and Love," and eadem, *Ladies Errant: Wayward Women and Social Order in Early Modern Italy* (Durham, NC: Duke University Press, 1998); Benson, *Renaissance Woman*; Finucci, *The Lady Vanishes*; Judith Bryce, "Gender and Myth in the *Orlando furioso*," *Italian Studies* 47 (1992): 41–50; Sartini-Blum, "Pillars of Virtue"; Constance Jordan, "Writing beyond the Querelle: Gender and History in *Orlando furioso*," *Renaissance Transactions: Ariosto and Tasso*, ed. Valeria Finucci (Durham, NC: Duke

Ludovico Ariosto inserted a substantial proem in which he forcibly asserts and illustrates the noteworthiness of women's accomplishments in all fields. Women's deeds, he claims, are comparable to and perhaps even greater than those of their male counterparts. Here are the first three stanzas of what turns out to be the longest such exordium in the poem:

> Since worthy women have labored day and night with long care and greatest diligence to acquire other gifts from among those that Nature does not give without human effort, and in the end have succeeded in producing works that are by no means obscure, if they had also given themselves over to those studies that render mortal virtues immortal, so that by themselves they were able to memorialize their own praises, and did not have to go begging for help from male writers [*scrittori*], in whose hearts resentment and envy [*astio e invidia*] gnaw, such that the good which might be said is often left unspoken, and as much evil as they know is everywhere heard [*'l mal, quanto ne san, per tutto s'ode*], then those women's names would rise up so high that perhaps virile fame never rose to such a degree. For many of these men, it is not enough that they share the work of making each other glorious throughout the world, they also study how to uncover everything that is unclean in women [*ch'anco studian di far che si discuopra / ciò che le donne hanno fra lor d'immondo*]. They

---

University Press, 1999), 295–315. For individual female characters and specific passages that concern sexuality and gender, see also Mario Santoro, "L'Angelica del 'Furioso': fuga dalla storia," *Esperienze letterarie* 3 (1978): 3–28, and idem, "Un'addizione esemplare del terzo *Furioso*: la storia di Olimpia," in idem, *Ariosto e il Rinascimento* (Naples: Liguori, 1989), 275–94; Peter DeSa Wiggins, *Figures in Ariosto's Tapestry: Character and Design in the "Orlando furioso"* (Baltimore: The Johns Hopkins University Press, 1986), esp. 161–204; Wiley Feinstein, "Bradamante in Love: Some Postfeminist Considerations on Ariosto," *Forum Italicum* 22 (1988): 48–59; Juliana Schiesari, "The Domestication of Woman in *Orlando furioso*" 42 and 43, or a Snake is Being Beaten," *Stanford Italian Review* 10 (1991): 123–43; Miranda Johnson-Haddad, "'Like the Moon it Renews Itself': The Female Body as Text in Dante, Ariosto, and Tasso," *Stanford Italian Review* 11 (1992): 203–15; Melinda Gough, "'Her filthy feature open showne' in Ariosto, Spenser, and *Much Ado about Nothing*," *SEL 1500–1900* 39 (1999): 41–67. See also note 9 below. For male sexuality and gender identity in the poem see McLucas, "Ariosto and the Androgyne"; Elizabeth Jane Bellamy, *Translations of Power: Narcissism and the Unconscious in Epic History* (Ithaca: Cornell University Press, 1992); Valeria Finucci, "The Masquerade of Masculinity: Astolfo and Jocondo in *Orlando furioso*, canto 28," in *Renaissance Transactions*, ed. eadem, 215–45; Marc Schacter, "'Egli s'innamorò del suo valore': Leone, Bradamante and Ruggiero in the 1532 *Orlando furioso*," *MLN* 115 (2000): 64–79.

(I mean the ancients) don't want to let women get on top and do as much as they can push them to the bottom [*Non le vorrian lasciar venir di sopra, / e quanto puon, fan per cacciarle al fondo*]. Almost as if the honor of women obscured their own, like fog the sun. (37.1–3)[4]

More impressive than the assertion of female merit — common in the contemporary (almost exclusively male) humanist discourse "in defense of women"[5] — is the aggressive exhortation to women to take up the pen on their own behalf.[6] More striking still is the reason given for this exhortation:

---

[4] This and all future citations are from Ludovico Ariosto, *Orlando furioso*, ed. E. Bigi, 2 vols., (Milan: Rusconi, 1982); translations are mine.

[5] On the Renaissance "defense of women" and the larger *querelles des femmes* to which it is connected, see Ruth Kelso, *Doctrine for the Lady of the Renaissance* (Urbana: University of Illinois Press, 1956); Ian McLean, *The Renaissance Notion of Woman* (Cambridge: Cambridge University Press, 1980); Joan Gadol Kelly, "Early Feminist Theory and the *Querelle des Femmes*," in eadem, *Women, History and Theory* (Chicago: University of Chicago Press, 1984), 65–109; Constance Jordan, "Feminism and the Humanists: The Case of Sir Thomas Elyot's *Defence of Good Women*," *Renaissance Quarterly* 36 (1983): 181–201, and eadem, *Renaissance Feminism: Literary Texts and Political Models* (Ithaca: Cornell University Press, 1990); Benson, *Renaissance Woman*. For pro-feminist writings in the courts of Ferrara and Mantova under the patronage of Isabella d'Este, see Conor Fahy, "Three Early Renaissance Treatises on Women", *Italian Studies* 11 (1956): 30–55; Werner Gundersheimer, "Bartolomeo Goggio: A Feminist in Renaissance Ferrara," *Renaissance Quarterly* 33 (1980): 175–200; Deanna Shemek, "In Continuous Expectation: Isabella d'Este's Epistolary Desire," in *Phæthon's Children: The Este Court and its Culture in Early Modern Ferrara*, ed. D. Looney and eadem (Tempe: MRTS, forthcoming). On the historical condition of women in the early modern period, see, inter alia, Joan Kelly, "Did Women Have a Renaissance?" in eadem, *Women, History and Theory*, 19–50; Christiane Klapisch-Zuber, *Women, Family, and Ritual in Renaissance Italy*, trans. L. G. Cochrane (Chicago: University of Chicago Press, 1985); Margaret L. King, *Women of the Renaissance* (Chicago: University of Chicago Press, 1991); Merry E. Wiesner, *Women and Gender in Early Modern Europe*, 2nd ed. (Cambridge: Cambridge University Press, 2000). See also the essays in *Rewriting the Renaissance: The Discovery of Sexual Difference in Early Modern Europe*, ed. Margaret Ferguson, Maureen Quilligan, and Nancy Vickers (Chicago: University of Chicago Press, 1986); and *Refiguring Woman: Perspectives on Gender and the Italian Renaissance*, ed. Marilyn Migiel and Juliana Schiesari (Ithaca: Cornell University Press, 1991).

[6] From Boccaccio's *De Mulieribus Claris* (1361) forward, the genre of defenses of women was largely carried out by men (*pace* Christine de Pizan). Literary treatments, including the *Decameron*, sometimes have female narrators speak for male authors. In book 3 of Castiglione's *Cortegiano* female characters instigate the debate, but men carry it out (Baldassare Castiglione, *Il libro del Cortegiano*, in *Opere di Baldassare Castiglione, Giovanni della Casa, Benvenuto Cellini*, ed. C. Cordié [Milan and Naples: Ricciardi, 1960]). Despite his overt position, of course, Ariosto does this as well.

male writers are guilty of a blind envy (*invidia*: 37.2.4, 6.8, 23.3; cf. 37.12.4, 20.1, and 20.2.8), toward women which consistently leads them to hide the other sex's accomplishments even as they appropriate all earthly glory to themselves and their brethren. And this exclusionary behavior is couched in an evidently sexualized language which places "men on top" and women "below" (3.5–6). The proem, in other words, clearly anticipates a number of key themes and problems central to feminist and gender studies in our own times: the systematic repression and exclusion of women by men; the use of invidious misogynist attacks to perpetuate a patriarchal regime; the formation of an elite "homosocial" community dedicated to the perpetuation of its own preeminence and constituted precisely through its exclusion of the sexually-defined other;[7] the positing of an empowering female writing as a partial remedy to male power-plays.

Moreover, the radical critique of male envy and the equally radical solution proposed in the proem is then dramatically borne out by the narrative episode which takes up the balance of the canto:[8] the tale of the rise and fall of the patriarchal, misogynist regime of the giant Marganorre, which translates into openly political terms the literary question raised at the outset. The explicit hinge between the proem and the story is the case of the woman-warriors,[9] Marfisa and Bradamante, whose deeds have remained too hidden, too secret (23–24). As the tale unfolds, connections multiply: the villainous giant has propagated a law that excludes women from his city *and* exposes

---

[7] Cf. Eve Kosofsky Sedgwick, *Between Men: English Literature and Male Homosocial Desire* (New York: Columbia University Press, 1985).

[8] Cf. Benson, *Renaissance Woman*, 139. For the signifying economy of Ariostan interlace, including discussion of the function of the proems and the "episodes," with bibliography, see A.R. Ascoli, *Ariosto's Bitter Harmony: Crisis and Evasion in the Italian Renaissance* (Princeton: Princeton University Press, 1987): 101–7, 295–301, 391–93; idem, "Il segreto di Erittonio," 53 and 70 n. 5; idem, "Faith as Cover-Up: Ariosto's *Orlando furioso*, Canto 21, and Machiavellian Ethics," *I Tatti Studies in the Renaissance* 8 (1999): 135–70; and idem, "Ariosto and the 'Fier Pastor': Form and History in *Orlando furioso*," *Renaissance Quarterly* 54 (2001): 487–522.

[9] For the topos of the "woman-warrior" see Lillian Robinson, *Monstrous Regiment: The Lady Knight in Sixteenth-Century Epic* (New York: Garland, 1985), 121–90; Margaret Tomalin, *The Fortunes of the Warrior Heroine in Italian Literature* (Ravenna: Longo, 1982), 94–117; Carol Rupprecht, "The Martial Maid and the Challenge of Androgyny," *Spring* (1974): 269–93; John McLucas, "Amazon, Sorceress, and Queen: Women and War in the Aristocratic Literature of Sixteenth-Century Italy," *The Italianist* 8 (1988): 33–55; Thomas Roche, "Ariosto's Marfisa or Camilla Domesticated," *MLN* 103 (1988): 113–33; Bellamy, *Translations of Power*.

them, literally ripping open their dresses to reveal the pudenda, "their secret things [le cose / secrete lor]" (27.7–8), just as male poets deliberately hide the good of women and show the bad. His defeat by Marfisa and Bradamante (accompanied by Ruggiero) leads to the establishment of a regime controlled by women, in which the traditional gender hierarchy is fully reversed. Here, an attack on the envious abuses of male poets; there, the defeat of political patriarchy. Here a counter-Republic of female letters; there, the foundation of a new *polis* where women rightly rule and men justly submit.

Before joining the substantial, though not uncontested, chorus of critics who see in the *Furioso* a genuine, even historic, innovation in the treatment of women,[10] however, let us consider a little more carefully the position that Ariosto — or at least his textual self, the notoriously ubiquitous narrative "I" of the *Furioso* — occupies in relation to a group, the envious male poets, with which he has an obvious affinity both by gender and by vocation. The potential "conflict of interest" of being a male author who indicts male authors as a class is clearly evident to the Ariostan narrator, who goes to some lengths to exempt himself and a number of others from the accusations of pervasive male blindness that he initially levels at his colleagues.

This process goes well beyond the fact that, simply in writing stanzas 1–3 of canto 37, the narrator has apparently achieved an insight that distinguishes him from a typical male perspective. Despite referring to invidious male writers in a universalizing present tense (used ten times in stanzas 2 and 3), he also deploys an aside to relegate the offenders to classical times ("I mean the ancients"), implying that things are different with him and other moderns. The point is then reinforced when, in the succeeding stanzas, he provides a list of *sixteen* contemporary male poets who celebrate women openly (7-13). The result — paradoxically — is that the radical critique of male misogyny is compromised and the stated justification for female authorship is potentially evacuated.

---

[10] Santoro, "'Rinaldo ebbe il consenso universale';" idem, "L'Angelica del 'Furioso';" idem, "Un'addizione esemplare"; Wiggins, *Figures in Ariosto's Tapestry*; McLucas, "Ariosto and the Androgyne"; Brand, "The Marganorre Episode"; Benson, *Renaissance Woman*; Jordan, "Writing beyond the Querelle"; Marilyn Migiel, "Olimpia's Secret Weapon: Gender, War, and Hermeneutics in Ariosto's *Orlando Furioso*," *Critical Matrix* 9 (1995): 21–44. However, Günsburg, "'Donna liberata?'," 19 and passim; Feinstein, "Bradamante in Love"; and Finucci, *The Lady Vanishes*, argue that Ariosto's pro-feminism is consistently undermined. For a "balanced" approach, see Durling, *Figure of the Poet*; Shemek, "Of Women, Knights, Arms, and Love," and *Ladies Errant*; and Sartini-Blum, "Pillars of Virtue."

Thus far we might conclude that the narrator is at worst guilty of a bland hypocrisy and at best is indulging in an unconvincing meliorism that flies in the face of his own initially darker perceptions. However, a more telling indication that the overt Ariostan feminism may be concealing some dark secrets of its own comes very near the beginning of the tale proper, when Marfisa and Bradamante encounter three women by the side of the road, squatting in a desperately embarrassed attempt to conceal the "the awful, shameful spectacle" (28.1) of those "secret things," which, the narrator says "as much as it can, Nature hides" (29.8). The representation of the women's plight alone suggests that the narrator may be playing a double game. Immediately after strenuously recommending that women expose their hidden talents and virtues to the light, and offering to do so himself (24), he brings before us women who must struggle vainly to keep the mark of their biological sex hidden from view. In other words, just like the other envious male poets, he is uncovering the "unclean [*immondo*]" of women for public spectacle (28.1).[11]

The situation is further complicated when the narrator deploys a curious mythological simile to describe the unhappy condition of three women:

They [Marfisa, Bradamante, and Ruggiero] came upon three women who had had their dresses shortened up to the navel by who knows what discourteous person, and who, for lack of any better way of concealing themselves [*celarsi*], sat on the earth [*sedean in terra*], and dared not stand up. / Like that son of Vulcan who came forth from the dust without mother into life, and whom Pallas gave to Aglauro — too bold in looking [*al veder troppo ardita*] — to be nurtured, kept his ugly feet hidden by sitting [*sedendo i brutti piedi nascosi*] on the quadriga first designed [*ordita*] by him, so those three young women kept their secret things hidden by staying seated [*le cose / secrete lor tenean, sedendo, ascose*] (26.3, 5–8; 27.1–8).

---

[11] That such a reading was possible apparently occurred to an early commentator of the canto, Girolamo Ruscelli (cited by Brand, "The Marganorre Episode," 36). My point, of course, is that the text creates a contrast between the narrator's condemnation of misogynist male writers at the outset, and his own later reference to the "immondo" of Ullania and her comrades. The characters are attempting, one supposes with mixed success, to keep their private parts from view (stanza 26, quoted below), but the text itself displays them as an "awful shameful spectacle" and represents them figuratively, as we will see more clearly below, through the comparison with Ericthonius's serpentine lower limbs.

The "son of Vulcan" refers periphrastically to a mythological character named Ericthonius. By saying that he "came out of the dust without mother into life," Ariosto alludes to his being the product of Vulcan's failed attempt to rape Pallas Athena, when the lame god of fire and forge ejaculated onto the thigh of the chaste goddess of weaving and wisdom. The sperm then trickled down to earth, where it gave rise to a monstrous son, namely Ericthonius, whose lower limbs ("ugly feet") were — in the versions of the myth which Ariosto follows most closely here — serpentine, and thus particularly susceptible to being interpreted as phallic.[12] However, as I will show as I proceed (see especially note 57 below and related text), the narrator deliberately complicates the issue by suggesting that snakes can also be a figure of a specifically female sexuality. After Ericthonius's birth, Pallas assumed responsibility for the child of which she was ostentatiously *not* the mother, giving him into the care of the over-curious nursemaid, Aglauro, whose illicit viewing of his lower body led to her petrification. The final element of the story alluded to by Ariosto is Ericthonius's invention of a covered conveyance, the "quadriga," to hide his deformity.

This is indeed a complex and perverse way of figuring the women's shame. For now, let me call attention to a number of elements that link the narrator ever more closely to the envious writers from whom he initially distinguishes

---

[12] The version of the myth closest to Ariosto's is that of Hyginus (*Fabulae*, 166; *Poetica Astronomica*, 2.13, in M. Grant, ed., *The Myths of Hyginus* [Lawrence: University of Kansas Publications, 1960]). Other important redactions that Ariosto might have known are Boccaccio (*Genealogia Deorum Gentilium Libri*, ed. V. Romano, 2 vols. [Bari: Laterza, 1951], 2:625); Fulgentius (*Mythologiarum Libri Tres*, in idem, *Opera*, ed. R. Helm, rev. J. Preaux [Stuttgart: Teubne, 1970], 2.11:51–52); and Apollodorus (*The Library*, ed. James Frazier, 2 vols., Loeb Classical Library [London: Heinemman, 1921]), vol. 2:3.14.6). Ovid (*Metamorphoses*, ed. and trans. F. J. Miller, 3rd ed., Loeb Classical Library 42 [Cambridge, MA: Harvard University Press, 1977], 2.552–62, 755–7) offers a different version of the myth, in which a serpent is seen lying next to the baby Ericthonius (561: "infantemque vident adporrectumque draconem"), but influenced the simile in other ways (see note 59 below). For additional information, see B. Powell, *Ericthonius and the Three Daughters of Cecrops*, Cornell Studies in Classical Literature 17 (Ithaca: The MacMillan Company, 1906).

The phallic connotations of serpentine imagery have, of course, been especially highlighted by Freudian critics and thus their invocation might seem anachronistic. I would argue, however, that the Ariostan narrator assumes that an image of a male character hiding the shame of his lower body would first have implied — as much for his readers as for a twenty-first century critic — the presence of male genitalia, however deformed, especially in light of the myth of attempted rape that lies behind the reference. As we will see, later references in the canto identify the hyperphallic figure of Marganorre with snakes as well.

himself, while continuing to imply that there is something truly monstrous in that envy:

i. all women are now shown to have something to hide;
ii. what they have to hide is shown to be intrinsic to their biological being — the "immondo" of their genitalia;
iii. the hidden quality being revealed is not merely grotesque, but in fact menacing (the threat of the petrification that befell Aglauro is transferred to their "cose secrete");
iv. rather than being given an autonomous, specifically female space of their own (as the proem suggests), the women are defined by comparison to a man (at least a male);
v. but where the shame of the women comes from the display of an intrinsic and normal part of their anatomy, the male point of comparison is a monster, implying (ironically) that men are the norm and women deformed versions of them, genitally and otherwise;[13]
vi. even in his monstrosity, Ericthonius's "shame" is specifically shown to be creative — he invents the "quadriga" (the four-horse chariot) — in a way that the women's is not — the best they can come up with is an undignified squatting.

Ericthonius's secret — his monstrous deformity — is, in other words, a figure not only for the women's predicament, but also for the underlying ambivalence of the Ariostan narrator toward the women he overtly praises. That ambivalence is itself twofold, in the sense that it points doubly toward the hidden monstrosity of female sexuality and toward the monstrosity of

---

[13] As is well known, one strain of Renaissance physiology, deriving from Aristotle, defined women biologically as incomplete males, even to the point of arguing that the vagina is simply a penis that has failed to extrude itself (cf. McLean; *Renaissance Nation of Woman*, 28–46; Thomas G. Benedek, "Belief about Human Sexual Function in the Middle Ages and Renaissance," in *Human Sexuality in the Middle Ages and Renaissance*, ed. Douglas Radcliff-Umstead [Pittsburgh: University of Pittsburgh Publications in the Middle Ages and Renaissance, 1978], 97–119; and Thomas Laqueur, *Making Sex: Body and Gender from the Greeks to Freud* [Cambridge, MA: Harvard University Press, 1990]). While Ariosto alludes to this point of view in general terms, I see no evidence that he subscribes specifically to this account of female genitalia.

the male representation of women and their sex. Above all, the simile establishes that the canto's pervasive discourse on gender, which is articulated first in poetic and linguistic terms, then in political, military, and legal ones, is founded upon a primordial assimilation of and distinction between the male and female genital bodies, which in turn engages Ariosto and his readers with the most fundamental cultural representations of gender and sexuality.

In what follows, I will attempt to demonstrate in some detail how this ambivalence plays out over the course of the canto, continuously interweaving an authorial exposé of the strategies by which male discourse excludes women with an oblique Ariostan repetition of those very strategies. The question that guides my analysis is what, precisely, the narrator refers to when he speaks of male *envy* [*invidia*] of women, and how that envy articulates itself in and around the representation of the "secret things" of the female and male bodies in the canto (and, presumably, in "history").[14] To begin with, it is easy enough to see, from the imagery of secrets and exposure, sight and blindness found in both the proem and the simile, that Ariosto is playing on the conventional etymology of *invidia* as *non videre*.[15] Envy, in this sense,

---

[14] As this essay was going to press, I learned that when Ariosto refers to the "secrete cose" of women, he is echoing the language of a significant late-medieval, early-modern physiological and medical tradition with a heavily misogynistic bent, one which refers doubly to the "objective" secrets of women's bodies and the "subjective" secrets about those bodies which women are accused of keeping hidden from men. The relevance of the tradition is thus not only to the specific exposure of women's bodies by Marganorre (and by Ariosto), but also to the Ariostan narrator's proposal that women "reveal themselves" in a writing of their own. A key, if not founding, text in this tradition is Pseudo-Albertus Magnus's treatise *De Secretis Mulierum* dating from the late 13th century, with echoes in numerous later Latin and vernacular works. See *Women's Secrets: A Translation of Pseudo-Albertus Magnus' 'De Secretis Mulierum' with Commentaries*, ed. Helen Rodnite Lemay (Albany: SUNY Press, 1992). See also Katharine Park, "Dissecting the Female Body: From Women's Secrets to the Secrets of Nature," in *Attending to the Early Modern Women*, ed. Adele Seef and Jane Donawerth (Newark: University of Delaware Press, 2000), 22–47. I am indebted to Professor Park as well for personal communications that made the relevance of this tradition to the case of Ariosto clearer to me.

[15] Drawing on the derivation of *invidia* from Latin *videre* ("to see"), Dante punishes the envious by turning their metaphorical blindness into a literal blindness (the eyes stitched shut) in the next (cf. *Purgatorio* 14.82–84). Aglauro, who is one of Dante's examples of envy (*Purgatorio* 14.139), appears in 37.27.4 as "Aglauro, too bold in looking." For Aglauro, see note 59 below. Canto 37 is pervaded with imagery of blindness and seeing, including references to (1) light and darkness: I.6, 3.8, 17, 24.3, 27, 34.7, 86.7; (2) hiding and uncovering: 3.3, 24.5, 24.7, 26.7, 27, 29, 33.3, 44.7, 49.4, 59–62; (3) seeing and blindness: 27.4, 28.1, 29.2, 32.4, 35.6, 36.6, 37.7, 54.1, 77.3.

is precisely a deliberate blindness to the being and value of another, in this case, the gendered other. However, the primary sense of desiring to possess what another possesses, or to be what the other is — which would then be the motive force behind envious self-blinding — is less clearly defined. To judge from the proem alone, it would simply be a matter of men fearing that women, as a group, would outdo them in many areas. The simile, however, suggests that text is more specifically concerned with the differentiated anatomical features (the male penis; the multiple female genital organs),[16] which are traditionally understood to be the basis for gendered differences. In other words, though the text begins by suggesting that the differences of gender are cultural (women could behave like men if only patriarchal society would let them), the shift of focus to genitalia tends to take us back in the direction of a naturalized vision in which biological sex and the phenomenology of gender are identical, and where, to return to our principal point, envy must be understood in terms of the sexed body.

Looking at the problem in this way, however, raises more questions than it answers. To a typical reader in the post-Freudian era, the concept of sexual envy is concentrated around the penis, and is attributed to women rather than to men.[17] In this account, women are said to understand their sexuality as a lack or absence and therefore to envy the penis, the substantial objectification of a plenary male sexuality and power. Given the cultural subordination of women to men in the Renaissance, one would suppose that then too, even without Freud's authority, women should have been the envious, not the envied. Still, male *invidia*, the desire to eclipse, but also to appropriate the female Other, not only as concerns the cultural traits of "gender," but, in fact, qualities linked directly to biological sex, is overtly posited as the canto's principal concern, although what, specifically, is envied in the "cose secrete" remains mysterious.

To understand these questions better, let us begin by following out the ways in which the canto articulates its explicit, pro-feminist, agenda in terms of emblematic references to female and male bodies, and in doing so establishes fundamental links between the sexed body of the individual person and the

---

[16] While Ariosto does not specify the "cose" that women are trying to hide, he does designate them plurally (cf. Luce Irigaray, *This Sex Which is Not One*, trans. Catherine Porter [Ithaca: Cornell University Press, 1985], esp. chap. 2, 23–33).

[17] See, for example, Sigmund Freud, "Some Psychical Consequences of the Anatomical Distinction Between the Sexes," in *The Standard Edition of the Complete Psychological Works of Sigmund Freud*, ed. and trans. James Strachey (London: The Hogarth Press, 1955), 19: 248–58. For a reading of the concept in relation to Ariosto, see Finucci, *The Lady Vanishes*, 208–12.

figuratively "gendered" political body which sets out to define and to regulate persons according to their genital sex. We will then revisit the parallel "counter-discourse" through which the narrator, playing out his own male *invidia*, qualifies and even subverts his explicit position. My conclusion, which will be amply illustrated in a closing return to the figure of Ericthonius, is that the canto operates through an extraordinarily sophisticated double process whereby women's bodies are defined in relation and subordinated to a male norm, while simultaneously men appropriate to themselves and patriarchy the monstrous imaginative powers that they associate with female corporeality. Whether, in the end, the canto represents a critical analysis of this situation, or a blind repetition, or in some sense combines the two, will be addressed in closing.

To begin understanding the discourse of the genital body in canto 37, we need to begin with an intratextual excursus into another episode to which the present one clearly responds. I refer to the fact that the principal of the three women whom Marfisa, Bradamante, and Ruggiero encounter is one Ullania, who first entered the poem in an earlier adventure featuring Bradamante, the so-called "fortress of Tristan" (Rocca di Tristano) episode in cantos 32–33 (esp. 32.79–108).[18] Not coincidentally, that episode was also one of the four major narrative additions to the 1532 edition of the Furioso,[19] and

---

[18] As with the other episodes of 1532, canto 37 was composed in close relationship with precise segments of the first *Furioso* (see Ascoli, "Fier Pastor," 514–15; idem, "Faith as Cover-Up," 166–7 and nn. 36–37; cf. Brand, "The Marganorre Episode," 39–40). The proem itself is an *amplificatio* of the encomium that opened the 20th canto from the first, 1516, edition forward (stanzas 1–3). The story of Marganorre systematically inverts the episode of the "femine omicide" (cantos 19–20; cf. Giuseppe Dalla Palma, *Le strutture narrative dell' "Orlando furioso"* [Florence: Olschki, 1984], 143–45; see also Carrara, "Marganorre," 6–7; McLucas, "Ariosto and the Androgyne," 244; Shemek, "Of Women, Knights, Arms, and Love"; Benson, *Renaissance Woman*, 131–34). The episode should also be seen in relation to the proximate developments in the careers of Bradamante and Marfisa (for canto 36, see Ascoli, *Ariosto's Bitter Harmony*, 369–71; for canto 38, see note 64 and related text). Cf. Brand, "The Marganorre Episode," 41–44.

[19] For the "Rocca di Tristano," see note 20. The other principal two additions are the Olympia episode (cantos 9, 10, and 11) and the episode of Ruggiero, Bradamante, and Leone (cantos 44–46). All four represent male domination of and/or violence toward women, as well as the possibility of redressing the balance in favor of the latter. For Olimpia, see note 46 below. On the gender question raised by the Ruggiero, Bradamante, and Leone episode, see McLucas, "Ariosto and the Androgyne," 82–97; Shemek, *Ladies Errant*, 118–19; Jordan, *Renaissance Feminism*; Schacter, "Leone, Bradamante and Ruggiero"; cf. Brand, "The Marganorre Episode," 37–39. Finally, the four additions share other themes — especially the politics of tyranny (Dalla Palma, *Strutture Narrative*, esp. 210-15) and the *ethos* of chivalric "fede" (Eduardo Saccone, "Appunti per una definizione dei *Cinque canti*," in idem *Il soggetto del "Furioso" e altri saggi tra*

notoriously offers a highly problematized vision of gender identity.[20] In canto 32, as in canto 37, Bradamante confronts a gender-specific law that is harsh on man and woman alike, this one the product of male jealousy, like envy a vice of possessiveness.[21] The rule of the place, established by Tristano in reproof of the discourteous behavior of the jealous boor Clodione (32.82–94), is that only the most powerful (male) knight and the most beautiful lady who present themselves may stay in the fortress each night. Bradamante creates a crisis in it because, while her strength establishes her as the "best knight" (she has defeated three male warriors), the beauty she reveals in removing her helmet qualifies her equally as the leading lady (beating out this same Ullania). The episode has, in fact, often been read as an androgynous apotheosis of Bradamante as both perfect (male) knight and ideal of female beauty,[22] and thus as another sign of Ariosto's "progressive" views on gender (32.79-108).[23] Particularly significant for our purposes is that Bradamante, when she realizes that Ullania is now going to be expelled, comes to her defense with an argument that seems to offer an uncanny anticipation of contemporary ideas of gender as "performance" rather than as effect of biological nature:[24]

Quattro e Cinquecento [Naples: Liguori, 1974], 119–56; idem, "Prospettive sull'ultimo Ariosto" *MLN* 98 [1983]: 55–69; cf. Ascoli, "Faith as Cover-Up"). On the revisions in general, see Lanfranco Caretti, "Codicillo" and "Storia dei *Cinque canti*," in idem, *Antichi e moderni* (Turin: Einaudi, 1976), 103–8, 121–31; Walter Moretti, *L'ultimo Ariosto* (Bologna: Patron 1977); Brand, "The Marganorre Episode"; Santoro, "Un'addizione esemplare"; Alberto Casadei, *La strategia delle varianti: Le correzioni storiche del terzo "Furioso"* (Lucca: Pacini Fazzi, 1988); Ascoli, "Fier Pastor," esp. 512–17. Indispensable for a comparison among the three editions is S. Debenedetti and C. Segre, eds., *Orlando furioso* (Bologna: Commissione per i Testi di Lingua, 1960).

[20] Feinstein, "Bradamante in Love"; Charles Ross, "Ariosto's Fables of Power: Bradamante at the Rocca di Tristano," *Italica* 68 (1991): 155–75; Finucci, *The Lady Vanishes*, 246–50; Shemek, *Ladies Errant*, 95-104; Jordan, "Writing beyond the Querelle."

[21] Cf. Carrara, "Marganorre," 8–9.

[22] Cf. McLucas, "Ariosto and the Androgyne," 224–33. For androgyny in the *Furioso* see also Rupprecht, "Martial Maid"; Günsberg, "'Donna Liberata',", 19–20; Bellamy, *Translations of Power*, 112–19, 157–59. For early modern ideas of androgyny, see Jerome Schwartz, "Aspects of Androgyny in the Renaissance," in *Human Sexuality*, ed. Radcliff-Umstead, 121–31; and Carla Freccero, "The Other and the Same: The Image of the Hermaphrodite in Rabelais," in *Rewriting the Renaissance*, ed. Ferguson et al., 145–58.

[23] For Bradamante as a positive figure, see Wiggins, *Figures in Ariosto's Tapestry*, 192–204; Benson, *Renaissance Woman*; Ross, "Ariosto's Fables of Power"; Jordan "Writing beyond the Querelle." For another view see Feinstein, "Bradamante in Love"; Finucci, *The Lady Vanishes*, esp. 229–53.

[24] Judith Butler, *Gender Trouble: Feminism and the Subversion of Identity* (New York and London: Routledge, 1990); eadem, *Bodies that Matter: On the Discursive Limits of Sex* (New York and London: Routledge, 1993).

> I, who undertake to defend this cause [Ullania's claim to shelter], say: whether or not I am more beautiful than she, I did not come here as a woman [*non venni come donna qui*], nor do I wish that my activities should be those of a woman now. But who is to say, unless I undress completely [*se tutta non mi spoglio*], whether I am or I am not what she is? And what one doesn't know, one shouldn't say, so much the less when someone else suffers for it. (32.102)

Bradamante's assertion, amounting to the claim that "clothes make the woman," strikes directly at any presumed equation between biological sex and the gender roles one happens to be performing.

Ullania's reappearance at this juncture — where she is once again saved by Bradamante from a humiliating situation based solely on her female identity — might seem to be calculated to reinforce the "culturalist" view of gender implied both by the events of canto 32 and by the proem to canto 37. However, rather than reinforcing the androgynous ideal, this episode tends to subvert it, precisely by stripping Ullania of clothing, which in the "Fortress" had been an essential refuge for the ambiguous sexual identity of Bradamante (cf. 32.102-3).[25] Marganorre's law apparently demystifies the earlier equivocation about gender identity, emphasizing the "organic" proximity of biological "sex" and cultural "gender."

While Bradamante and Marfisa are not specifically subjected to the same humiliation as Ullania, they are, nonetheless, symbolically caught up in the display of female sexual organs. The key moment comes in their response to the "spettacolo" of the three women:

> The awful, shameful spectacle [*spettacolo enorme e disonesto*] made one and the other of the magnanimous woman-warriors take on the color that — in the gardens of Paestum [*giardin di Pesto*] — the rose becomes in springtime. (28.1-4)

The blushes of the two *guerriere* conform to the culturally prescribed behavior for women. The passage, however, is not just culturally but also genitally sexed, again through the allusive simile, in its own way as loaded as the preceding image of Ericthonius. The rose, especially when plucked, is of course a traditional image of the hymen, as in the extended simile in which Sacripante imagines himself plucking Angelica's hypothetical "rose" at the very beginning

---

[25] Cf. 26.80 and Wiggins, *Figures in Ariosto's Tapestry*, 190. On the "masquerade" of women as men in the *Furioso*, see Finucci, *The Lady Vanishes*.

of the poem (1.42.1–3). The garden is thus not only the traditional scene of sexual activity, but itself a figure of female sex specifically.[26] The identification is sealed by placing this rose in the gardens of "Pesto," Paestum. There is, to begin with, an echo of a traditional euphemistic figure for human genitalia as (male) "mortar" and female "pestle" ("pesto"; cf. *Decameron* 2.10.37; Author's Conclusion 5). More important still is an intertextual reference to the *Georgics* of Virgil, where the "biferique rosaria Paesti" ("rose-beds of twice-blooming Paestum"; 4.119) are explicitly under the supervision of Priapus, god of the phallus ("tutela Priapi" ["guardian Priapus"]; 4.111), and to Propertius, where the "odorati victura rosaria Paesti" (*Elegies*, 4.5.61) are intimately linked with the concession of sexual favors by young women.[27]

At the same time as the image of the garden is used to emphasize the biological sex of the woman warriors, it also creates a hinge between the defining locus of bodies sexed female and the political typology of the "corpus politicum" or "body politic," with the potential implication that there is a social and political form that derives from, or at least corresponds closely to, the sexed identity of the female person. This is particularly evident in the image of the three women seated on the ground (26.8; cf. 27.4, 8) in a valley (26.3) and sorrowing (25.5; 26.4) which echoes the female personification of Jerusalem at the beginning of Lamentations:

> How the city sits alone [sedet sola] that was once full of people! She who was the mistress [domina] of peoples is made as it were a widow [vidua] (Lamentations 1:1, cf. Lamentations 2:10).

Jerusalem, of course is the typological city-garden par excellence, for the Hebrews a symbol of the ordered realm of law which constitutes a home alternative to Eden lost (cf. Lamentations 2:6), and by Christians consistently etymologized as "visio pacis" (vision of peace), a typological figure for

---

[26] The idea of the garden as figure of female sexuality can be easily traced through a series of biblical references (for example: Eden as the scene of Adam's "seduction"; the *hortus conclusus* of the Song of Songs) and classical topoi (Page Dubois, "'The Devil's Gateway': Women's Bodies and the Earthly Paradise," *Women's Studies* 7 [1980]: 43–58; cf. A. Bartlett Giamatti, *The Earthly Paradise and the Renaissance Epic* [Princeton: Princeton University Press, 1966]. Compare Boccaccio's "Valley of the Ladies" (*Decameron* VI.concl.).

[27] *Georgics*, in *Virgil: Eclogues, Georgics, and Aeneid I-VI*, ed. and trans. H. R. Fairclough, Loeb Classical Library (Cambridge, MA: Harvard University Press, 1986); *Elegies*, in. *Propertius*, ed. and trans. H. E. Butler, Loeb Classical Library (Cambridge, MA: Harvard University Press, 1976).

paradisal peace in the transcendent "City of God."[28] The recollection of this passage in particular, which was cited more than once by Dante in describing his own native city-garden, Florence, as an abandoned widow,[29] is especially apt in the present context for three reasons. First, it links these women, and their sexual organs, to the prominent cluster of widows in the canto: notably Vittoria Colonna, her classical double Artemisia, and, we will find shortly, Drusilla. Second, the law of Marganorre resulted in the exile of the "tribe" of women from their city, on analogy with the Hebrews taken into captivity by the Babylonians. Finally, as we will now see, it sets them up in typological opposition to Marganorre's city, identified as a sexualized anti-Jerusalem. Having initially centered attention on female genitalia and their symbolic corollary in the political domain, the canto shifts focus almost immediately to politicized figures of the male organ, with a similar, or even more evident, tendency to create an identity between biology and politics. To put it bluntly, Marganorre and his realm are indirectly but surely defined in phallic terms. The all-male city has at its center a raised "sasso" (a free-standing cliff or small butte: Devil's Tower might give the idea), on top of which is a towering fortress (98.2–8). The long, hard, cylindrical shape of this strikingly phallic combination of nature and architecture stands out because it is placed in a decidedly non-mimetic context, given the absence of the walls and/or moat typical of virtually all Italian Renaissance towns.[30]

The fortress-tower is a domicile specifically suited to Marganorre (92.8) not only because he is lord of the place, but also because it mirrors his own dimensions. He is specifically said to have "a body of giant stature [*gigantea statura*]" (41.5). Moreover, precisely at the moment when he falls into the misogynist rage that leads to the founding of his city, he is compared to a serpent:

---

[28] See, for example, Guibert of Nogent, *Ad Commentarios in Genesim*, in PL 156.25D–26A; Isidore of Seville, *Etymologiarum Sive Originum Libri XX*, ed. W. Lindsay (Oxford: The Clarendon Press, 1966), 8.1.6. See Ascoli, *Ariosto's Bitter Harmony*, 268–69, for Ariosto's parody of Jerusalem as city-garden in cantos 33–34.

[29] For example, in Epistle 11 and *Vita Nuova*, chap. 28 (cf. chap. 30, and *Purg.* 6.113–14). See Nancy Vickers, "Widowed Words: Dante, Petrarch, and the Metaphors of Mourning," in *Discourses of Authority in Medieval and Renaissance Literature*, ed. K. Brownlee and W. Stephens (Hanover, NH: University Press of New England, 1989), 97–108; and cf. Ronald L. Martinez, "Mourning Beatrice: The Rhetoric of Threnody in the *Vita Nuova*," MLN 113 (1998): 1–29.

[30] Cf. Ronald L. Martinez, "Ricciardetto's Sex and the Castration of Orlando: Anatomy of an Episode from the *Orlando furioso*," unpublished typescript; also Finucci, *The Lady Vanishes*, 282 n. 10.

> Like a serpent [*serpe*] held fast in the sand by a pole vainly snaps its fangs... such was Marganorre,... far crueler than any serpent,... against the bloodless body [of Drusilla] (78.1–2, 7–8)

The image, of course, carries a sexual charge not merely because of generically sexualized and at times specifically phallic association with serpents, but also because it links Marganorre imaginatively to the "ugly feet" of Ericthonius.

Finally, the misogynist statute that now underpins the giant's patriarchal rule of a city populated only by men is ostentatiously inscribed on another totemic object, a pillar placed in the center of a piazza next to a church (119.1–4).[31] By this point it is not difficult to conclude, given both the sexually-specific nature of the law that is inscribed and the multiplication of similarly shaped objects in the canto, that the choice of this particular vehicle for this specific purpose was determined by its phallic shape. In other words, the pillar is no arbitrary, functionalist vehicle of a legal signified; rather it has the character of a simulacrum of that which lies behind the law of Marganorre, namely, the regime of the "phallus," expressed as "the law of the father," in a proto-Lacanian sense.[32]

An opposition, then, is created between the shameful appearance of the "impure" genitals of women and the ostentatious display of penis-surrogates. And it is an opposition that runs not only between private female and male bodies, but also between two concepts of the city as public space: the "city-garden" of Jerusalem, gendered female, and something that begins to look like its traditional nemesis, Babylon-Babel, the male gendering of which is marked by its famous tower, evoked by the "rocca" at the center of town. Marganorre is undoubtedly designated as a giant not only to emphasize his phallic stature, but also to link him with Nimrod, builder of Babel, who is consistently turned into a giant by the exegetical tradition.[33] Ariosto is

---

[31] Sartini-Blum has also discussed phallic imagery associated with pillars in the *Furioso*. As far as canto 37 is concerned, she speaks only about the proem ("Pillars of Virtue," 12). Cf. note 53 below.

[32] Juliet Mitchell and Jacqueline Rose, eds., *Feminine Sexuality: Jacques Lacan and the École Freudienne* (London: Macmillan, 1982), 74–85.

[33] E.g., Dante's Nimrod in *Inferno* 31.46-81. Ariosto's first description of Marganorre (37.41.3) verbally echoes Dante's characterization of the giants (*Inferno* 31.55–7): Ariosto, ed. Bigi, 1540 n. 41.2. On Renaissance gigantology see Walter Earl Stephens, *Giants in Those Days: Folklore, Ancient History, and Nationalism* (Lincoln, NE: University of Nebraska Press, 1989). The typology is central to the *Furioso*: Rodomonte, the archpagan, is identified as Nimrod's

clearly stressing the metaphors of sexual embodiment or "incorporation" by which political and ecclesiastical authorities of patriarchy designate themselves: e.g., the Church as the Bride of Christ (traditional allegorization of the literal and often graphic love story of the Song of Songs); the city as a woman mourning the loss of her husband-leader; and so on.[34]

The "climax" of this sequence of imagery comes in a complex simile that figures Marganorre's defeat, and with it the apparent collapse of his regime and the triumph of the women and a new form of politics:

> Like an alpine stream [*torrente*] that is swollen with pride [*che superbo faccia*] by long rains or melted snow — at times comes rushing ruinously down and drives before it trees and rocks and fields and harvests, but then the moment comes when his proud head slumps [*orgogliosa faccia gli cade*], and his powers are so taken from him that a young boy, a wench [*una femina*], can cross him anywhere, often with dry feet [*piede asciutto*], / just so it was that Marganorre had once made everyone tremble, wherever his name was heard, but now someone has come along to break the horn of such pride [*spezzato gli ha il corno / di tanto orgoglio*], and his powers so tamed, that even babes can scorn him, and anyone can pluck his beard or pull out his hair. (110.1–8, 111.1–6)[35]

Marganorre's defeat at the hands and sword of Marfisa is clearly imaged as a collapse from phallic gianthood into a cross between post-coital exhaustion and emasculation. The torrent reduced to a trickle, the "broken horn" and the "face" that falls; the depilatory and other humiliations that he now suffers

---

ancestor and carries his sword and his serpentine armor (cf. 46.119). He is also the builder of a tower (see 29.31–33), beside which Bradamante defeats him, stripping him of his invulnerable armor, in a sexually charged battle (35.40–57, esp. 46 and 50). This symbolic "castration" is what permits Ruggiero to defeat him easily in the poem-ending duel. His serpentine armor links him to Ericthonius and Marganorre (37.78) both. On Nimrod and Babel in the *Furioso*, see Jane Tylus, "The Curse of Babel: The *Orlando furioso* and Epic (Mis)Appropriation," *MLN* 103 (1988): 154–71; Ascoli, *Ariosto's Bitter Harmony*, esp. 254, 351–53, 371.

[34] For the human body as metaphorical template for institutions, see Ernst Kantorowicz, *The King's Two Bodies: A Study in Medieval Political Theology* (Princeton: Princeton University Press, 1957); and Leonard Barkan, *Nature's Work of Art: The Human Body as Image of the World* (New Haven: Yale University Press, 1975). For a cogent critique of the *corpus politicum* as specifically male, see Adriana Cavarero, *Corpo in Figure: Filosofia e Politica della Corporeità* (Turin: Feltrinelli, 1995).

[35] Cf. 37.92.1–6. An earlier image of Marganorre as a tree knocked over by the wind reinforces this one (106).

at the hands of children and, especially, the defenseless women he once dominated: all this suggests that the "tamed... powers" are specifically gendered male and sexualized.

With the defeat of both Marganorre and "phallocratic" patriarchy, the woman-warriors are able not only to redress past abuses allowing the women who once lived in the city to return to their homes — but also in fact to install an entirely new matriarchal regime, which, following the symbolic logic of embodied cities, should replace (male) Babylon with (female) Jerusalem, the law of the phallus with that of the womb:

> Before leaving, the woman-warriors [*guerriere*] made the city's inhabitants swear that husbands will give to wives rule of the city and of all things, and that anyone who dares oppose will be castigated with severe penalties [*pene severe*]. In short, what elsewhere is given to the husband, here is made statutory of the wife [*quel che altrove è del marito, / che sia qui de la moglie statuito*]. (115)

Nonetheless, in spite of the absolute victory of the women over a patriarch symbolically reduced to a desiccated, hairless castrato, it is not finally clear how much progress has been made over the course of the canto toward eradicating the invidious patriarchal system of representation and power denounced in the first three stanzas of the proem.

It is time now to turn back to the misogynist "counter-discourse" subtending the narrator's avowed feminism, whose presence we have already observed in the proem and in the Ericthonius simile. Let me begin with the exordium. We have already considered the opening passage, as well as the subsequent attempt to exempt contemporary male poets from its indictment. The balance of the proem is taken up with amplifying, qualifying, and illustrating the exhortation to women to take charge of their own destinies through writing, and, above all, with celebrating the poetic career of Vittoria Colonna — the best-known female poet of the day — as an example for other women writers to imitate.[36] The novelty and importance of Colonna's poetic project is brought home by the attribution to her of "a sweet style, whose better I do not hear [*dolce stil, di che il meglior non odo*]" (16.6). The echo of Bonagiunta da Lucca's celebration of Dante's "sweet new style [*dolce stil novo*]" in *Purgatorio* 24.57 transfers the categories of a heretofore exclusively

---

[36] Cf. Benson, *Renaissance Woman*, 137–38; Ordine, "Vittoria Colonna," 60–66 and passim. [See also V. Stanley Benfell's essay in this collection. –*ed.*]

male lyricism of idealizing love to a female poet, bringing along the implication of radical newness. Furthermore, by aligning himself with the Dantean Bonagiunta, whose sincere tribute to Guinizelli from the perspective of purgatorial afterlife unveils palinodically that *envy* which motivated the historical Bonagiunta's attacks on the "father" of the "sweet new style,"[37] the Ariostan narrator puts himself in the place of one who has known envy, but has now been converted away from it.

Nonetheless, as John McLucas first argued several years ago,[38] Colonna's exemplary function is profoundly compromised even as it is asserted:

> ... Shall I remain silent about all [women poets] or choose one from among so many? / I will choose one, and I will choose her such that she will be so far beyond envy [*invidia*] that no other [woman] can take it badly if I omit them and praise her alone. This one has not only made herself immortal with the sweet style, whose better I do not hear, but anyone of whom she speaks or writes she is able to bring forth from the tomb, and make them live eternally [*trar del sepolcro, e far ch'eterno viva*] (15.7–8, 16.1–8)
>
> Vittoria is her name; and it is quite suitable to one who was born among victories [*nata fra le vittorie*] and to one who — ever decorated with victories and triumphs [*di trofei sempre e di trionfi ornata*] — whether she stays [with her birth family] or goes [to her husband] [*o vada o stanzi*], has victory [*vittoria*] with her, either before or after [*o dietro o inanzi*]. This one is another Artemisia, who was lauded for her piety toward her Mausolus; in fact, she is greater still, in that it is a much lovelier work to draw a man out of the earth than to bury one in it [*por sotterra un uomo, trarlo di sopra*]. / If Laodamia, ... and many others deserve praise for having wished — at their husbands' deaths — to be buried with them, what greater honor is owed to Vittoria who drew forth her consort [*ha tratto il suo consorte*] from Lethe.... (18.1–8, 19.1–8)

---

[37] See Gianfranco Contini, ed., *Poeti del Duecento*, 2 vols. (Milan and Naples: Ricciardi, 1960), esp. 1:257–59, 2:481–83. For Bonagiunta's *tenzone* with Guinizelli in *Purgatorio* 24, see Giuseppe Mazzotta, *Dante, Poet of the Desert: History and Allegory in the 'Divine Comedy'* (Princeton: Princeton University Press, 1979), esp. 198–99. See also Ronald L. Martinez, "The Pilgrim's Answer to Bonagiunta and the Poetics of the Spirit," *Stanford Italian Review* 3 (1983): 37–64; Teodolinda Barolini, *Dante's Poets: Textuality and Truth in the "Commedia"* (Princeton: Princeton University Press, 1984), 85–123.

[38] McLucas, "Ariosto and the Androgyne," 237–39.

Not only does the narrator present numerous male poets before beginning the celebration of a single woman author,[39] but he also calls specific attention to the fact that he is "remaining silent" about many others (15.1–16.4), actually echoing the language used of the invidious "antiqui" (2.5).

Most to the point, Colonna's poetic project, as Ariosto represents it, hardly matches the female poetics proposed in stanza 2, since it consists not in a celebration of her own or other women's deeds at all, but rather in a lament and encomium of her late husband, Alfonso D'Avalos, with whose family Ariosto had a patronage relationship (cf. 15.28–29).[40] Her poetry, like the Mausoleum of Artemisia, is both a tomb for the beloved male object and a means of resurrecting it (him) as a famous name (16–20) in accordance with humanistic norms, which, however, were discredited for (male) poetry in general during Saint John's exegesis of the lunar allegory in canto 35.[41]

Even Vittoria's own name participates in the process of deflecting women's achievements and writings back in the direction of the patriarchal world of husbands and fathers. The "victories" signified by her first name are, in fact, not her own (18.1–4). The narrator emphasizes that they belong to the paternal family from which she derives and the family of the husband into which she has entered ("whether she stays or goes"; "either before or after") and she is said to be "decorated" by them, cosmetically as it were. In other words, the narrator's encomium focuses on the dependent place of women in a patriarchal economy within which they pass from the control of one man to another, from father to husband.[42] The process of reappropriating the famous woman into the patriarchal system continues through the curious associations that cluster around her surname. In the immediately preceding list of modern male poets is a reference to Luigi Gonzaga and the poems written

---

[39] McLucas, "Ariosto and the Androgyne," 238.

[40] McLucas, "Ariosto and the Androgyne," 240.

[41] For the consistently ironic treatment of the humanist motif of fame in the *Furioso*, see Ascoli, *Ariosto's Bitter Harmony*, 64–68, 199–221, and passim. On the lunar episode, see Patricia Parker, *Inescapable Romance: Studies in the Poetics of a Mode* (Princeton: Princeton University Press, 1979), 44–53; David Quint, *Origin and Originality in Renaissance Literature* (New Haven: Yale University Press, 1983), 81–92; Ascoli, *Ariosto's Bitter Harmony*, 287–94; Sergio Zatti, *Il "Furioso" fra epos e romanzo* (Lucca: Pacini Fazzi Editore, 1990), 142–49. Cf. Ordine, "Vittoria Colonna," 78–82; and Sartini-Blum, "Pillars of Virtue," 15. Ariosto may have had specific verses of the historical Colonna in mind. See, for example, sonnet 12 in the *Rime Amorose* (in Vittoria Colonna, *Rime*, ed. A. Bullock [Bari: Laterza, 1982]), which is comparable to *Furioso* 37.17–20.

[42] Cf. Jordan, "Writing beyond the *Querelle*."

in honor of his wife, Issabella Colonna, whose "columnar" constancy is reflected in her patronymic (9–11, esp. 11.5). That the greatest of modern female poets, Issabella's relative Vittoria, also bears the name "Colonna" from her male forebears is not mentioned explicitly, though it was obvious to Ariosto's courtly contemporaries. The connection is reinforced by the reference to Vittoria's being "decorated with trophies and with triumphs" (18.3), with a patent allusion to the Roman martial tradition of a triumphal column or pillar (cf. 119.5). McLucas goes further to suggest that this totemic object — long, tall, straight, and cylindrical — has a specifically phallic implication.[43] Given the subsequent proliferation of genital and especially phallic imagery in the canto, notably including the pillar ("colonna"; 119.2, 120.2) on which Marganorre's law is inscribed, I have to agree.

To summarize: the proem's architectural and military imagery of triumphal columns and elaborate tombs brings women, at least in name, back within the city and the political life from which male envy, nominally and otherwise, is at first said to have excluded them. In this sense, the proem clearly anticipates the political concerns of the Marganorre episode that follows. At the same time, however, the very language of Ariosto's celebration of women's language tends first to continue the invidious exclusion of women in favor of men as authors and objects of verse and, second, to reduce what women's names and verses we do hear of to male categories, male subjects, and, indeed, male organs. Against the radical claims of the first three stanzas, those that follow imply that it is women who envy and emulate men, rather than the reverse. In fact, when the danger of the "invidia" of a woman's accomplishment is raised again in the discussion of Isabella Colonna it is now attributed to other women rather than to men, with the further implication that it could be directed violently against the male narrator himself (15.1–8, 16.1–4, esp. 16.2).

The Marganorre episode does, as we have already begun to see, consistently focus attention on female agency and on communities either exclusively populated by women (the little village where the wives, sisters, and daughters of the male inhabitants of Marganorre's city have been sent) or dominated by them (as in the new city founded by Bradamante and Marfisa). Here too, however, there are invidious undercurrents at work. I will now consider three relevant moments in turn: (1) the "city of women" where the woman-warriors learn of the tyranny of Marganorre; (2) the story of the

---

[43] McLucas, "Ariosto and the Androgyne," 22, 237–39, 244–45.

vengeful murder of Marganorre's son by Drusilla which led to the founding of his all-male phallocracy and his misogynistic law; (3) the foundation of a "gynocracy" by Marfisa and Bradamante after the fall of Marganorre and his regime.

After encountering Ullania and her attendants, but before confronting "Marganorre il fellon" himself, the warriors stop in the village where the exiled women live, and learn of the nature and origins of the giant's vile rule. While the female inhabitants of the village are explicitly treated as victims of tyrannical injustice, the narrator, again, inserts an illustrative mythological comparison that, again, virtually contradicts his overt position:

> They found a little village placed on the ridge of a steep hill. They looked around and saw every place filled with women: some young, some old, but in such a crowd no face of a man appeared. / Jason, and the Argonauts who came with him, marveled no more at the women who killed their husbands [*le donne che i mariti morir fenno*], as well as sons, fathers, and brothers, so that in all the island of Lemnos no more than two virile faces were to be seen [*di viril faccia non si vider dui*], than did Ruggiero here, and those who were with him. (35.1–2, 5–8; 36.1–6)

Women who have suffered bitterly from an exclusionary male violence are, strangely, compared to "misandronous" women who pitilessly slaughter men.[44] The simile thus reinforces the obscure (female) menace already present in the comparison of the exposed genitals of the three women to the petrifying power of Ericthonius's nether parts. Moreover, as we are about to see, it previews a critical counter-discourse subtending the story of Drusilla's apparently justifiable murder of her new husband.

Once established in the little "city of women," the two woman-warriors and Ruggiero hear an account of the origins of this exile and the custom of humiliating or killing all women who happen into the giant's domain. Marganorre, it is said, was always evil by nature (44.5–8; cf. 41.1–4); the tale, however, does not offer direct evidence for this affirmation. Rather, the genesis of his active misogyny is attributed to the violent deaths of his two beloved sons, Cilandro and Tanacro, especially that of the latter (37.44–85). With evident parodic reference to the stil-novist and Neoplatonic motif of the ennobling love of an "angelic woman," the two young men were exemplars

---

[44] McLucas, "Ariosto and the Androgyne," 242.

of chivalric goodness up until the moment when they — one after the other — fell in love (46–47). The story of Cilandro is told in a few words: his inept attempt to steal a lady from her consort ends with his death at the hands of the other knight (48–50). The story of Tanacro is instead told at length and in detail (51–79). He too falls in love with a lady, Drusilla, who is already married. In order to avoid the sad destiny of his brother, however, he treacherously kills the husband (Olindro) and then constrains the desolate widow to second nuptials. Unfortunately for him, Drusilla's obsessive desire for revenge is more than a match for his own transgressive love. Realizing the need for secrecy and treachery in accomplishing her purpose (since as a woman and a stranger in a foreign patriarchy she has no other resources), she outwardly shows a "a happy face [*viso giocondo*]" (69.7) and assents to a wedding on one, apparently innocuous, condition. In order to appease the spirit of her dead first husband she invokes a custom of drinking from a chalice of wine blessed by the priest and then carried by the bride to her new groom — a custom that she spuriously attributes to her (grammatically feminine) "patria" or "fatherland" (60–64). Into this wine she contrives to pour poison with which she successfully brings about the murder of Tanacro and her own suicide. Before dying, she proudly boasts of her hatred and of her vengeance before Tanacro, Marganorre, and all the rest of those who came to witness the marriage, and she offers Tanacro's imminent death as a "sacrifice [*sacrificio*]" (63.7, 72.7) to the dead Olindro. Having witnessed the death of his second and last son, Marganorre goes mad with an obsessive hatred of all women (76–85).

Although the two sons are to blame for their own deaths, and although Marganorre's generalized response against all women is disproportionate to the events that set it off, nonetheless the purity and justice of Drusilla's revenge is ostentatiously contaminated in a number of ways. To begin with, an unexpected pathos is evoked in the reader by the scene of a devoted father — Marganorre — who loses both his dearly beloved sons (45, 76–77), and who finds himself overcome simultaneously by "love, pity, disdain, sorrow, and anger [*Amor, pietà, disdegno, dolore et ira*]" (77.1).[45] Given that from the outset the giant was represented as the personification of inherent and unmotivated evil, we must take account of this strong suggestion of more comprehensible origins for his misogynist behavior. At the same time, Drusilla's

---

[45] I would still agree with Benson's (*Renaissance Woman*, 141) rejection of attempts to turn Marganorre's "tragedy" into the canto's dramatic center.

vengeful murder of her bridegroom is not presented in an entirely positive light. For example, it recalls the parallel wedding-day homicide performed by Olimpia — not without implied narratorial criticism — in another of the added episodes of 1532.[46] Particularly striking is the fact that Drusilla asks for the complicity of an aged nurse, with the specific promise that she will be protected from eventual punishments, but then leaves her completely exposed to the rage of Marganorre (88–91).[47] In the end, all the protagonists — Tanacro, Drusilla, and Marganorre himself — seem to be equally the victims of that universal folly that afflicts all the inhabitants of the Ariostan "forest [*selva*]" (cf. 24.1–2). On the one hand it becomes increasingly difficult to assign moral blame to someone consumed (as Marganorre is) by an irresistible passion — and on the other it becomes just as impossible to attribute ethical superiority to someone (like Drusilla) who is ready to contaminate the best of causes with the worst of means.

The ambiguity of Drusilla — suspended between victimization and violent agency — is in fact given an institutional and even cosmic dimension that ties her, subversively, to the canto's thematics of gendered institutions, especially to the "corpus mysticum" of the Church. In a notable departure from his sources,[48] Ariosto displaces the scene of revenge from the clearly pagan

---

[46] For the parallels between Olimpia and Drusilla, see Carrara, "Marganorre," 2–5; Dalla Palma, *Strutture Narrative*, 143–45; and Finucci, *The Lady Vanishes*, 281–82 n. 10. Olimpia is, like Drusilla, ostensibly an example of faithfulness, victimized by male treachery. On closer inspection, however, she (1) is directly responsible for the deaths of all her male relatives; (2) murders the bridegroom who was imposed on her against her will; and (3) does all this in order to keep faith blindly with her unworthy fiancé, Bireno. See Wiggins, *Figures in Ariosto's Tapestry*, 116–26; Barbara Pavlock, *Eros, Imitation, and the Epic Tradition* (Ithaca: Cornell University Press, 1990), 149–70; as well as Finucci, *The Lady Vanishes*, 147-68, who rightly emphasizes the problematic attitude of the Ariostan narrator toward Olimpia. Among those who read the character more positively are D. S. Carne-Ross, "The One and the Many: A Reading of *Orlando furioso*," *Arion* n.s. 3 (1976): 146–219; Santoro, "Un'addizione esemplare"; and Migiel, "Olimpia's Secret Weapon."

[47] Cf. Brand, "The Marganorre Episode," 42.

[48] Plutarch, *Mulierum Virtutes*, in *Moralia*, trans. F. Babbitt, 11 vols., Loeb Classical Library (London: Heinemann, 1931), 3:551–55 (257E–258C); Francesco Barbaro, *De Re Uxoria*, ed. A. Gnesotto, in *Atti e Memorie della R. Accademia di Scienze, Lettere, ed Arti in Padua* n.s. 32 (1915–1916): 2.1; Castiglione, 3.25–28. See Pio Rajna, *Le fonti dell' "Orlando furioso,"* ed. F. Mazzoni (Florence: Sansoni, 1900; repr. 1975), 518–26, for Ariosto's blend of sources; see also Brand, "The Marganorre Episode," 35–37. Another significant change from the sources has the protagonist's name turn from "Camma" to "Drusilla," perhaps linking her to the poisoner empress, Livia Drusilla (cf. Ascoli, "Il segreto di Erittonio," 62–63 and n. 47).

environment of the sources into a "temple [*tempio*]" which seems instead to be a Christian church (89.5). This alteration shines a new and unpleasant light on Camma/Drusilla's suicide, which for pagan Stoicism would present no difficulties, but in a Christian context becomes an abominable sin. Moreover, in this new context the poisoned cup of wine shared by Drusilla and her unfortunate groom becomes a desecration of two different sacraments: that, obviously, of marriage, as well as that of the Eucharist.[49] Both sacraments, obviously, involve the (re)constitution of normatively male bodies (in marriage, two bodies mystically become one, with man as the "head"; in communion Christ's body is made present again) and, thus, in this sense too Drusilla is symbolically launching a stealth attack on the traditional Christian concepts of community gendered male.

That Tanacro is explicitly "sacrificed" to Olindro in fact constitutes a grotesque refraction of Christ the Son's self-sacrifice to fulfill God the Father's law, in which the living participate precisely through the communion cup. By enforcing her own revenge, through means which travesty divinely instituted sacraments, Drusilla usurps the role of the Eternal Father who alone, biblically, is capable of true justice. That justice, of course, is meted out in the two realms of the afterlife, Hell and Heaven, and it is no accident that with her dying words Drusilla first imagines herself in Hell, enjoying the eternal torments of Tanacro though damned herself, and then in Paradise reunited with her adored Olindro. In short, Drusilla is not only a woman who interposes herself between a father and a son, disrupting the order of earthly patriarchy, but also a symbolic threat to the patriarchal cosmos of the Christian God, who is at once, and self-sufficiently, Father and Son.[50] The opposed eschatological alternatives that Drusilla imagines could be said to define the divided attitude of a canto that overtly celebrates but then secretly condemns the violent initiative of a woman oppressed by men.

A defining moment in this systematic travesty of gendered Christian typologies comes somewhat earlier in the tale, as Drusilla plots her revenge. Even as she is inwardly consumed by violent hatred, she outwardly acquiesces to Tanacro's proposal that she should now marry the murderer of her

---

[49] Parodies involving the Eucharist and other spiritually symbolic chalices are common, abundant, and savage in the *Furioso*, for example in canto 21 (Ascoli, "Faith as Cover-Up," esp. 160–62); and in cantos 42–43 (Ascoli, *Ariosto's Bitter Harmony*, 327, 337). Cf. Sartini-Blum, "Pillars of Virtue," 20 n. 19.

[50] Another version of this reversal appears in canto 21 (Ascoli, "Faith as Cover-Up," 161–62 and n. 32).

beloved husband. As the narrator says, at this moment "her demeanor simulates peace [*simula il viso pace*]" (60.1). This expression is, in fact, a straightforward adaptation of the Latin phrase "visio pacis" (vision of peace), which, as we noted earlier, is the traditional etymological exegesis of the name "Jerusalem," the city-garden which prefigures paradisal peace. Drusilla is thus allusively connected to the typology of the sacred city-garden, gendered female, which seemingly anticipates the refounding of Marganorre's city by the woman-warriors. Given the context of simulation, and subsequent violence, however, the reference is clearly parodic, and tends to subvert the prospect of any idealized community gendered female.

The tale of Drusilla, in other words, acts proleptically to subvert the political utopia of the proem. As we will now see, it also retrospectively taints the poetic utopia of the proem, as her wifely revenge becomes a nightmare version of Vittoria Colonna's devotion to *her* dead husband. The implicit structural echoing is brought out first by the apparently incidental mention of the "columns [*colonne*]" on which the ark is set for this noble wedding (68.4), but then emerges more plainly as Drusilla suddenly abandons her pose as dutiful bride: "now here the sweet style [*dolce stil*] and mild changes in her" (70.3–4). Why should the deceptive and deadly "sweet style" of Drusilla so clearly recall the neo-Dantean "sweet style" of Vittoria Colonna, with which she nominally resurrects her beloved husband (37.18–20)? The implication is that women are as likely to put a new spouse in the tomb, literally and treacherously, as they are to resurrect an old one poetically and devotedly. Is the insinuation justified by the narrative facts? In the case of Drusilla the evidence is, as we have seen, equivocal. In the case of Vittoria, the explicit evidence runs exactly counter to the invidious implication. Thus the ultimate effect of this misogynist background noise is potentially double. On the one hand, it undercuts the explicit celebration of women; on the other, it undercuts the narrative celebrator himself, whose explicit "piety" toward women clearly conceals a dark and unmotivated envy.

The implicit return through the figure of Drusilla to Vittoria Colonna prepares the way for another recall at precisely the critical moment when the woman-warriors decide to replace Marganorre's regime with a gynocracy. I noted earlier that the law of the regime is inscribed on a phallic object that both expounds and embodies phallocratic patriarchy:

> The bold woman-warriors saw there, in a piazza next to a temple [*tempio*], a column [*colonna*], upon which the impious tyrant had had

written his cruel and mad law [*scriver la legge sua crudele e pazza*]. Imitating the example of a trophy [*trofeo*], they attached to it the cuirass and helmet of Marganorre, and next to them they had had written the law [*scriver fenno la legge*] that they now gave to the place. They lingered on long enough so that Marfisa had her law placed on the column [*fe' por la legge sua ne la colonna*] contrary to that which had once been carved there [*v'era incisa*] promising death and shame to every woman. (119.1–8; 120.1–4)

There is no doubt that this passage demands to be read in relation to the proemial encomium to Vittoria Colonna. Not only is the word "colonna" repeated twice, but its adaptation by the woman-warriors for use as a *trophy* of their victory over the giant specifically echoes the triumphalist associations given to her name (cf. 18.3).

At first, however, it might seem that progress has been made here. Whereas in the proem the victories with which the female poet par excellence is associated are not her own but those of her male relatives, here the celebration is of a "vittoria" won by and for women, which in turn gives rise to a city in which women rule and men submit. The matter, however, is not that simple. It seems particularly strange that when the women come to replace the male order with their own, they do not, as one might expect, cast down the pillar and replace it with a less ostentatiously masculine symbol of rule (effecting the same symbolic "castration" on it as they did with Marganorre's person). Instead, they link themselves symbolically to the triumphalism of classical patriarchy. Then they simply erase the words that codified Marganorre's law, and replace them with others that put women on top and men beneath them, inverting the gendered hierarchy of the prior arrangement, but leaving its underlying structure intact (one gender dominating the other with a continuing threat of overt violence). In other words, women may be empowered, but only in distinctly male terms, remaining decidedly "phallocentric" in their "statutory" rule.[51]

A final example comes with the punishments meted out to Marganorre for his misdeeds. Put in the care of the old nurse who abetted Drusilla's vengeance, and whom the giant had persecuted nearly unto death, Marganorre is stripped naked (like his female victims), enchained, and then subjected to

---

[51] Shemek, "Of Women, Knights, Arms, and Love," 96 reaches a similar conclusion. Cf. Benson, *Renaissance Woman*, 139–47 passim; Finucci, *The Lady Vanishes*, 289 n. 26.

the keen pricks of her sharpened goad until he turns "rosy red [*rubicondo*]" (118.6; cf. 108). This "contrapasso" submits him to the same sexual humiliation, the same markedly "phallic" violence, to which so many women were earlier subjected on his orders. In the end, Ullania herself forces him to climb to the top of a high tower, which is either similar to the one that marks his city as both Babelic and phallic, or identical with it, and then sends him leaping out the window and down to a messy death below: "one day she made him jump down from a tower [*giù d'una torre*] — and he made no greater leap in all his days" (121.6). In the context of this story and this canto, which from the myth of Ericthonius onward has continually called our attention to male and female genital organs, Marganorre's death takes the comic-symbolic shape of an ejaculation (cf. 19.69).

It is not, then, by concealing the deeds of women that the Ariostan narrator expresses his own version of male envy. Rather, by representing the female appropriation of military power and political authority as patently male and phallic, he subverts any attempt to affirm a properly female identity.[52] One might say, in fact, that women are made to undergo a "castration" in reverse, since a male member is symbolically added. In other words, from Vittoria Colonna forward, the female protagonists in the canto are consistently converted into "phallic women," a fact "embodied" in the column which bears the new gynocratic law.[53] The effect is to imply that, in fact, it is women who envy, and seek to possess, the male phallus, rather than men envying women and their organs.

In retrospect, the phallic reification of all female agency invests even the initial call for the creation of a female poetics. This point emerges through yet another echo linking Colonna's poetry to the pillar of patriarchal Law. The regime of Marganorre, we are told, is based on "a law, than which the worse one neither hears nor reads [*una legge / di cui peggior non s'ode nè si legge*]" (82.7-8). The allusion to that poetic style "than which the better I do not hear [*di che il meglior non odo*]" (16.6) is obvious, as is the retrospectively

---

[52] Thus, as Barbara G. Spackman observes in another context: "the fascination of the phallic mother ... is more reassuring than not for the fetishizing male fantasy" (*Fascist Virilities: Rhetoric, Ideology, and Social Fantasy in Italy* [Minneapolis: University of Minnesota Press, 1996], 22). For the "phallic woman" in general terms, see Mary Jacobus, "Judith, Holofernes, and the Phallic Woman," in eadem, *Reading Woman: Essays in Feminist Criticism* (New York: Columbia University Press, 1986), 110–36.

[53] Sartini-Blum ("Pillars of Virtue," 10–13) equates other Ariostan pillars with the "phallic woman" (cf. notes 31 and 52 above).

subversive effect on the encomium to the woman-poet.[54] In other words, it is not only the dream of a female *polis* that is "masculinized" at the end of the canto, but also the proposal for a poetry proper to women.

What should further interest us here is the rhyming nexus established between the reading of texts ("si legge") and the phallic Law ("una legge"). This link suggests the strong ideological charge of writing, its capacity for reproducing and reinforcing the premises of patriarchal society, even in contradistinction to the intentions of whoever is writing (woman or man as may be). This point also brings into focus the significance of something noticed earlier, namely that the law of Marganorre is transmitted by means of an architectural mimesis: the pillar not only states the law, it represents it, symbolically reproducing its phallic character.[55] Poetry, which has at its command the symbolic and mimetic language par excellence, becomes the privileged vehicle for disseminating that law and its emanations: the writings of Colonna are equivalent to the writings on the column, and both are nothing other than effects of Ariosto's male-authored poem.

At this point we are still left with a significant problem in understanding both the character of the Ariostan treatment of women and of the relationship between biological sex and gendered structures of power. On the one hand, the whole of the canto reveals that the Ariostan narrator, and perhaps Ariosto himself, are not the enemies but the exponents of an envious male misogyny. On the other, the explicit naming of male envy in the proem and the dramatization of its mechanisms throughout the canto allows a reader to reach such a conclusion, implying a genuine ideological critique of patriarchy and an innovative reflection on gender identity. This conundrum in turn brings us face to face with a chastening fact, namely that our analysis, though it has revealed the phenomenology of male envy in action, has not brought us any closer to understanding what men are supposed to envy in women. Rather we have followed the evasive dynamic of the canto, which deflects attention consistently onto the "unclean" of women, on the one hand, and their (envious) attempts to possess the phallus, on the other.

---

[54] An apparent opposition between the "worser" law and the "better" style is compromised by an intermediate term, namely the treacherously "sweet style" of Drusilla, and by Colonna's identification with the "colonna" of phallocentric law.

[55] This point is reinforced by the use of the word "statuito" ("established," "created as a legal statute") at a crucial juncture (37.115.8; cf. 68.1), suggesting an equivalence between the "statute" and the "statue," not to mention the gigantic "statura" of Marganorre (48.5). The word "legge" appears more frequently: 37.82.7–8, 83.2, 103.7, 104.6, 117.7, 119.4 and 8, 120.2.

Indeed, by suggesting that the biological penis of the individual man and the symbolic phallus of patriarchal power are not the same — that women use a "phallic" language and exercise a "phallic" power that is indistinguishable from the language and laws of men — the narrator implicitly exonerates the sex to which he belongs from the crimes of which he accused it.

The narrator, in other words, has exposed the "secrete cose" of women, while keeping the reader blind to his own secrets and those of other envious men. Or so it might seem, until we turn our attention back to the remarkable simile in which Ullania and her companions are compared to a male monster, Ericthonius:

> Like that son of Vulcan who came forth from the dust without mother into life, and whom Pallas gave to Aglauro — too bold in looking [*al veder troppo ardita*] — to be nurtured, kept his ugly feet hidden by sitting [*sedendo i brutti piedi nascosi*] on the quadriga first designed [*ordita*] by him, so those three young women kept their secret things hidden by staying seated [*le cose/ secrete lor tenean, sedendo, ascose*]. (27)

When I first considered this passage, I emphasized the way in which it reflects back upon the women themselves, suggesting that there is something intrinsically monstrous in female biology, that even at their most deformed men are more creative than women, and that, finally, women cannot (as proposed in the proem) be understood "on their own terms," but rather must always be defined in relation to the hierarchically superior male (body).

This is not, however, the only way to read the passage. What if, instead, we read it as a commentary on men and their appropriation of what belongs to women? That is, what if we consider not what it means to compare the women to Ericthonius, but rather what it means to introduce a male monster who can be assimilated to women, who in some sense expresses the hidden truth about what men envy in women? The emphasis then would not fall on the "natural" deformity of women defined according to their sex, but rather on the hidden monstrosity of men as they define themselves in relation to the otherness of Woman.

Let us begin with the fact that the myth of Ericthonius's birth is precisely one of male parthenogenesis: of procreation accomplished by sperm alone, without benefit of female participation. On the one hand, of course, this reinforces the motif of male efforts to separate themselves from women: not only the poets' exclusion of female deeds from their writing, but also

Marganorre's attempt to create an all-male city. On the other, in order to accomplish such a separation, men have to become like women, have to take on their enviable power of bringing forth life out of their bodies. Ericthonius, in this light, represents an admittedly deformed complement to the woman-warrior's appropriation of the phallus: he is the figure of what might happen if the fantasy of male uterus-envy was made real.[56]

This assimilation of male physiology to female is, in fact, specifically "embodied" by Ericthonius's serpentine lower body. While a modern reader of Freud might assume that because the focus is put on Ericthonius's lower body, because that lower body is serpentine, and because it is male, what is being hidden is the phallus, and what is being expressed is the normativity of male genitalia with respect to female. There is no doubt that the canto does tend to support such a reading, for example by comparing the phallic Marganorre to a serpent.[57] Clearly, however, the "mimetic" basis of the simile, beyond the simple fact of concealment, is that Ericthonius's "secrete cose" look more like a woman's genitalia than a man's, first of all because they are *multiple*, and then because, in fact, they clearly link Vulcan's deformed son to a much better known story of monstrous *female* power: the myth of Medusa, the snaky-haired Gorgon.[58] The most fundamental parallel between the two mythical monsters, of course, is the inverted specularity between the serpents that adorn Medusa's head and those that take the place of Ericthonius's lower limbs, legs and otherwise. As a corollary, the myth of Ericthonius, like that of the Medusa, is one of disastrous and petrifying sight: Aglauro ("too bold in looking") peers into the box that hides her charge and is driven mad, or, in some versions of the fable, notably Ovid's, is turned to stone, just like the

---

[56] For "womb envy," see E. Feder Kittay, "Womb Envy: An Explanatory Concept," in *Mothering: Essays in Feminist Theory*, ed. J. Trebilcot (Totowa, NJ: Rowman & Allanheld, 1983), 94–128; and "Rereading Freud on 'Femininity' or Why Not Womb Envy?," in *Hypatia Reborn: Essays in Feminist Philosophy*, ed. A. Y. Al-Hibri and M. A. Simons (Bloomington: Indiana University Press, 1990), 192–203. I am indebted to Julia Hairston for these references.

[57] McLucas ("Ariosto and the Androgyne," 241) makes the case that the serpentine feet are phallic, and links them to numerous other convincingly "phallic objects" in the poem (Marfisa's sword [19.67–69]; Bradamante's lance [35.40–54]). Cf. Schiesari, "The Domestication of Woman." A case can be made, however, that classical serpent imagery is ambivalently genital, between male and female. Consider, for example, the myth of Tiresias, in which the mating of two serpents effects a metamorphosis from male to female bodies, and back again (Ovid, *Metamorphoses* 3.322–331). Cf. notes 60–61 below.

[58] Cf. McLucas, "Ariosto and the Androgyne," 241; Finucci, *The Lady Vanishes*, 166–67 and 297 n. 15.

Gorgon's victims.[59] It then remains only to recall the obvious fact that the Medusa's hair, from classical times to the present, has borne obvious symbolic relationship to the female pubic zone.[60] In other words, by juxtaposing

---

[59] For Aglauro, see Ovid, *Metamorphoses* 2.552–561, 735–832; Dante, *Purgatorio* 14.139 (cf. notes 12 and 15 above). In Ovid, the sight of Ericthonius only precipitates what happens later (755–757). Other versions (e.g., Hyginus) have Aglauro and her sisters driven mad by the sight of Ericthonius. According to Ovid, whom Ariosto follows in this at least, Minerva punished Aglauro's excessive desire to *see* with the torments of *Envy* (whose effects are linked to a serpentine poison: see 760ff, esp. 768–772, 777, 784–785, 881) leading to her petrification by Mercury (830–832). From the other side, one of the traditional etymologies of Medusa's name links her to the thematics of invidious blindness: "quod videre non possit" (Mazzotta, *Dante, Poet of the Desert*, 277–78 and note). Finally, Fulgentius (*Mythologiae* 2.11) etymologizes Ericthonius as "certamen invidiae" (battle of envy).

[60] Nancy Vickers, "'The Blazon of Sweet Beauty's Best': Shakespeare's *Lucrece*," in *Shakespeare and the Question of Theory*, ed. P. Parker and G. Hartman (New York: Methuen, 1985), 95–115, shows how the Medusa myth gathers together political, sexual and poetic problems (109–12; cf. Ascoli, *Ariosto's Bitter Harmony*, 67 and n. 166–67). Most contemporary discussion starts with S. Freud, "Medusa's Head," in *Complete Psychological Works*, ed. Strachey, 18:273–74; cf. idem, "The Infantile Genital Organization of the Libido," in *Works*, 19:144 and n. For the Medusa as a figure of monstrous "alterity" in the classical era, see Jean-Pierre Vernant, *La mort dans les yeux: figures de l'autre en Grèce ancienne* (Paris: Hachette, 1985). For the relevance of Freud's discussion of Greek myths to their cultural context, see Philip Slater, *The Glory of Hera* (Boston: Beacon Press, 1968), esp. 17–20, 308–38. I am indebted to Slater's critique of Freud's interpretation of the Gorgon's power as the fear of castration. For Slater, rather than the absence of the penis it may be the "presence" of the vagina itself (or rather, the curly hairs that cover it) which incites such a strong reaction. See also Neil Hertz, "Medusa's Head: Male Hysteria under Political Pressure," *Representations* 4 (1983): 27–54; and Catherine Gallagher, Neil Hertz, et al., "More about Medusa's Head," *Representations* 4 (1983): 55–72. For the crucial, polemical role of the myth of the Medusa in contemporary feminist discourse, see first of all Hélène Cixous, "The Laugh of the Medusa," in *New French Feminisms*, ed. E. Marks and I. De Courtivron (Amherst, MA: University of Massachusetts Press, 1980), 245–64. See John Freccero, "Medusa: The Letter and the Spirit," *Yearbook of Italian Studies* 2 (1972): 1–18, for the erotic force of the Medusa in Dante (see also Robert Durling, "Introduction," in idem, ed. and trans., *Petrarch's Lyric Poems* [Cambridge, MA: Harvard University Press, 1976], 29–30); and J. Freccero, "Medusa and the Madonna of Forlì: Political Sexuality in Machiavelli," in *Machiavelli and the Discourse of Literature*, ed. A. Ascoli and V. Kahn (Ithaca: Cornell University Press, 1993), 161–78, esp. 172–78. Both Freccero, "Medusa: The Letter and the Spirit," 7, and Mazzotta, *Dante, Poet of the Desert*, 277–78, discuss Fulgentius's etymology of Medusa as "quod videre non possit" ("that which cannot be seen": *Mitologia* 1.21, ed. Helm, rev. Préaux, 33) in relation to the problem of interpretive blindness. For Spackman, in a reading of D'Annunzio that applies equally to the theme of male envy in canto 37, the real danger of the Gorgon is not that men might see *her*, but rather that she would see (through) them (*Fascist Virilities*, 101). For Medusa in the *Furioso*, see also Miranda Johnson-Haddad, "Ovid's Medusa

Ericthonius' "secret things" with the women's, Ariosto ensures that the Gorgon's genitally-based powers will be transferred from them to "him."[61]

The link between Ericthonius and Medusa is made stronger still by the pivotal role that Pallas Athena plays in both myths. Medusa, originally a beautiful young woman, became monstrous only after being raped by Neptune in the temple of Pallas, an event echoed in Vulcan's failed rape attempt. Pallas then sponsored and aided Perseus's quest to destroy the Gorgon, in direct and striking contrast to her behavior with Ericthonius whom she entrusts to the daughters of Cecrops for nurturing. Finally, the head of Medusa ends up mounted upon the terrifying aegis, the war-shield of Jove that Pallas bears on his behalf, under which Ericthonius had been placed by her for safekeeping.[62] This last event provides us with a vivid heuristic image of the process by which the Ericthonius simile serves the double function of, on the one hand, exposing and neutralizing the terrifying threat that female sexuality poses to men, and on the other, of appropriating its power for men. Medusa, of course, is defeated by a man, Perseus, precisely by exposing her to her own image, mirrored in his shield, while he himself has made sure not to see her. He then appropriates her power for himself by mounting it on that shield, and using it against his various enemies.[63] That this shield then morphs into Jove's aegis, borne by Pallas, elevates the process to cosmic dimensions.

---

in Dante and Ariosto: The Poetics of Self-Confrontation," *Journal of Medieval and Renaissance Studies* 19 (1989): 211-25; Finucci, *The Lady Vanishes*, 136–38, 158–67, and passim.

[61] Freud, "Medusa's Head," speaks of the "technical rule" by which the multiplication of phallic symbols always refers to castration. The appropriateness of such an interpretation for Ericthonius is reinforced by the fact that his birth arises from the sexual failure of his father, Vulcan (famous in any case for his unhappy marriage to the goddess of love, and for a potentially symbolic limp). I tend, however, to believe that while the identification of Ericthonius's private parts with those of the women may reflect a fear of symbolic castration, it is also a gesture of appropriation of positive female power (see the previous note).

[62] In Hyginus's second version (*Poetica Astronomica*, 2.13), both of the principal versions of the myth of Ericthonius are recounted — that he was a monster with serpentine feet and that (as also in Ovid; cf. note 12 above) he had human form but was protected by Pallas's serpent, which had descended from the aegis for this specific purpose. Immediately thereafter is told the story of Jove's gift of the aegis — with Medusa's head mounted upon it, to Pallas, creating a direct connection between the two myths that Ariosto almost certainly knew.

[63] Freud, "Medusa's Head," 273–74; see also Hertz, "Medusa's Head," esp. 30–31, 51 n. 9. The aegis actually appears in the *Furioso* in the guise of Atlante's shield (see Ascoli, *Ariosto's Bitter Harmony*, 166). For the allusive presence and function of Perseus in the *Orlando Furioso*, see Marianne Shapiro, *The Poetics of Ariosto* (Detroit: Wayne State University Press, 1988), chap. 3; Ascoli, *Ariosto's Bitter Harmony*, 248–50.

Pallas herself can be seen as another, less obviously monstrous, symbol of the same phenomenon, and one more directly evoked by Ariosto's text. One of the most puzzling features of the Medusa/Ericthonius comparison is why a female goddess would, on the one hand, persecute a woman (her priestess in fact) who was raped by a male god, and on the other solicitously protect a male whose birth is linked to an attempt to rape her. The "realistic" answer is found in the specificity of Pallas's own mythical identity. She herself is the product of male parthenogenesis, having — notoriously — sprung full-grown from the head of Jupiter without benefit of heterosexual intercourse. Her career is, in fact, defined by her subordination to her father, whom (as we have just seen) she serves faithfully as shield-bearer. One way of reading this myth is to see Pallas as defining the figure of the "phallic woman" whose powers — military, intellectual, and creative — are enviously imitative of men's. Ariosto presents us very explicitly with a version of this scenario in the following canto (38), when Marfisa — the "phallic woman" par excellence of the *Furioso* — who famously proposes to make her sword do the work of the male member (19.67–69; cf. note 57) — confesses to Carlomagno that her rivalry with the male *cavalieri* has been spurred on by *invidia* (38.13.2, 16.1, 17.3).[64]

As we have already seen, however, this kind of reading is one offered from a male perspective to mask something very different: the appropriation of women's bodies and powers for the purposes of patriarchy (and, indeed, Marfisa then subordinates herself to the patriarch, Carlo, as daughter to father [17.1–2, 19.8, 20.2]). Seen in this light, Pallas's surprising solicitousness toward Ericthonius could be allegorized as the love of a personified and feminized male imaginary for its own monstrous fantasies. She herself can be understood as a figure for the male appropriation of female wisdom and creativity, not to mention power.

This brings us back, at last, to Ariosto and the envious poets, and to the role that Ericthonius plays in mediating their relationship to the women they at once exclude and pillage. As noted briefly at the outset, Ericthonius is identified as a creator, the inventor of the "quadriga" (four-horse chariot) which enables him to move about in spite of his lack of normal limbs. This is not so surprising, since he is, of course, the son of the artisan-god par excellence,

---

[64] Since Marfisa's conversion is already in place in the first edition of the poem, the thematics of *invidia* in canto 38 may be seen, paradoxically, as a source for the topic as developed in canto 37. See notes 15, 59, and 60 above.

Vulcan, who often appears as a poet or artist figure in the early modern period, and, more cogently here, the protegé of Pallas, the weaver-goddess, who is also traditionally associated with artistic creation (e.g, Ovid, *Metamorphoses*, 6.1–145). In this sense he enters implicitly into analogical relation with the male poets, including Ariosto himself. Attention is called to this parallel by the use of the word "ordita," to "warp" or "weave," and, by extension, to create an orderly design. Ariosto uses this word frequently in a figurative sense: to refer to secret plots and, above all, to the interlaced textuality of his own work.[65] In other words, Ericthonius is positioned as a relay between the women with "secret things" exposed, and the envious poets, including the Ariostan narrator, to whom he is implicitly linked. His function is to transfer the qualities of the former to the latter, a point that is emphasized by the use of a female deity, and a metaphor taken from an art traditionally female (weaving is the one activity of Pallas that is traditionally specific to her gender) to mediate further his connection to the male poets. From this perspective, it seems particularly important that at the culminating moment of the poem Ariosto will choose to figure his own art, at once encomiastic and subversive, in terms of the woven tapestry of a woman, the prophetess Cassandra.[66]

The real secret of Ericthonius, then, is that he constitutes the hidden male counterpart to the phallic woman: an imaginary man with female genitalia — which now appear as the true object of male fear, and male envy. Unlike the phallus, which is constantly on display in the canto, as throughout the public world of patriarchal politics, the multiple powers associated by the text with female genitalia are covert and self-concealing: to see them is to be blinded by them. They correspond, figuratively, to Drusilla's stealth attack on patriarchy, rather than to Marganorre's blunt assault on all women, or, for that matter, to the defeat of Marganorre himself by the phallic woman-warriors. More to the point, they correspond, figuratively again, to the narrator's multiply indirect strategy throughout the canto: using an assumed mask of feminism to hide an oblique attack on women, and then using his portrait of female aspiration to phallic power as a blind for male appropriation of powers specific to women: the capacity to create new life from within the body, but also to "petrify," sexually and otherwise, the male imagination, and, finally, to generate potent figures of discourse through which domination can be exercised and extended.

---

[65] Ascoli, *Ariosto's Bitter Harmony*, esp. 161–62; cf. Durling, *Figure of the Poet*, 117–18.
[66] Ascoli, *Ariosto's Bitter Harmony*, 389–92.

This strategy fits into a discourse on power the name of which, but not its means or effects, was unknown to Ariosto. The phallocratic realm of Marganorre — and the successor, and equally phallocentric, gynocracy of Marfisa and Bradamante — are based on a traditional understanding of power administered through rigid and explicit laws backed by the threat of force. The secret of Ericthonius, a secret simultaneously exposed and concealed by the narrator, is that the most effective form of power is one that operates obliquely by co-opting those whom one wishes to dominate and appropriating their oppositional forces to one's own ends. Such power — which one might be tempted to call "ideology" — operates not through explicit law or violence, but through the very values, concepts, and above all, linguistic discourses that shape and constrain our understanding of ourselves and our place in the world. If, drawing on the figurative associations traditionally assigned to biological genitalia, we can call the first explicit type of power phallic, I might be tempted to call the second "vaginal," or "uterine." [67] In doing so, however, I certainly risk being accused of the same sort of categorical appropriation that the Ariostan narrator undertakes, and implicitly attributes to patriarchal society in general.

How then, finally, is one to understand the position occupied by a man, Ariosto, or myself, for that matter, who attempts to analyze the workings of male oppression and appropriation of women? There is a sense in which the logic that the canto employs in defining the mechanisms through which male envy operates also suggests that, in principle, the biological sex of a person should make no difference. The canto, in fact, can be read as pursuing a systematic analysis of the (biologically determined) sex vs. (culturally imposed) gender distinction. We begin with a proem that seemingly suggests that traditional distinctions between men and women are the constructions of a male-dominated culture that can be overturned by changes in behavior (men start celebrating women; women start writing for themselves). That position is then apparently reversed as the narrator focuses attention on the mark of biological sex in women, and creates an apparent identity between a male person (Marganorre) and a phallocratic state (identifying penis and phallus). This view, too, is in turn overthrown as it becomes evident that women can exercise a power that is obviously "phallic," while men can figuratively, apotropaically,

---

[67] I am thinking primarily of what Jacques Derrida, "La loi du genre/The Law of Genre," *Glyph* 7 (1980): 176–232, has called "invagination," the enfolding and enclosing of women and men alike within categories and assumptions that turn over the force of female metaphors and language into the collective keeping of male poets and their masters.

appropriate a power that is gendered female, returning us to a modified, and far from "progressive," version of sexual difference as discursive construction. We arrive, then, at something of an impasse: while biological sex consistently disappears behind its figurative emanations, those figures are just as consistently mobilized in the service of a specifically male social order in which biologically male subjects dominate biologically female ones.

The conclusion toward which our argument, and Ariosto's poem, finally pushes us, is that *there are in fact no women to be seen* in this canto: Vittoria Colonna, Drusilla, Marfisa, and Bradamante are all as much the parthenogenic products of an individually and culturally male imagination as are Pallas or Medusa. The extreme version of the opening indictment of invidious male poets who blindly conceal the accomplishments of women would be a poem — in some sense this poem — which substitutes the imaginary simulacra of women for the real thing. Of course, if the canto's analysis of how sexed bodies can appear only in figurative form is generalizable, this critique would be true of any text that attempted to define the body politics of women and men: only the nature of the fantasy would change, not the fact that it is a fantasy. What is intriguing and perhaps distinctive about Ariosto's representation of the male imagination as it plays over the bodies of women is that it treads a remarkably fine line between "performing" and describing its subject matter. There should be no doubt by now that canto 37 gives expression to insidiously misogynistic desires; no doubt, either, that the canto points toward the complex phenomenology of domineering male envy, including its own participation therein. In the end, and after all, Ariosto does not truly set out to expose the "cose secrete" of the women, which are not described in detail, and which in any case disappear immediately back into a figurative discourse of sexualized power.[68] What he does expose, instead, is Ericthonius's secret, the monstrous secret of the male imagination.

Albert Russell Ascoli
University of California, Berkeley

---

[68] Here I follow Judith Butler's reconsideration of the sex/gender distinction and her claim that the biological "fact" of sex is already a discursive construct, always folded into the ideology of gender (*Bodies that Matter*). On the specific "constructions" of genital sex in the early modern period, see note 13 above. Given the importance that this idea has played in some readings of early modern sex differentiation, I should note that while Ariosto clearly deploys the traditional notion of female physiology as an incomplete version of the male body, he does not, to my knowledge, directly refer to the notion that the vagina is an inverted penis.

Translating Form
Gender, Genre, Identity

Desire in Language and Form: Heloise's Challenge to Abelard

Marcelle Thiébaux writes in *The Writings of Medieval Women*, "Of all the forms available to women writers, none has been so necessary and congenial over the centuries as the letter."[1] Although this is particularly true in the case of Heloise, twelfth-century scholar, abbess, and letter writer, she, however, was not the most ordinary of medieval women writers.[2] Whether the author of the letters is either Heloise or another, it is evident that the "Heloise" of the letters constructs a definition of herself which is completely dependent upon her own relationships, both past and present, with Abelard.[3]

Although most current debate has focused on the authenticity of these letters, there has been some discussion of the relationship of the two protagonists in the letters. Most writers in this debate maintain that Heloise was trapped in a man's world, both as a cloistered nun and as a letter writer;

---

[1] Marcelle Thiebaux, *Writings of Medieval Women* (New York: Garland Press, 1987), xiv. Professor Joan Ferrante of Columbia University runs *Epistolae*, an e-database of letters to and from women in the medieval west, fourth through the thirteenth centuries [http://db.ccnmtl.columbia.edu/ferrante/about2.html].

[2] A favored niece of her uncle, Fulbert, a canon in Paris, Heloise received a considerable education, and later correspondence suggests that she was fluent in Latin, Greek, and Hebrew. Her letters also reflect her education, for they follow the rules of letter writing as set forth in the *ars dictaminis*, or school texts which set forth the traditional rules for the epistle. On her status as an author see Christopher Baswell, "Heloise," in *The Cambridge Companion to Medieval Women's Writing*, ed. Carolyn Dinshaw and David Wallace (Cambridge: Cambridge University Press, 2003), 161–71.

[3] There has been much debate among scholars as to the authenticity of these letters. This discussion is not intended to add directly to this debate. For a concise history of the controversy, see Glenda McLeod, "'Wholly Guilty, Wholly Innocent': Self-Definition in Heloise's Letters to Abelard," in *Dear Sister: Medieval Women and the Epistolary Genre*, ed. Karen Cherawatuk and Ulrike Withaus (Philadelphia: University of Pennsylvania Press, 1993), 82.2; and Constant J. Mews, *The Lost Love Letters of Heloise and Abelard: Perceptions of Dialogue in Twelfth Century France* (New York: St. Martin's Press, 1999), 47–53.

constrained to the formal epistle tradition, she used the letters to rebel and to express to Abelard her long-repressed desire.[4] For example, Peggy Kamuf studies the letters as the source for "narratives which stage the confrontation of a specific and active woman's desire with a social or symbolic order that represents no place for such a desire."[5] Linda Kauffman also sees Heloise's letters as an attempt to rebel:

> ... in all the texts in my study, passion is transgressive, woman is disorder, and discourses of desire are repressed. Their speakers are literally exiled or imprisoned or metaphorically 'shut up' — confined, cloistered, silenced. To speak of the mixing of genders and genres as a transgression of some inexplicable law is not mere hyperbole .... Transgression lies in telling, for each discourse in my book combines writing and revolt, defiance and desire. The writing is the revolution.[6]

I agree with Kauffman that the epistle is a form of tyranny over Heloise, but I believe that Heloise chooses to subvert her own prison, to turn it into a tool to strengthen the hold Abelard already has on her.

On the other hand, several critics do not address at all the important role the epistle as a genre plays in the complex relationship portrayed in them. Altman and Thiébaux do focus on Héloïse's epistolarity. Little connection is made, however, between the structure of the letter and its content, other than the fact that the letter was a convenient medium for her debate with Abelard. Nye does not discuss the importance of the epistle at all, but sees the letters as a philosophical argument between a male philosopher and his female student, in which Heloise, the student, proceeds to challenge Abelard's 'masculine' philosophies. Mews presents the idea that in these letters Heloise is continuing a philosophical debate that she and Abelard had begun

---

[4] See the following: Janet Gurkin Altman, *Epistolarity: Approaches to a Form* (Columbus: Ohio State University Press, 1982); Peggy Kamuf, *Fictions of Feminine Desire: Disclosures of Heloise* (Lincoln: University of Nebraska Press, 1982); Linda S. Kauffman, *Discourses of Desire: Gender, Genre, and Epistolary Fictions* (Ithaca: Cornell University Press, 1986), 19–20; Andrea Nye, "A Woman's Thought or a Man's Discipline? The Letters of Abelard and Heloise," *Hypatia: A Journal of Feminist Philosophy* 7 (1992): 1–22; Katharina Wilson and Glenda McLeod, "Textual Strategies in the Abelard/Heloise Correspondence," in *Listening to Heloise: The Voice of a Twelfth-Century Woman*, ed. Bonne Wheeler (New York: St. Martin's Press, 2000), 121–42.

[5] Kamuf, *Fictions of Feminine Desire*, xviii–xix.

[6] Kauffman, *Discourses of Desire* 19–20.

Desire in Language and Form: Heloise's Challenge to Abelard

years before.[7] However, we can see Heloise continually trying to utilize these same philosophies to translate the desire of her past relationship with Abelard into the present relationship. I suggest that since the only relationship Heloise has known with Abelard has been one in which he was her superior (either teacher, lover, or husband), she seeks the same type of relationship within these letters. To that end, she uses the epistolary form to encourage Abelard to recognize his "debt" and responsibility to her as a position of authority, since she can no longer hope for his erotic desire.

Throughout her correspondence, Heloise attempts to draw Abelard into a discussion of the past by bringing up recurrent images of her own self. A study of the letters will show how she refuses to forget her past relationships with Abelard, fusing the prior roles of lover, wife, and mother with her present role of sister in Christ. She presents a self-image of a hypocritical and guilty woman needing to be disciplined, as a woman who is inferior to Abelard, and, throughout the letters, she argues that Abelard should recognize his authority over her. This subordinate self-image is self-perpetuating and dependent upon her desire for Abelard. Since Heloise's desire is the driving force behind her self-image, she uses not only the verbal description of herself to drive Abelard into a position over herself, but also the epistle itself, which becomes more than a convenient medium for their discussion. Indeed, Heloise, constrained as she is, manipulates the epistle as a genre that enforces her own self-image and forces Abelard to recognize it as such.

Heloise's Self-Image

Heloise's multi-faceted portrayal of self-image in her letters is seen most succinctly in the salutation in her first letter to Abelard:

> Domino suo immo patri, coniugi suo immo fratri, ancilla sua immo filia, ipsius uxor immo soror, Abaelardo Heloisa.
>
> [To her master, or rather her father, husband, or rather brother, his handmaid, or rather his daughter, wife or rather sister; to Abelard, Heloise.] [8]

---

[7] Mews, *Love Letters*, 55.

[8] All citations of the letters, unless otherwise noted are from: J.T. Muckle, C.S.B., "The Personal Letters Between Abelard and Heloise," *Mediæval Studies* 15 (1953): 47–94; here 68. All translations are from *The Letters of Abelard and Heloise*, trans. Betty Radice (Baltimore: Penguin, 1974); here 109.

In this salutation, Heloise presents the mix of roles she once held and now holds in relation to Abelard. He was once her teacher or "dominus," but now as spiritual advisor of her convent, he is her father. He was once her husband, but now they have both taken vows, and he is become her brother. She uses relative terms to define her own roles in this relationship; once she was his student or handmaid, now she is his spiritual daughter. Once she was his wife, now she is his sister. Glenda McLeod describes how this salutation explains "that while Abelard may regard the past as dead, Heloise experiences her life as a continuum" ("Self-Definition," 65). She explains further that the past "colors the present and helps shape her life" (66). This blending of the roles of past and present causes the paradoxical description of self in these letters to Abelard.

The overriding paradox is the continual switch between Heloise's public and private lives: "In loving Abelard, then, Heloise's actions were condoned by both interior and exterior sources; the public and private aspects of her identity were united" (McLeod, "Self-Definition," 70). This love for Abelard, however, is of two natures. There is the public, chaste love which she has for Abelard, a love which a sister in Christ may have for her brother. The second love is a more private love, the love of a woman for her lover. Heloise addresses both loves within a single paragraph. She first reminds Abelard of their love for each other as spiritual brother and sister:

> Unde non mediocri admiratione nostrae tenera conversationis initia tua iam dudum oblivio movit quod, nec reverentia Dei nec amore nostri nec sanctorum patrum exemplis admonitus, fluctuantem me et iam diutino moerore confectam vel sermone praesentem vel epistola absentem consolari tentaveris. (ed. Muckle, 70; trans. Radice, 112)

> [And so in the precarious early days of our conversation long ago I was not a little surprised and troubled by your forgetfulness, when neither reverence for God nor our mutual love nor the example of the holy Fathers made you think of trying to comfort me, wavering and exhausted as I was by prolonged grief, either by word when I was with you or by letter when we had parted.]

The love she mentions here, "amore nostri," sandwiched as it is between a reverence for God and the example of the Church Fathers, suggests the chaste love which can and should exist between a monk and a nun. The next line, however, contrasts this relationship with their prior relationship as lovers, which, according to Heloise, is possibly more important:

> Cui quidem tanto te maiore debito noveris obligatum, quanto te amplius nuptialis foedere sacramenti constat esse astrictum et eo te magis mihi obnoxium, quo te semper ut omnibus patet immoderato amore complexa sum. (ed. Muckle, 70; trans. Radice, 113)

> [Yet you must know that you are bound to me by an obligation which is all the greater for the further close tie of the marriage sacrament uniting us, and are the deeper in my debt because of the love I have always borne you, as everyone knows, a love which is beyond all bounds.]

This second love, which for Heloise is a greater reason for Abelard to offer her some words of consolation, is the love they shared as lovers, and later as husband and wife. This "immoderatus amor" remains with Heloise, defining her role as wife and lover, while their mutual chaste love supports her role as his sister in Christ.

Heloise perpetuates this dual role in her second letter to Abelard, where she offers the following as the true incentive for her behavior:

> In omni autem (Deus scit) vitae meae statu, te magis adhunc offendere quam Deum vereor; tibi placere amplius quam ipsi appeto. (ed. Muckle, 80; trans. Radice, 134)

> [At every stage of my life up to now, as God knows, I have feared to offend you rather than God, and tried to please you more than him.]

Heloise recognizes here both the roles of wife of Christ and wife of Abelard. Of the two masters she has had, it is the master of her past, Abelard, whom she still recognizes as her true lord and inspiration. Because of this confusion of roles, Heloise is plagued by feelings of guilt and hypocrisy. She knows that she should be faithful to God, but she is still living her life for Abelard. Immediately after this passage, she requests from Abelard support, healing, and grace. Unfortunately, Abelard cannot offer these things. As her self-defining roles blend, she expects from her past husband, Abelard, the power which is offered only by her present "husband," Christ.

Likewise, in defining herself, Heloise's public role as abbess of Abelard's monastery and her private role as his former lover blend. Referring to her self, Heloise mixes her references, sometimes referring to herself alone, and at other times referring to the convent as a whole. For example, in the following passage, Heloise mentions the former private injuries Abelard had inflicted on her, but then asks for words of comfort and guidance for the whole convent:

> ... dum eius mederi vulneribus cuperes, nova quaedam nobis vulnera doloris inflixisti et priora auxisti. Sana, obsecro, ipsa quae fecisti qui quae alii fecerunt curare satagis. Morem quidem amico et socio gessisti et tam amicitiae quam societatis debitum persolvisti. Sed maiori te debito nobis astrinxisti quas non tam amicas quam amicissimas non tam socias quam fillias convenit nominari vel si quod dulcius et sanctius vocabulem potest excogitari. (ed. Muckle, 69; trans. Radice, 111)

> [... in your desire to heal his wounds you have dealt us fresh wounds of grief as well as reopening the old. I beg you, then, as you set about tending the wounds which others have dealt, heal the wounds you have yourself inflicted. You have done your duty to a friend and comrade, discharged your debt to friendship and comradeship, but it is a greater debt which binds you in obligation to us who can properly be called not friends so much as dearest friends, not comrades but daughters, or any other conceivable name more tender and holy.]

As Heloise demands of Abelard words to heal old wounds, the debt he formerly owed to Heloise alone has become payable now to the entire convent. This replacement of the entire convent for herself in her relationship with Abelard is evidence of her mental confusion of the past with the present, the private with the public. In the same letter, Heloise succinctly makes the demand that he repay to her alone the debt which he owes the entire convent:

> Atque ut ceteras omittam, quanto erga me te obligaveris debito pensa ut quod devotis communiter debes feminis unicae tuae devotius solvas. (ed. Muckle, 70; trans. Radice, 112)

> [Apart from everything else, consider the close tie by which you have bound yourself to me, and repay the debt you owe a whole community of women dedicated to God by discharging it the more dutifully to her who is yours alone.]

Desire in Language and Form: Heloise's Challenge to Abelard

Heloise is still mixing the public and private relationships she has with Abelard: since Abelard can no longer pay the "marital debt" he owes to a wife, he can at least offer spiritual guidance.[9] In this passage, however, it is a debt owed no longer to her solely, but to the entire convent. But she does not let him forget the debt he owes her personally, or his inability to pay it; instead she suggests that he can pay off this debt by offering some *words* to her alone. The constant replacement of self for the convent, and the convent as a whole for herself, reflects Heloise's perception of her past role as wife blended with her present role as abbess.

Heloise's blended roles represent a confused view of the different episodes of her life. This confusion is nonexistent in her mind, however, for they all share one thing in common: a distinct relationship to Abelard. When either first as a pupil, or as a lover, wife, and now abbess of the convent under his patronage, Heloise is dependent upon Abelard. This dependence allowed Heloise constant contact with a man who offered her at different times knowledge, both physical and emotional love, protection (literally, for Fulbert's anger forced Heloise to flee in a nun's habit to stay with Abelard's sister in Brittany), and eventually financial and spiritual support and guidance. Because the object of her dependence never changes, she allows her different relationships with him to blend and to become one.

Related to her blended roles of abbess and wife are the self-concepts of the chaste nun mixed with the image of the hypocritical harlot. Many times throughout her letters, Heloise discusses her conflicting positions as an abbess displaying her internal impurity before God, while men commend her for her outward purity:

> Castam me praedicant qui non deprehendunt hypocritam. Munditiam carnis conferunt in virtutem, cum non sit corporis, sed animi virtus. Aliquid laudis apud homines habens, nihil apud Deum mereor, qui cordis et renum probator est, et in abscondito videt. (ed. Muckle, 81; trans. Radice, 133)

---

[9] For more on the marriage debt and medieval theology, see Michael Sheehan, "Maritalis Affectio Revisited," and Erik Kooper, "Loving the Unequal Equal: Medieval Theologians and Marital Affection," in *The Olde Daunce: Love, Sex and Marriage in the Medieval World*, ed. Robert R. Edwards and Stephen Spector (Albany: SUNY Press, 1991), 32–43, 44–57 respectively.

[Men call me chaste; they do not know the hypocrite I am. They consider purity of the flesh a virtue, though virtue belongs not to the body but to the soul. I can win praise in the eyes of men but deserve none before God, who searches our hearts and loins and sees in our darkness.]

Just as Heloise is unable to put away her past roles as lover and wife of Abelard, she is unable to sever herself from the feelings of passion which accompanied those roles. These passionate longings and desire are still within her private thoughts and feelings. Because these desires remain, she retains still her former idea of self. When the role of the chaste abbess is placed on top of this former idea of self and its corresponding desires, Heloise can resolve this confusing self-image only by naming herself "hypocrite" — requiring discipline and governance from Abelard and Christ.

Plagued with this hypocrisy, Heloise discusses her public role as a chaste lover of God, who according to Abelard should be elevated above himself on the part of a Bride of Christ, as contrasted with her private role as an inferior, adulterous, lustful, and destructive harlot. These public and private images are highly complex and interrelated. Heloise recognizes early in the first letter that she accepted this public image as a chaste and holy woman solely out of a lustful desire for Abelard:

> Et solus es qui plurimum id mihi debeas et nunc maxime cum universa quae iusseris in tantum impleverim ut cum te in aliquo offendere non possem me ipsam pro iussu tuo perdere sustinerem. Et quod maius est dictuque mirabile, in tantam versus est amor insaniam ut quod solum appetebat, hoc ipse sibi sine spe recuperationis auferret, cum ad tuam statim iussionem tam habitum ipsa quam animum immutarem ut te tam corporis mei quam animi unicum possessorem ostenderem. (ed. Muckle, 70; trans. Radice, 113)

[You alone have so great a debt to repay me, particularly now when I have carried out all your orders so implicitly that when I was powerless to oppose you in anything, I found strength at your command to destroy myself. I did more, strange to say — my love rose to such great heights of madness that it robbed itself of what it most desired beyond hope of recovery, when immediately at your bidding I changed my clothing along with my mind, in order to prove you the sole possessor of my body and my will alike.]

Desire in Language and Form: Heloise's Challenge to Abelard

Heloise recognizes her lustful love, "quod solum appetebat," for Abelard as the sole cause for her chaste lifestyle. This hypocrisy becomes, for her, the defining mediator between the roles of the past and the present. By defining herself above all other things as a hypocrite, Heloise has found a way to sustain both the private and the public roles, the roles of the past and the present.

As Abelard's lover in the past, Heloise was the highest of all women, but now she resides below all others:

> O me miserarum miserrimam, infelicium infelicissimam, quae quanto universis in te feminis praelata sublimiorem obtinui gradum, tanto hinc prostrata graviorem in te et in me pariter perpessa sum casum! (ed. Muckle, 78; trans. Radice, 129)

> [Of all wretched women, I am the most wretched, and amongst the unhappy I am unhappiest. The higher I was exalted when you preferred me to all other women, the greater my suffering over my own fall and yours, when I was flung down.]

Her role as hypocrite allows her to see this change in events, but still cling to the former role as lover. It is this continual identification with her old roles which sustain the overall role as hypocrite. In addition to her continual self-definition as hypocrite, Heloise gives other examples of why she must now accept her inferior status.

Heloise's sense of inferiority and guilt is also evident in her comparison of self with biblical women who destroyed their lovers. She mentions Eve, Delilah, and Job's wife as examples of women who, like herself, had brought about the downfall of their lovers or husbands. Although she realizes that she did not harm him willingly, Heloise blames herself for Abelard's mutilation:

> Deprehensis in quovis adulterio viris haec satis esset ad vindictam poena quam pertulisti. Quod ex adulterio promerentur alii, id tu ex coniugio incurristi per quod iam te omnibus satisfecisse confidebas iniuriis. Quod fornicatoribus suis adulterae, hoc propria uxor tibi contulit. (ed. Muckle, 79; trans. Radice, 130)

> [The punishment you suffered would have been proper vengeance for men caught in open adultery. But what others deserve for adultery came upon you through a marriage which you believed had made amends for

all previous wrongdoing; what adulterous women have brought upon their lovers, your own wife brought on you.]

Heloise uses this image of the guilty wife to prove her ultimate inferiority to Abelard and the necessity for discipline. She adds to this guilt of her husband's injury, and the role of transgressor to her self-portrait. Female desire's destructive tendency, according to Heloise, ends ultimately in Abelard's castration as a payment for both of their sins. She mentions his castration several times throughout the letters. In the first letter she mourns how this one act robbed her in robbing him. In the second letter, she mourns that he alone was punished for their sins: "Solus in poena fuisti, duo in culpa" [You alone were punished though we were both to blame] (ed. Muckle, 79; trans. Radice, 130). Peggy Kamuf argues that Abelard's castration is the incident which Heloise is unable to understand and therefore fit into her self-image:

> For Abelard, the break which eludes Heloise is to be found in the significance of his castration. Through this healing wound, this punishment which is a grace, this destruction which is a preservation, Abelard has been given a way out of the fiction.... (*Fictions of Feminine Desire*, 41)

Heloise never leaves this fiction, but continually blames herself for their sin and Abelard's ultimate punishment. Because she cannot view Abelard's castration as a healing wound, she remains in the fiction of her many past roles. She has never put aside her role of lover, and when the role of the chaste abbess is placed on top of this earlier role and still-present desire, Heloise allows present roles to blend with those of the past. Within this confusion of roles, Heloise's desire of the past becomes linked to her present roles, where her present needs translate past desires.

This self-image of the hypocritical, destructive woman is like that of the blended image of wife/lover and sister/daughter, for the image is dependent upon Abelard's role in the events of the past. She herself chooses to become the destructive lover in her letters, because at least in that role she can still acknowledge their past sexual desire. She cannot see, as Abelard does, that the castration is a source of healing and change. Although it is only out of love for him that she took vows in the first place, she continues in them because it is what *he* desires of her — but she does so only as a hypocrite in need of further discipline. The vows have brought about only an outside purity; inwardly, she still remembers and burns with the former love they once shared.

Heloise's Letters

Heloise's language, as noted above, continually perpetuates her own self-interest. She focuses throughout her letters on the many different roles she once played or still plays in Abelard's life. In all of these situations she places herself beneath him and in need of his authority. The most succinct example of her use of language, as well as the most evident attempt of Heloise to force Abelard to retain his position over her, is the salutation of the first letter discussed above. The salutation in his response challenges Heloise directly:

> Heloisae, dilectissimae sorori suae in Christo, Abaelardus, frater eius in ipso. (ed. Muckle, 73; trans. Radice, 119)

> [To Heloise, his dearly beloved sister in Christ, Abelard her brother in Christ.]

With this answer, Abelard defies Heloise's attempt to force him to resume his position over herself. He places Heloise's name before his own, placing Heloise in a superior or equal position. The titles he assigns to Heloise and himself are also verbal challenges. He avoids the titles which suggest any relationship in which he would have control, or responsibility, over Heloise, although he acknowledges himself a spiritual leader. Instead, he chooses only one of the pairs of terms Heloise had used, that of brother and sister, where they can be seen as equals. Furthermore, this sibling relationship is specified as one mediated by Christ, who sanctifies and transforms any previous relationship they may have had.

In the next letter, Heloise challenges Abelard's placement of her name before his own in his salutation. She refers to the *ars dictaminis* which had set forth the rules for epistolary correspondence. According to these rules, her name should always follow Abelard's because of her inferiority before him. In her argument, she recounts each role she has had and still has in relationship to Abelard:

> Miror, unice meus, quod praeter consuetudinem epistolarum, immo contra ipsum ordinem naturalem rerum, in ipsa fronte salutationis epistolaris me tibi praeponere praesumpsisti, feminam videlicet viro, uxorem marito, ancillam domino, monialem monacho et sacerdoti diaconissam, abbati abbatissam. (ed. Muckle, 77; trans. Radice, 127)

> [I am surprised, my only love, that contrary to custom in letter-writing and, indeed, to the natural order, you have thought fit to put my name before yours in the greeting which heads your letter, so that we have woman before man, wife before husband, handmaid before master, nun before monk, deaconess before priest and abbess before abbot.]

In this list, Heloise sums up all the many roles she has played, and argues that in the case of each she is inferior and subject to Abelard. She does not, however, list the one relationship in which they could be considered equals, the one title that Abelard had actually used in his salutation, that of brother and sister. She rejects Abelard's attempt to equalize their relationship, an act that would limit her own self-interests because her strategy is dependent upon the idea that Abelard believes he has a responsibility to her and can govern her body still. Heloise continues, instead, to insist that her name, according to both the laws of men and *natural order,* should be placed only after his own.

It is not only in the salutation that Heloise attempts to use the epistle as a tool to force Abelard to retain his place over herself. Indeed, she utilizes the rules of the epistolary genre to reinstate her own constructed self-image. Abelard, however, constantly undermines her efforts by avoiding the rules and any discussion of them. Heloise remains embodied within the constraints of the epistle, her own chosen genre, which she uses as a vehicle for discursive desire. As Albrecht Classen points out, the epistle has always been seen as the one outlet the medieval woman had recourse to for self-expression.[10] For Heloise, however, it is more than the accessibility of the genre, but the rules of the genre itself which make it a logical choice for her correspondence with Abelard. For Heloise, the letter allows her to remain within the relationship she once had with Abelard, who exercised power over her as instructor, master, and husband — and owed her a "debt" in each of these relationships. The rules and functions of the epistle were set out in the *ars dictandi,* medieval textbooks written, as far as we know, exclusively by men describing how each letter should be written, often including specific samples of these letters.[11]

---

[10] Albrecht Classen, "Female Epistolary Literature from Antiquity to the Present: An Introduction," *Studia Neophilologica* 60 (1988): 3–13, here 3.

[11] Martin Camargo, *Ars Dictaminis, Ars Dictandi,* Typologie des Sources du Moyen Âge Occidental 60 (Turnhout: Brepols, 1991), 20. See also Giles Constable, *Letters and Letter Collections,* Typologie des Sources du Moyen Âge Occidental 17 (Turnhout: Brepols, 1976). Also see now Juanita Feros Ruys, "*Eloquencie vultum depingere*: Eloquence and *dictamen* in the Love Letters of Heloise and Abelard," in *Rhetoric and Renewal in the Latin West 1100–1540: Essays in Honour of John O. Ward,* ed. Constant J. Mews et al. (Turnabout: Brepols, 2003), 99–112.

Desire in Language and Form: Heloise's Challenge to Abelard 101

These textbooks are believed to have appeared in France in the early twelfth century, when Heloise was beginning her own education (Camargo, *Ars Dictaminis*, 20). Heloise certainly was aware of these rules, as she attempts to draw Abelard into a discussion of his own infraction of them in their correspondence. Within these textbooks, the parts of the letter, standardized no later than 1140, were set out as such: *salutatio, exordium, narratio, petitio*, and *conclusio*. The *salutatio* often received the majority of the explanation within the text, for it was believed to perform a necessary social function in setting forth the social status of both the sender and receiver.[12] Heloise's claims, that Abelard should follow these rules and place his name before her own, as he is her ecclesiastical superior, are predicated on her continued efforts to force Abelard into a disciplinary role as her teacher.

The other part of the letter which Heloise develops to her own end is the *narratio*. The *narratio* referred to the main body of the letter, and was described by several particular *virtutes* — *brevitas, claritas, varietas* (*Ars Dictaminis*, 24). Also to be followed were the rules concerning *cursus*. Camargo explains, "*Cursus* refers exclusively to the rhythm of sound, specifically to cadences at the end (or sometimes in the middle) of *clausulae*" (*Ars Dictaminis*, 25). Although there were some differences, the *cursus* was quite uniform throughout Europe, and its rules were established for several centuries before they were set forth in the *ars dictandi*.

In his study of the *cursus* of both Heloise and Abelard, Peter Dronke shows that Heloise used a proportion of "slow" to "swift" cadences quite opposite to those used by all the major northern French writers of her day.[13] She chose to conclude more than 25 percent of her sentences with a *tardus* cadence, as opposed to 16 percent ending with a *velox*. This usage of cadences is, indeed, not French, but is in keeping with the practices of the early twelfth-century Italian teacher of letters, Adalbertus. Abelard answers Heloise with a similar tendency toward *cursus* (18 percent *tardus* to 16 percent *velox*), although his usage is not as marked (Dronke, *Women Writers*, 111). Linguistically, Heloise follows a different set of rules, expecting and desiring to be corrected by Abelard, her former instructor. Abelard, however, refuses to make it an issue, and, indeed, seems to follow her example more

---

[12] Camargo explains: "They modified the *genera dicendi* (*stilus altus, medius, humilis*) in order to devise a social hierarchy in which both secular and ecclesiastical persons were classified as *superiores/sublimi, pares/mediocres*, or *inferiores/infimi*" (*Ars Dictaminis*, 22).

than to pull away from it. Dronke implies that Abelard may even have been influenced by Heloise's writing practices (*Women Writers*, 111).

It might be objected that Heloise was only following the rules of the epistolary form, and not manipulating it to benefit herself. Heloise's epistolary form, however, forces Abelard to retain his position over her while soliciting his correction of an "error" obvious enough to catch his attention. Heloise was no longer to possess Abelard physically, but she was attempting to continue the erotic struggle through questions of literary decorum. To explain this tactic fully, we must first discuss the nature of Heloise's desire for Abelard, and understand exactly what she desires of him.

Heloise's Desire

By looking at René Girard's model of triangular desire, Heloise and Abelard's relationship, both before and after the "calamitous" event, makes more sense. Girard uses the triangle as a spatial metaphor to demonstrate how desire involves a subject (the desirer), an object (the desired), and a mediator. The mediator is a "model" for the subject.[14] By following the model or mediator, the subject can approach the desired. The base of the triangle is a straight line, representing the desire directed to an object by a subject. Girard explains, "The mediator is there, above that line, radiating toward both the subject and the object" (*Deceit, Desire*, 2). If the mediator is merely an idea or object, then the model is rather simple, for the mediator never interferes with the desire of the subject for the object. Girard calls this "external mediation." The model becomes more complex when the mediator becomes a person who enters the construct with a secondary desire directed toward the same object. The mediator with his desire becomes a rival to the subject for whom he mediates. Girard describes this rivalry as "internal mediation" (*Deceit, Desire*, 7-9).

The desire demonstrated by Heloise for Abelard can be demonstrated using Girard's model. Just as Heloise describes herself within roles she played in both the past and the present, her expressed desire is also rooted in both the past and present. In all her descriptions of desire, the object of her desire remains the same: to have Abelard, either mentally, emotionally, or physically.

---

[13] Peter Dronke, *Women Writers of the Middle Ages* (Cambridge: Cambridge University Press, 1984), 110.

Desire in Language and Form: Heloise's Challenge to Abelard

It is the mediators of her desire that change with the change in circumstances from past to present, and as these mediators change, that aspect of Abelard which Heloise desires to possess also changes.

Heloise's original desire was fired by other women whom she saw as rivals (or mediators) who envied her for Abelard's affections:

> Quae coniugata, quae virgo non concupiscebat absentem et non exardebat in praesentem? Quae regina vel praepotens femina gaudiis meis non invidebat vel thalamis? (ed. Muckle, 71; trans. Radice, 115)
>
> [Every wife, every young girl desired you in absence and was on fire in your presence; queens and great ladies envied me my joys and my bed.]

As she describes his fame, she mentions the many other women who desired his physical presence. These women acted as mediators for Heloise's physical desire for Abelard. This desire changed as Heloise's relationship with Abelard changed to take in different mediators.

As she writes these letters, Heloise expresses a present desire as well. She still asks for Abelard, but specifies now that he write to her a word of comfort:

> ... in quo modo potes tuam mihi praesentiam reddas consolationem videlicet mihi aliquam rescribendo. (ed. Muckle, 73; trans. Radice, 117)
>
> [I beg you to restore your presence to me in the way you can — by writing me some word of comfort....]

This desire is still to have Abelard, but since his physical love is no longer possible, his words become her surrogate. This desired object fits her present role as the chaste abbess of Abelard's convent. It also fits Girard's model of triangular desire. In this instance, it is the friend of Abelard to whom the *Historia Calamitatum* is addressed who mediates this desire. Early in the beginning of her first letter, Heloise chides Abelard for having sent words of consolation to a friend, although he had never done the same for her and her sisters, to whom the debt was greater. She then expresses her own desire to receive some words of consolation, or even discipline, from Abelard.

Although the mediators have changed, Heloise's basic desire has not. Instead, it has been translated across temporal and social boundaries. She still desires to have Abelard in whichever form she can. Her desire is illustrated temporally, belonging to either Heloise's past or present; the different mediators dictate the difference in time. Heloise blends the different forms of her desire, as she blends her different self-images, demanding at least Abelard's words in return for her memories of his body and her continued transgressive desire:

> Memento, obsecro, quae fecerim et quanta debeas attende. Dum tecum carnali fruerer voluptate, utrum id amore vel libidine agerem incertum pluribus habebatur. Nunc autem finis indicat quo id inchoaverim principio. (ed. Muckle, 73; trans. Radice, 117)
>
> [Remember, I implore you, what I have done, and think how much you owe me. While I enjoyed with you the pleasures of the flesh, many were uncertain whether I was prompted by love or lust; but now the end is proof of the beginning.]

This blend of desires parallels the confusion of roles discussed earlier that Heloise presents in her letters. It becomes clear that in her own personal construction, she has never stopped being Abelard's lover and believes she deserves that which she desired as his wife — now translated into discourse as his sister in Christ.

Important to note in this model of triangular desire is the lack of Abelard's reciprocal desire for Heloise. Heloise does not request that Abelard love her erotically in return; he is only an object to be desired. Heloise allows no room for his sexual desire in her construct — only his continued attention. In fact, she admits that his desire no longer exists:

> Concupiscentia te mihi potius quam amicitia sociavit, libidinis ardor potius quam amor. Ubi igitur quod desiderabas cessavit quicquid propter hoc exhibebas pariter evanuit. (ed. Muckle, 72; trans. Radice, 116)
>
> [It was desire, not affection which bound you to me, the flame of lust rather than love. So when the end came to what you desired, any show of feeling you used to make went with it.]

With this realization, Heloise distinguishes between Abelard's own past and present roles. She *appears* to make clear that she understands that Abelard no longer holds the same roles as he once did. This understanding, however, reflects the fact that Heloise may very well be blending the past with the present intentionally, as Linda Kauffman suggests:

> Yet there is every reason to believe that it is Heloise herself who provides the evidence of her double life, that she is the one making a conscious effort to expose it. The device of drawing attention to her own duplicity is itself a strategy of doubleness, for on the one hand, she writes as abbess seeking spiritual guidance, but at the same time she wants to combat Abelard's apparent indifference, to end the silence of ten years, and to engage him actively in amorous correspondence. (*Discourses of Desire*, 73)

This consciousness is evident both in the handling of Abelard's different roles, and in the distinction she makes between his desire of the past and the lack of such desire in the present.

Although Heloise recognizes that Abelard does not hold the same desire for her as he once did, she makes this distinction between the present and the past only in connection to him. In her own desiring self, past is present, and she discursively insists at all times upon her roles as lover, wife, and abbess. Her desire reflects this blend of roles, for she continually desires Abelard, although the mediators of that desire may change. At the end of her second letter to Abelard, however, Heloise leaves a clue that she may understand the inescapable nature of her own desire, and desire in general:

> Quocumque me angulo coeli Deus collocet, satis mihi faciet. Nullus ibi cuiquam invidebit, cum singulis quod habebunt suffecerit. (ed. Muckle, 82; trans. Radice, 135–36)

> [In whatever corner of heaven God shall place me, I shall be satisfied. No one will envy another there, and what each one has will suffice.]

Heloise wishes in the end to find a small corner in heaven where there will be no envy, and, therefore, no desire. This seems at first a strange wish for a woman who has just poured out her heart to the man she loves, and for whom she has, through it all, refused to relinquish her desire. Using the Girardian model of triangular desire, however, one can see why Heloise desires to be away from any envy. Triangular desire requires a mediator who provides a model for the subject. The subject builds his/her desire for the object in accordance to and rivaling with the mediator's own desire for the object. This rivalry is based on the subject's envy for the object.

Heloise defines her own desire in terms of envy as well. The mediators of her past desire were the women who "burned" for her beloved Abelard. The mediator of the present desire is the recipient of the *Historia Calamitatum*, whose relationship and correspondence with Abelard she herself envies. Her wish for any corner in heaven that will be devoid of envy reflects an understanding that desire is built upon the envy of a mediator. Without any envy, Heloise's own desire disappears. Her roles of lover, wife, and abbess are all related to Abelard, and her desire is for his authority and attention. If she can escape this desire, Heloise would be able to free herself from both the past and present roles which rule over her.

Heloise's Success

Thus Heloise's own consciousness of her desires is evident in her recognition of the role envy plays in the situation as well as in her understanding of Abelard's own freedom from the erotic roles of their past. She *seemingly* grants to Abelard this freedom to move beyond desire, but retains for herself the blended roles of chaste nun and hypocritical harlot as a way to force him to remain a figure of authority and discipline in her life. This consciousness is also evident in her deliberate usage of the epistolary form, placing constant pressure on Abelard to enter into a discussion of rules and to take up a position of linguistic superiority and spiritual governance over her — for that is the desired result of each of these conscious ploys. Her self-definition as a hypocrite is also a demand for chastisement and correction from Abelard.

The question, then, is did Heloise succeed at all in her attempt to force Abelard into a position of responsibility over herself? Rhetorically, she achieved perhaps only minor success. Abelard avoids any responsibility to her within his own letters, for he translates all her demands for attention, instruction, and correction into prayers for his *own* safety and health. In the end, however, Heloise wins from Abelard the only concession he can sanction, as is evident in Heloise's introduction to her third letter: she receives the chastisement she desires. She puts away her images of past and present, and comes to accept Abelard's position of spiritual advisor as the only relationship he will allow:

> Ut enim insertum clavum alius expellit, sic cogitatio nova priorem excludit cum alias intentus animus priorum (sic) memoriam dimittere cogitur aut intermittere.
>
> [As one nail drives out another hammered in, a new thought expels an old, when the mind is intent on other things and forced to dismiss or interrupt its recollection of the past.][15]

With an aptly violent metaphor, Heloise, in effect, puts behind her all of her past desire and adopts the submissive role of student awaiting Abelard's instruction (a reprisal, of sorts, of her first role with him). The sexual metaphor of the new thought being "hammered in" symbolically portrays Heloise's translation of their former physical relationship into this newer "spiritual" one. She realizes that Abelard will recognize his superiority over herself only when she accepts their present relationship as priest and abbess. Abelard responds with a long letter that explains the history of religious women and sets forth the rules she and her convent should follow (ed. Muckle [1955], 253–81). Heloise accepts these rules,[16] for with them, she has succeeded in some small way in forcing Abelard back into her life as an authority and teacher.

Suzanne Wayne
THE PENNSYLVANIA STATE UNIVERSITY

---

[14] René Girard, *Deceit, Desire, and the Novel*, trans. Yvonne Freccero (Baltimore: Johns Hopkins University Press, 1965), 2.

[15] J. T. Muckle, C.S.B., "The Letter of Heloise on Religious Life and Abelard's First Reply," *Mediæval Studies* 17 (1955): 240–81, here 242.

[16] See also T.P. McLaughlin, C.S.B., "Abelard's Rule for Religious Women," *Mediæval Studies* 18 (1956): 240–92.

Translating Petrarchan Desire in Vittoria Colonna and Gaspara Stampa

> Hast du der Gaspara Stampa
> denn genügend gedacht, daß irgend ein Mädchen,
> dem der Geliebte entging, am gesteigerten Beispiel
> dieser Liebenden fühlt: daß ich würde wie sie?
> Sollen nicht endlich uns diese ältesten Schmerzen
> fruchtbarer werden? Ist es nicht Zeit, daß wir liebend
> uns vom Geliebten befrein und es bebend bestehn:
> wie der Pfeil die Sehne besteht, um gesammelt im Absprung
> *mehr* zu sein als er selbst. Denn Bleiben ist nirgends.
> — Rilke, *Duino Elegies*

> [Have you memorialized
> Gaspara Stampa so fully, that now any woman
> whose beloved has eluded her might feel, thanks to this lover's
> heightened example: "If only I could be like her?
> Couldn't this oldest of sufferings finally be for us
> more fruitful? Isn't it time that lovingly
> we freed ourselves from our lover and, trembling, endured it:
> as the arrow endures the bowstring, to be collected in its leap-off
> into more than itself? For staying put is nowhere."]
> — trans. Galway Kinnell and Hannah Liebmann

In his *The Civilization of the Renaissance in Italy* (1860), Jacob Burckhardt made a claim that has become commonplace in discussions of Renaissance culture: one of that culture's distinctive features was the development of the individual. In the Middle Ages

> Man was conscious of himself only as a member of a race, people, party, family, or corporation — only through some general category. In Italy

this veil first melted into air; an *objective* treatment and consideration of the State and of all the things of this world became possible. The *subjective* side at the same time asserted itself with corresponding emphasis; man became a spiritual *individual*, and recognized himself as such.[1]

Burckhardt's Renaissance individual views him- or herself as independent of the institutions and ideas without which a medieval man or woman simply had no sense of self. In the Renaissance, therefore, the self becomes autonomous. This view of Renaissance individualism has more recently been questioned, as many critics have discovered that the Renaissance sense of self proves to be far more scattered and fragmented, far more tied to institutions and religious beliefs than Burckhardt assumed.[2] Despite his oversimplification, however, Burckhardt points to a crucial issue for Italian writers in the early modern period: the status of the self and its dependence on others for self-definition. In this essay I will investigate how narratives of the self appear in the lyric poetry of Renaissance Italy, suggesting that we can understand lyric desire in the Renaissance, which owes so much to Saint Augustine — at least as filtered through Petrarch — as the desire for the completion, or at least containment, of the self, for a self-fashioning that can finally cease within some kind of stable identity. I will concentrate on two female poets — Vittoria Colonna and Gaspara Stampa — both Petrarchan poets who sought different solutions to the problem of fragmented desire and a divided self in Petrarch. Ultimately, these two poets seek stability through various strategies of containing the tension that exists at the very heart of the Petrarchan narrative. Whereas Colonna heals Petrarch's split self by positing a Neoplatonic bridge between her love for her husband and her love for God, Stampa begins to portray the development of a more autonomous self, a self that breaks free of its dependency on one individual male beloved in order to define itself more freely.

---

[1] Jacob Burckhardt, *The Civilization of the Renaissance in Italy*, trans. S. G. C. Middlemore (New York: Random House, Modern Library, 1995), 100; emphasis in original.

[2] Perhaps the best known example is Stephen Greenblatt, *Renaissance Self-Fashioning: From More to Shakespeare* (Chicago: University of Chicago Press, 1980). He begins by stating that "my starting point is quite simply that in sixteenth-century England there were both selves and a sense that they could be fashioned" (1) but ends with the admission that his conclusions are "more tentative, more ironic than I had originally intended" (256).

The language of desire in Renaissance lyric poetry must not be misunderstood to be a simple translation of erotic longing into poetic form. Often, and especially with Petrarch, the desire for the beloved becomes a way of considering metaphysical and existential issues at the heart of personal identity. Petrarch found ample precedent for using desire as a language of the self in his predecessor Dante. In Virgil's discourse on desire in *Purgatorio* XVIII, for example, Dante clarifies that desire is "spiritual motion," the movement of the soul:

> così l'animo preso entra in disire,
>   ch'è moto spiritale, e mai non posa
>   fin che la cosa amata il fa gioire. (31–33)
>
> [thus the captive soul enters into desire, which is spiritual motion, and it never rests until the loved thing makes it rejoice.][3]

This passage owes a great debt to Saint Augustine, who located all human motivation in the movement of desire. Petrarch relied greatly on Augustine, and was no doubt influenced by the saint's location of metaphysical questioning in the language of eroticism.[4] In book three of his *Confessions*, for example, Saint Augustine opens with an account of his life in Carthage:

> To Carthage I came, where a whole frying-pan full of abominable loves (*sartago flagitiosorum amorum*) crackled round about me, and on every side. I was not in love as yet, yet I loved to be in love (*amare amabam*), and with a more secret kind of want, I hated myself having little want. I sought about for something to love, loving still to be in love: security I hated, and that way too that had no snares in it: and all because I had a famine within me, even of that inward food (thyself, O God) though that famine made me not hungry. For I continued without all appetite towards incorruptible nourishments (*eram sine desiderio alimentorum incorruptibilium*), not because I was already full, but the more empty.[5]

---

[3] I cite the Petrocchi text as reproduced in Dante Alighieri, *The Divine Comedy: Purgatorio*, ed. Charles S. Singleton (Princeton: Princeton University Press, 1973). This and all other unattributed translations are my own.

[4] See Peter Brown, *The Body and Society in Late Antiquity* (New York: Columbia University Press, 1988), 405–8.

[5] Saint Augustine, *Confessions*, trans. William Watts (Cambridge, MA: Harvard University Press, 1912), 98–99.

Augustine locates the origins of erotic desire in the longing for God, though this source is not initially recognized. The restlessness that the soul feels even upon attaining the desired object leads to a rejection of that object as unsatisfying, ultimately leading to the recognition that all things except God fail to satisfy the longing that defines the soul's existence. The desire for the beloved, for Augustine, thus becomes a misplaced longing for God, and one that cannot satisfy. Augustine's narrative of his life traces the gradual discovery of the desire for God, and how that single desire replaced or subsumed all others; he rejects the notion of an autonomous self, a notion that for him is a blasphemous delusion. The self finds its full meaning and the satisfaction of its desires only in surrendering to God; our identity is inextricably bound up in the divine, and any attempt to deny this fundamental truth leads only to despair.

Another influential outgrowth of Augustine's self-portrayal is the way in which he embeds his portrayal of the self within narrative. As Paul Ricoeur points out, for Augustine humans are temporal creatures, and — rejecting the movement of celestial bodies as a way of accounting for time — he can only make sense of temporality as an inner movement of the soul, a movement that exists within narrative. Thus, when Augustine attempts to describe this inner movement in book eleven of the *Confessions*, he compares it to the recitation of a psalm, in which the present text being recited quickly recedes into the past but is recalled in the anticipation of the remainder of the psalm to come, a motion of the mind analogous to the human anticipation of the future. Similarly, when he accounts for the self and its relationship to God, he treats that self as a character within a teleological narrative.[6] Augustine's notion of the self, that is, is always temporal, and temporality is always and only comprehensible within narrative.

Augustine's conception of selfhood and its relation to both desire and narrative infuses Petrarch's vernacular poetry. As Teodolinda Barolini has

---

[6] See Paul Ricoeur, *Time and Narrative*, trans. Kathleen McLaughlin and David Pellauer (Chicago: University of Chicago Press, 1984), 1:5–30. Ricoeur goes on to argue that all of our meditations on temporality necessarily occur within narrative: "A constant thesis of this book will be that speculation on time is an inconclusive rumination to which narrative activity alone can respond" (6). For a more general consideration of the idea of time in Augustine, see J.M. Quinn, "Time," in *Augustine through the Ages*, ed. Allan Fitzgerald et al. (Grand Rapids: Eerdmans, 1999), 832–38; for a detailed reading of the relevant chapters in book eleven of the *Confessions* see idem, *A Companion to the Confessions of St. Augustine* (New York: Peter Lang, 2002), 689–735.

argued, Petrarch's vernacular collection poses particularly acute problems of the relation between time and narrative in the juxtaposition of the individual lyric — a seeming attempt at atemporality — and the collection, which embeds the discrete lyrics into a sequence that explicitly evokes narrative conventions.[7] This joining of lyric and narrative further complicates Petrarch's portrayal of desire in his description of his longing for the beloved Laura. John Freccero, in his well-known study "The Fig Tree and the Laurel," argues that Petrarch takes the Augustinian model of desire and selfhood only to twist it, with the aim of creating "a totally autonomous portrait of the artist, devoid of any ontological claim." Rather than forming a narrative of conversion, Petrarch presents us with a collection "whose real subject matter is its own act and whose creation is its own author." Freccero centers his discussion on the laurel tree and the figure of Laura; Petrarch deprives his beloved of any referentiality so that she can serve "as an Archimedean point from which he can create himself."[8] The result is an autonomous self, which directly contradicts the Augustinian conception of a self dependent on and moving toward God. According to Freccero, then, Petrarch's poetry takes an idolatrous and atemporal turn inward, with the aim of eternalizing the poet that creates it. Desire becomes a state (static rather than dynamic) against which the poet can write, and thus create, himself as an eternal creation, not a lack that indicates the self's isolation and meaninglessness in the absence of God.

Freccero's analysis indeed provides a powerful way to account for Petrarch's use of the laurel and of his enduring desire for Laura, but it ignores Petrarch's repeated attempts to repudiate Laura and her laurel tree. This competing desire conflicts — throughout the collection — with the nascent humanist desire for fame and eternal life through poetry that Freccero identifies. Indeed, we can see the conflict between them as early as the initial poem of the *Rerum vulgarium fragmenta*.[9] This poem was composed specifically to introduce

---

[7] See Teodolinda Barolini, "The Making of a Lyric Sequence: Time and Narrative in Petrarch's *Rerum vulgarium fragmenta*," *MLN* 104 (1989): 1–38.

[8] John Freccero, "The Fig Tree and the Laurel: Petrarch's Poetics," *Diacritics* 5 (1975): 34–40, here 34, 39.

[9] I use the Latin title instead of the more common vernacular titles *Canzoniere* and *Rime sparse* since this is the title given in Petrarch's autograph manuscript. As will become clear in the following discussion, I dispute the reading of Petrarch as the first Renaissance individual with a unified sense of self. I have been particularly influenced in my reading of the collection by Giuseppe Mazzotta, "The *Canzoniere* and the Language of the Self," in idem, *The Worlds of Petrarch* (Durham, NC: Duke University Press, 1993), 58–79; and, especially, Barolini, "The Making of a Lyric Sequence."

the collection; it has commonly been viewed as palinodic (especially in the sixteenth century), as it seems to retract many of the poems concerned with Petrarch's "primo giovenile errore" ["first youthful error"] and ends on a note of repentance with "'l conoscer chiaramente / che quanto piace al mondo è breve sogno" ["the clear knowledge that whatever pleases in the world is a brief dream"].[10] The first poem thus appears to posit an Augustinian narrative of conversion, in which the early sins are denounced in the light of the new self, now turned to God. The poem itself resists such a reading, however, both by its position (since the poem initiates the collection, it cannot effectively "retract" what comes after it) and its language; the opening quatrain is particularly revealing:

> Voi ch'ascoltate in rime sparse il suono
> di quei sospiri ond'io nudriva 'l core
> in sul mio primo giovenile errore,
> quand' era *in parte* altr'uom da quel ch'i' sono. (emphasis mine)

> [You who hear in scattered rhymes the sound of those sighs with which I nourished my heart during my first youthful error, when I was *in part* another man from what I am now.]

Petrarch's conversion remains partial, an incomplete turning away from his error; in Augustinian terms, a partial conversion is no conversion at all. Instead, therefore, of recounting his Augustinian change, he yearns for it, for a new fashioning of the self, but is unable to attain it. His terming his own poems "scattered rhymes" reinforces the impression that this poetic self is divided, unable to come to a unity. Thus, while it is true that the Augustinian narrative of conversion posited in the poem never comes to fruition, neither does Petrarch fully turn from it. His collection of poetry is best understood as a narrative of partial turnings, inward and then upward toward God only to turn inward again. Petrarch drains the narrative of the self of its final teleology but never repudiates it; he points toward its end but never actually attains it.

This conflict between competing notions of the self that Petrarch adumbrates in the very first poem of the collection is pervasive throughout the

---

[10] Citations from and translations of Petrarch are from *Petrarch's Lyric Poems: The Rime Sparse and Other Lyrics*, trans. and ed. Robert M. Durling (Cambridge, MA: Harvard University Press, 1976).

remaining 365 poems. In the interest of space, I will refer to only one of the most famous and explicit instances of these conflicting desires: the paired sonnets 61 and 62. In the first of these, Petrarch appropriates the biblical form of beatitude in order to praise and bless all things associated with Laura — especially the poetry that has arisen from his desire for her:

> et benedette sian tutte le carte
> ov'io fama l'acquisto, e 'l pensier mio,
> ch' è sol di lei sì ch'altra non v'à parte. (61. 12–14)
>
> [and blessed be all the pages where I gain fame for her, and my thoughts, which are only of her, so that no other has part in them!]

In the following poem, however, the poet immediately repents of these thoughts and attempts to bring his desires back to Christ: "reduci i pensier vaghi a miglior luogo, / rammenta lor come oggi fusti in croce" ("lead my wandering thoughts back to a better place, remind them that today you were on the Cross" [62.13–14]). The *Secretum* — with its dialogue between an Augustinus urging conversion and a Franciscus resisting and clinging to his beloved — serves as an apt dramatization of this split in Petrarch's sense of his self. Petrarch thus is caught between alternate conceptions of the self: an Augustinian conception, where the self is moving along a journey directed towards God, where he must recognize his utter reliance on God and direct all thoughts to Him, and a nascent humanist conception, where the self is more autonomous. In this sense, Petrarchan desire expresses itself as the desire for wholeness, but one that is caught between two competing unities with the result that the self is scattered between them.[11] The resulting split also fractures his narrative, which moves haltingly toward one end and then another. As we move to the sixteenth century, we will see both Colonna and Stampa interrogate the disparate self of Petrarch's poetry while attempting to find new ways of unifying his narrative through the imposition of alternate teleologies.

Both Colonna and Stampa were Petrarchan poets, in accordance with the dominant form of versifying in the sixteenth century. The preeminence

---

[11] Cf. Thomas Greene's argument that Petrarch attained a great *flexibility* of self, a lateral freedom that was truly new: "The Flexibility of the Self in Renaissance Literature," in *The Disciplines of Criticism: Essays in Literary Theory, Interpretation, and History*, ed. P. Demetz et al. (New Haven: Yale University Press, 1968), 241–64.

of Petrarchism is in large measure due to the influence of Pietro Bembo, who in the *Prose della volgar lingua* argued for the canonization of Petrarch and Boccaccio as models for vernacular imitation; he thus translated the humanist practice of *imitatio* — the process of learning to compose through imitation — from Latin to Italian. The result was a century of lyric poetry dominated by Petrarchism, not only in Italy but throughout Europe. Renaissance *imitatio* in both Latin and the vernacular was not, of course, a doctrine of slavish imitation; it is perhaps best understood as "heuristic imitation," in Thomas Greene's definition: "Heuristic imitations come to us advertising their derivation from the subtexts they carry with them, but having done that, they proceed to *distance themselves* from the subtexts and force us to recognize the poetic distance traversed."[12] Pietro Bembo himself, for example, in his exchange of letters with Giovan Francesco Pico, argued that imitation should proceed in three phases: imitating (*imitari*) an exemplary author, equaling or catching up to him (*assequi*), and finally overtaking him (*praeterire*).[13] Imitation becomes a way of finding one's own poetic voice.

Pietro Bembo's choice of Petrarch's Italian verse as a model of vernacular poetic composition depended primarily on questions of style. Unlike Dante's *Commedia*, which Pietro, in the *Prose della vulgar lingua*, has his brother Carlo compare to "un bello e spazioso campo di grano, che sia tutto d'avene e di logli e d'erbe sterili e dannose mescolato" ["a beautiful and spacious field of grain, which is mixed throughout with oats and darnel and sterile and noxious plants"],[14] Petrarch's lyric poems avoid extremes and constitute the best single standard for vernacular poetry. Despite Bembo's insistence on style, however, the imitation of Petrarch also entailed an imitation of Petrarchan subject matter, which meant an imitation of Petrarchan narrative. Petrarch became important not only for his poetic accomplishments but also for the poetic account of his life, particularly the moral standing he attained in later years, where, many sixteenth-century commentators found, an Augustinian

---

[12] Thomas M. Greene, *The Light in Troy: Imitation and Discovery in Renaissance Poetry* (New Haven: Yale University Press, 1982), 40; emphasis in original.

[13] See the discussions of Bembo's theory of imitation in G. W. Pigman III, "Versions of Imitation in the Renaissance," *Renaissance Quarterly* 33 (1980): 1–32; William J. Kennedy, *Authorizing Petrarch* (Ithaca: Cornell University Press, 1994), 82–102; and Martin L. McLaughlin, *Literary Imitation in the Italian Renaissance* (Oxford: Clarendon Press, 1995), 262–74.

[14] Pietro Bembo, *Prose della Volgar Lingua, Gli Asolani, Rime*, ed. Carlo Dionisotti (Milan: TEA, 1966), 178.

piety brought him to reject his earlier poetry for poems of religious fervor.[15] Bembo thus tells us that he favors Petrarch's *stil canuto*, his mature style that developed following the death of Laura, which, as William Kennedy has pointed out, proved a common evaluation of Petrarch's vernacular poetry in the *cinquecento*, a judgment that often mingled stylistic with moral concerns.[16] Petrarch presented not only a stylistic model, that is, but also a model of the self, one which he progressively fashioned and then recounted within a teleological narrative. Interestingly, however, in practice most poets, including Bembo, abandoned this image of the later Petrarch and turned to the poems prior to Laura's death as the basis for imitation. This choice betrays, perhaps, a realization that the image of Petrarch's self as they perceived it in the later poems was largely a misleading construct; the poems following Laura's death, like those preceding it, show a self caught and split between two alternatives. Many Petrarchists thus imitated Petrarch but were able to construct a more unified sense of self than their canonical model. Colonna presents us with an exemplary instance of this practice.

Vittoria Colonna was the best known female poet of her time (some twenty editions of her poetry were printed during the sixteenth century), and one whose poetry was encouraged and approved by Pietro Bembo himself. Translating the language of Petrarchism across gender lines, of course, opened up certain opportunities but also brought difficulties, as it was not socially acceptable for women to speak openly of sexual desire, even if that desire could be understood as a metaphor for other concerns. Female poets thus had to employ strategies that while allowing them to imitate Petrarch also allowed them to transform Petrarchan convention in a way that would prove socially blameless.[17] Nevertheless, the proliferation of female Petrarchan

---

[15] See Luigi Baldacci, "Il Petrarca specchio di vita," in idem, *Il Petrarchismo italiano nel cinquecento* (Milan: Ricciardi, 1957), 45–74.

[16] See Kennedy, *Authorizing Petrarch*, 99–101. He notes, for example, the comments of Brucioli that Petrarch's early poetry was lacking, "non havendo cosi bei pensieri, ne cosi chiaro ingegno, e alte rime, e cosi buono giudicio." Similarly, Daniello wrote that Petrarch was not a great poet early in life: "Fu poco, non havendo ne cosi bei pensieri, ne cosi chiaro ingegno, e alte rime, e cosi buon giudicio, il quale suol crescere insieme con gli anni" (101).

[17] The degree to which Petrarchism was a patriarchal and therefore oppressive discourse is debated. For the view that it relegates women to a silent and scattered presence, see Nancy J. Vickers, "Diana Described: Scattered Women and Scattered Rhyme," in *Writing and Sexual Difference*, ed. Elizabeth Abel (Chicago: University of Chicago Press, 1982), 95–109; for the view that "within its culture, Petrarchism is a venue in

poets in the sixteenth century shows the general openness of Petrarchism to female appropriation, a fact noted by Bembo himself.[18] Additionally, Colonna's status as the wealthy and noble widow of the marquis of Pescara placed her in an unusual situation for a woman of sixteenth-century Italy in that it offered her a degree of independence not normally accorded to women. Her poetry, however, resists appearing as the product of an independent self, as she draws on Petrarchan narrative and lyric conventions to portray herself as dependent. The very first poem of her *Rime Amorose*, for example, disclaims responsibility both for writing the poetry and for any merit it possesses. Colonna writes only in order to ease her pain ("Scrivo sol per sfogar l'interna doglia" ["I write only to ease the inner pain"] [1]), because she cannot help herself ("'l grave pianto / è tal che tempo né ragion l'affrena" ["the weighty grief is such that neither time nor reason restrains it" (10–11)]). She claims for her poetic output both immediacy and spontaneity; her poetry is a diary of her emotions. Her grief supplies her entire subject and her style.

> Amaro lacrimar, non dolce canto,
> foschi sospiri e non voce serena,
> di stil no ma di duol mi danno vanto. (12–14)[19]
>
> [Bitter weeping, not sweet song, dark sighs and not a serene voice, make me vaunt not my style but my grief.]

---

which female aspiration is detectably more welcome than elsewhere, and ... probably did more to encourage than to inhibit female literary activity," see Gordon Braden, "Gaspara Stampa and the Gender of Petrarchism," *Texas Studies in Literature and Language* 38 (1996): 115–39. I tend to find Braden's conclusion persuasive: "Stampa's case indeed seems to me to show how comparatively ungendered, in potential if not in practice, the expressive resources of Petrarchism were, how readily useful they were for female self-fashioning" (129). Indeed, my argument makes this basic assumption, along with the obvious qualification, however, that the possibilities for female self-fashioning were limited by outside forces and pressures.

[18] In the opening of book three of the *Asolani*, Bembo suggests that women who write, occupying their free time "negli studi delle lettere e in queste cognizioni," should not pay attention to what men say about them, since the world will eventually praise them for it. See Bembo, ed. Dionisotti, 458–59.

[19] All citations of Colonna's poetry refer to *Rime*, ed. Alan Bullock (Rome and Bari: Laterza, 1982).

Colonna thus opens her collection with a modesty topos, assuring the reader that the poet recognizes her own dependence upon her husband, even after his death.[20] Indeed, in a later poem she affirms that she is tied to her husband just as faithfully in death as in life: "tempo non cangiò mai l'antica fede; / il nodo è stretto ancor com'io l'avolsi" ("time has never changed my ancient faith; the knot is as tight as when I tied it" [45.5–6]). And in poem 53, she draws on traditional nautical imagery to consider her fate since death has taken her husband, from whom she derived her sense of identity:

> Provo tra duri scogli e fiero vento
> l'onde di questa vita in fragil legno;
> l'alto presidio e 'l mio fido sostegno
> tolse l'acerba morte in un momento. (1–4)

[I experience the waves of this life in a fragile vessel, between hard rocks and fierce wind; bitter death took the lofty garrison and my faithful support in one moment.]

While Stampa claims that her identity is determined and governed by her husband even after his death, her sense of self ultimately — to continue her own nautical metaphor — is in danger of foundering. She ends the poem on a note of uncertainty, claiming that she knows neither where she should go nor who she is; death seems the most attractive option ("Almen se morte il ver porto m'asconde, / mostrimi il falso suo, ché chiare e amene / ne parran le sue irate e turbide onde" ["If death at least hides from me the real port, let him show me his false one, so that his turbid and angry waves will still appear bright and serene"(12–14)]). In the *Rime Amorose*, then, Colonna attempts to construct a self on a Petrarchan model in which the beloved becomes a focus for the construction of the poet's identity. With the death of the beloved, however, that identity breaks down, since the end of her desire

---

[20] Bullock groups Colonna's love poetry into two: (1) the "collection" presented in the manuscript that he labels F1, found in the Biblioteca Nazionale Centrale in Florence, which shows "un evidente desiderio di stabilire un svolgimento ben definito dei vari momenti emotive attraversati da Vittoria dopo la morte del marito"; and (2) other love poems not contained in that manuscript. Since my interest lies in the *narrative* that Colonna constructs, I limit my attention to the collection found in F1, and I assume that the ordering is Colonna's and thus can be read as a conscious attempt to construct a Petrarchan narrative of the self. See *Rime*, ed. Bullock, 325–28.

lies beyond any narrative that she is able to construct. Colonna eventually turns to the Augustinian model, the second pole of divided Petrarchan desire, in order to write. The poems that result from this shift are collected in her *Rime Spirituali*.[21]

The first poem of this collection asserts her conversion and explicitly describes her turn towards Christ as the assumption of a new poetics, one in which the very act of writing is personified so that she writes the body of her Lord:

> Poi ch 'l mio casto amor gran tempo tenne
> l'alma di fama accesa, ed ella un angue
> in sen nudrio, per cui dolente or langue
> volta al Signor, onde il rimedio venne,
> i santi chiodi omai sieno mie penne,
> e puro inchiostro il prezïoso sangue,
> vergata carta il sacro corpo exangue,
> sì ch'io scriva per me quel ch'Ei sostenne.
> Chiamar qui non convien Parnaso o Delo,
> ch'ad altra acqua s'aspira, ad altro monte
> si poggia, u' piede uman per sé non sale;
> quel Sol ch'alluma gli elementi e 'l Cielo
> prego, ch'aprendo il Suo lucido fonte
> mi porga umor a la gran sete equale.

[Since my chaste love for a long time inflamed my soul with a desire for fame, and it nourished a serpent in my breast, it — grieving and languishing — turns to the Lord, from whom comes the remedy [cf. Psalm 120:1], let the holy nails now be my quills and his precious blood my undiluted ink, the sacred, bloodless body my writing paper, so that I write for myself that which He sustained. Here it is not right to call Parnassus or Delos, for I aspire to other waters, lean on another mountain, where human feet cannot climb of themselves [cf. Psalm 17:34];

---

[21] Bullock makes a convincing case that the edition of the *Rime Spirituali* published by Vincenzo Valgrisi in Venice in 1546 represents a text based on an autograph manuscript. He bases his own edition on this 1546 text, and I assume, therefore, that the ordering in the Bullock edition represents Colonna's ordering. See Bullock's comments on pages 359 ff. of his edition.

Translating Petrarchan Desire 121

> I pray that Sun that illuminates the elements and the Heavens, that when he opens His clear fountain he offers me drink equal to my great thirst [cf. John 4:7–15].]

This poem recalls in subtle ways Petrarch's first poem, "Voi ch'ascoltate"; both poets refer to an earlier love as being in some way nourished in the heart ("un angue / in sen nudrio"), and both claim palinodic force for the poem. Colonna's sonnet, however, makes the case for an actual, that is a complete, conversion on the Augustinian model. Its position as the initial poem in a series of religious *rime* effectively introduces a new subject matter and a new poetics, as it signals the shift away from the humanist poetics in which fame is a chief good, towards a poetics centered on Christ, where Colonna's poetic identity, down to her pen, ink, and paper, is defined as the Lord's. The concluding tercets point to a new model of poetic inspiration, away from Petrarch's laurel tree and ancient, classical models toward a biblical model of inspiration, signaled by the numerous scriptural echoes that Colonna places in the poem.

Despite this new beginning, however, the sonnet also demonstrates clear ties to the *Rime Amorose*. In both collections, Colonna appeals to a masculine beloved, and she refers to both as "Sole" and "Signore." Many would view this continuum as a narrative of Neoplatonic ascent, in which the human beloved leads to God.[22] For my purposes here, however, I wish to read the two collections as a joining together of the two poles of Petrarchan desire through a narrative of conversion. Colonna moves from the love of the earthly beloved to desire for her heavenly God, and her Neoplatonic leanings allow her to posit continuity between the two, a continuity missing in Petrarch, who always sees his two desires as conflicted. Colonna ultimately writes an Augustinian self, in which her identity proves to be completely dependent on God, and where her poetic identity as well is subsumed; her only validation and definition come through the divine. Later in the *Rime Spirituali*, for example, she describes the process of writing in this way:

---

[22] See Dennis McAuliffe, "Neoplatonism in Vittoria Colonna's Poetry: From the Secular to the Divine," in *Ficino and Renaissance Neoplatonism*, ed. Konrad Eisenbichler and Olga Pugliese (Toronto: Dovehouse Editions, 1986), 101–12. McAuliffe argues that Colonna should be understood as an intensely spiritual poet and not within the "context of competitive Petrarchism" (111). I agree with this assessment but would still argue that Colonna nevertheless understood and narrated her spiritual struggles and theological preoccupations within a Petrarchan framework (as the only framework available to her in writing sonnets) and thus must be seen within that context, if not within the literary *querelles* of the time.

> movo la penna, mossa da l'amore
> interno, e senza ch'io stessa m'aveggia
> di quel ch'io dico le Sue lodi scrivo.   (46.12–14)

[I move the pen, moved by inner love, and unaware myself of what I say, I write His praises.]

Colonna continues to claim the immediacy she portrays in her *Rime Amorose*; now, however, her "unthinking" verses come through divine inspiration, since her pen is moved by inner love.[23] She creates a continuity between both the subject matter and the method of her two collections, and in doing so she transforms Petrarch's narrative of a self caught between alternate possibilities into a more unified progression from earthly to divine love. She ultimately embraces, however, an Augustinian model of self-formation, one where she can realize her true self only after recognizing her reliance on God. This dependence on others persists throughout her poetry: first she relies on her husband, even after his death, and then on Christ. Colonna's poetry heals the split in Petrarch's verse by returning to an earlier solution, one that Petrarch could never bring himself to accept.[24]

For much of her lyric collection, Stampa appears to fit into a similar Petrarchan model; she writes a Petrarchan verse in which she declares her total dependence on her beloved. And indeed, during much of the history of Stampa's reception readers took her at her word. Stampa's status in the sixteenth century differs widely from Colonna's; her poetry was published following her death in 1554 in a single edition by her sister,[25] and the poetry seems to have been forgotten until Antonio Rambaldo di Collalto — a

---

[23] This tercet echoes Dante's description of his own *dolce stil novo* in *Purgatorio* 24: "I' mi son un che, quando / Amor mi spira, noto, e a quel modo / ch'e' ditta dentro vo significando" (52–54). Both instances recall the iconography of a biblical evangelist writing according to the Holy Spirit's dictates.

[24] As Janet Levarie Smarr points out, however, the problem is complicated by the fact that Colonna is female. Thus Colonna resolutely avoids any sensual language regarding her beloved, even though he is now dead and was her husband, concentrating instead on his military glory; she does dwell, however, on Christ's naked body in order to emphasize his human vulnerability to pain and suffering. See "Substituting for Laura: Objects of Desire for Renaissance Women Poets," *Comparative Literature Studies* 38 (2001): 1–30.

[25] Stampa's poems did circulate individually, and occasionally they made their way into printed collections. See Fiora A. Bassanese, *Gaspara Stampa* (Boston: Twayne, 1982), 35–40.

descendant of Stampa's lover Collalto di Colaltino — had her poems published in the eighteenth century as a form of praise to his ancestor and hence to his family. Since that time, critics have often praised the collection's "immediacy" and "spontaneity," which has proved a backhanded compliment at best, since implicit in this praise is the assumption that the spontaneity of women writers stems from their inability to exercise the kind of rational control that male writers are assumed to possess.[26] More recently, however, critics have convincingly argued for a self-conscious and careful Petrarchan poet.[27] Indeed, here I will argue that the organization of her collection supports this view; the narrative teleology portrays a poet who ultimately refuses Neoplatonic consolations and Augustinian teleology and moves toward the construction of a more autonomous poetic identity.[28]

---

[26] This view was first articulated by Collalto in his edition of Stampa's poetry. In his introduction, he argues that in a couple of sonnets in which Stampa begins with *voi* but concludes with *tu* the change can be chalked up to a lack of careful revision: "la qual cosa non si dee attribuir ad altro, che a non aver rilette una seconda volta con attenzione le opere sue." See *Rime di Madonna Gaspara Stampa; con alcune altre di Collaltino, e di Vinciguerra Conti di Collalto: e di Baldassare Stampa*. (Venice, 1738), xviii. The most influential statement of this position, however, is found in Benedetto Croce, who argues that Stampa's poetry is spontaneous in a matter fitting for a woman ("come si conveniva a donna"), which is to say passionately rather than rationally. He also goes on to state that her collection of poems "è nient'altro che l'epistolario e il diario del suo principale e grande amore": *Poesia popolare e poesia d'arte* (Bari: Laterza, 1967), 368–69. The question was further complicated by Abdelkader Salza, who edited the modern, critical edition of her poems. Convinced that she had worked as an upper-class courtesan in Venice, he rearranged the order of her collection so that it would conclude with a group of religious poems and thus form a narrative of a repentant sinner. The critical consensus now seems to be that Stampa was a Venetian *virtuosa* or professional musician rather than a courtesan. See Gaspara Stampa — Veronica Franco, *Rime*, ed. Abdelkader Salza (Bari: Laterza, 1913). For a general overview of the reception history, see Bassanese, *Gaspara Stampa*, 25–33.

[27] See, for example, Luigi Rosso, "Gaspara Stampa e il petrarchismo del '500," *Belfagor* 13 (1958): 1–20; Bassanese, *Gaspara Stampa*; Patricia Phillippy, "Gaspara Stampa's *Rime*: Replication and Retraction," *Philological Quarterly* 68 (1989): 1–23; Braden, "Gaspara Stampa and the Gender of Petrarchism."

[28] There is compelling evidence that Stampa *was* concerned with the organization of her collection. The first poem, like Petrarch's first sonnet, was clearly written later than many of the other poems and was written in order to introduce the collection. She also, like Petrarch, wrote anniversary poems, in which she describes the time that has lapsed since she first saw and fell in love with her beloved. It also seems clear, however, that she died before she could complete the final ordering of her collection, as the last eighty to ninety poems do not have the same narrative force as the earlier poems. The

A good example of the "passive" Stampa, who defines herself solely in terms of her beloved, can be found in the seventh poem of her *Rime*. The poem begins with an invitation to the ladies ("donne") to come to know her lord, and she lists his features — a compendium of positive traits, which is qualified by her assertion that the beloved has proved "empio in amore" ("cruel in love"). In the sextet she then "mirrors herself" to her female readers, defining herself as a creature of grief, whose identity depends upon her beloved:

> un albergo di fé salda e costante,
> una, che, perché pianga, arda e sospiri,
> non fa pietoso il suo crudel amante. (12–14)[29]
>
> [a lodging of solid and constant faith, one, who, though she weeps, burns, and sighs, does not make her cruel beloved compassionate.]

In a later poem in the collection, when she doubts Collaltino's continuing affection, she begins to invoke death, to repudiate herself, since, as she tells us "perché cosí non so quel ch'io mi sia" ("because thus I know not what I am, even to myself" [84.14]). These poems present us with a Petrarchan lover, who looks to her beloved for fulfillment and who can define herself only as the lover of her beloved.

The extremity of her proclaimed dependence, however, has led some critics to suggest that she actually invokes this Petrarchan model in order to subvert it. In spite of the praise of the beloved, the speaking lover's absolute

---

problem is further exacerbated in modern editions, which have all been based on Abdelkader Salza's critical edition, which, as discussed above, presents a changed ordering of the poems in order to reinforce Salza's idea of Stampa as a courtesan who repents late in life. In the original edition of the poetry, there is a clear division at poems 220 and 221 (poems 246 and 247 in Salza's edition). Whereas the earlier poems are not differentiated in terms of presentation, these two poems — addressed to Henry II, king of France, and Catherine de' Medici — are separated from the rest of the collection, as they are surrounded by artistic embellishment and, unlike the other poems in the edition, have a title indicating to whom they are addressed (e.g. for poem 220: "AL CRISTIANISSIMO RE DI FRANCIA, HENRICO SECONDO"). I assume, therefore, that these poems indicate some kind of actual shift in the collection; I will thus treat the first 219 poems of the first edition as a unit and assume that their ordering was determined by Stampa herself. I will not consider any of the poems that follow 220 and 221. For the first edition of Stampa's poetry, see *Rime di Madonna Gaspara Stampa* (Venice, 1554).

[29] All citations of Stampa's poetry are taken from Salza's edition, though I will note when Salza's ordering differs from that found in the first edition.

fidelity and dependence works to call into question the beloved's idealization and throw into high relief the poet's fidelity and worth.[30] She uses the resources of Petrarchism and the societal subjecttion of women ultimately to counter that subjection. Much like Petrarch's use of Laura as a figure against which he can begin to define himself, Stampa uses Collaltino in order to write herself, and she ultimately finds that her identity does not depend on his relation to her, only on her relation to him, and she finally moves beyond him altogether so that her identity depends only upon her relation to "love." Poem 159 presents a useful example.

> Quella febre amorosa, che m'atterra
> due anni e piú, e quel gravoso incarco
> ch'io sento, poi ch'Amor mi prese al varco
> di duo begli occhi, onde l'uscir mi serra,
>   potea bastare a farmi andar sotterra,
> lasciar lo spirto del suo corpo scarco,
> senza voler ch'oltra i suoi strali e l'arco,
> altra febre, altro mal mi fesse guerra.
>   Padre del ciel, tu vedi in quante pene
> questo misero spirto e questa scorza
> a tormentare Amor e febre viene.
>   Di queste febri o l'una o l'altra smorza,
> ché due tanti nemici non sostiene
> donna sí frale e di sí poca forza.

[This amorous fever, which has grounded me for two years and more, and this heavy burden that I feel, since Love took me in the pass with two beautiful eyes, and prohibits my exit, would suffice to drive me underground, to leave the spirit divested of its body, without further need of his bow and arrows, another fever, another evil to make war against me. Father in heaven, you see in what great pain Love and fever come to torment this wretched spirit and frame. Of these fevers, extinguish one or the other, for a woman so frail and with so little strength cannot sustain two such enemies.]

---

[30] See, in particular, Justin Vitiello, "Gaspara Stampa: The Ambiguities of Martyrdom," *MLN* 90 (1975): 58–71; and Fiora A. Bassanese, "Gaspara Stampa's Poetics of Negativity," *Italica* 61 (1984): 335–46.

The poem draws on poem 62 of the *Rerum vulgarium fragmenta*, a sonnet that I briefly discussed above. The opening of the sextet recalls the opening of the Petrarchan original ("Padre del Ciel"), and Stampa's poem — like Petrarch's — is an anniversary poem, commemorating the passage of time since the speaker fell in love. Petrarch's poem forms the second of a pair of sonnets, the first celebrating Laura and all that she represents, the second yearning to break free of her in an Augustinian conversion: "piacciati omai col tuo lume ch'io torni / ad altra vita et a più belle imprese" ("let it please you at last that with your light I may return to a different life and to more beautiful undertakings" [5–6]). Stampa's poem, however, lacks all of the conversionary desire of Petrarch's; she seeks relief from one of her tormentors, but she does not look to turn away from her beloved in order to bring it about.[31] Instead, her suffering becomes a way for her to define herself. Although her identity is rooted in the social conception of woman as weak and without strength ("donna sí frale e di sí poca forza"), her prayer to rid herself of one of two potent enemies actually serves to underscore her emotional strength, a strength that her beloved, who refuses to demonstrate the same emotional courage and fidelity, lacks.

The first poem of the *Rime* also serves as a useful example of how Stampa creates her own unique kind of Petrarchan poetry. The poem, imitating Petrarch's first poem, was written to introduce the collection. "Voi ch'ascoltate in queste meste rime" ("You who hear in these mournful verses"), the opening line of this sonnet, recalls Petrarch's "Voi ch'ascoltate in rime sparse il suono." Once again, however, Stampa invokes Petrarch, thus creating similarity, in order to establish difference; she shows, by placing her poems directly against their model, precisely where they deviate from the authoritative subtext. Just as Petrarch's poem portrays the split self that will define his poetry, so Stampa's first poem begins to construct the self that Stampa will portray throughout her collection. The poem presents Stampa as an exemplary figure, defined by her sorrow, but who may serve as a role model for other women. It quickly becomes evident that the palinodic tendency of Petrarch's poem is absent; unlike her predecessor, Stampa does not regret her first, youthful error. Instead, she imagines, in the sextet, that her readers will seek to embrace similar errors, and she describes their asking

---

[31] Bassanese also notes that Stampa's prayer is "not redemptive or contrite": *Gaspara Stampa*, 77.

themselves: "perché tant'amor, tanta fortuna / per sí nobil signor a me non venne" ("why have such love and such a fate for such a noble lord not come to me" [12–13])? Petrarch tells us that he now realizes that because of his love for Laura, he became "the talk of the crowd" ("al popol tutto / favola fui" [9–10]), which he now regrets ("di me medesmo meco mi vergogno" [11]). Stampa, on the other hand, *seeks* for glory in addition to pardon ("gloria, non che perdon"), in stark contrast to Petrarch's desire for pity ("pietà"). As we discussed above, Petrarch's opening poem maps out the split self, torn between conflicting desires and antithetical conceptions of self-formation, a split crystallized by the claim that the poet differs "in parte" from his earlier self. In Stampa's poetry, however, that split has disappeared; instead we see a unified self, who finds its meaning in grief, in its *reaction* to the love brought about by the beloved, but not necessarily the beloved himself. Ultimately, Stampa uses Petrarchan convention as a way of realizing and defining herself as one who *willingly* chooses to embrace desire and its attendant suffering, who writes and forms herself against those norms, pushing them so that she ceases to find her identity in some other person.[32]

The narrative force of this model of the self becomes clear later in the collection. In poem 208 (206 in the first edition), Stampa, having repudiated her first love for Colaltino, finds herself in love again and concludes that she is a creature of love. She begins the sonnet by stating that Love has made her so that she lives continuously in fire ("Amor m'ha fatto tal ch'io vivo in foco"), and thus is similar to both the salamander, which was thought to live in fire, and the phoenix: "quale / l'altro di lei non men stranio animale, / che vive e spira nel medesmo loco" ("like that other no less strange animal, that lives and breathes in the same place" [2–4]). This mythical bird also served as a frequent theme for Petrarch. In a number of poems, Petrarch compares Laura to the phoenix, especially after her death, when she died

---

[32] In an unpublished thesis, Amy R. Insalaco has argued persuasively that Stampa — early on in the collection — attempts to create a sexual metaphor of female writing equivalent to the metaphor of a phallic pen writing on a virginal and female page commonly used to represent the act of a man writing. Instead, she finds Stampa drawing on the metaphor of childbirth, substituting *pena* (pain) for pen (*penna*) as a female equivalent. Stampa refers specifically to the virgin birth as a model, which of course does not require a human male in order to procreate. See A.R. Insalaco, "Pain for Pen: The Procreative Metaphor in Gaspara Stampa's *Rime* II and VIII" (Master's thesis, Brigham Young University, 1999). An article based on her thesis is now forthcoming in *Quidditas*.

and then was reborn in heaven.[33] But of greater interest to us here is poem 135, a canzone where he compares the phoenix to himself. In this poem Petrarch works through a series of comparisons, in which the lover's situation and the beloved herself are compared to mythical creatures and magical objects in order to illustrate the lover's strange condition. He begins by noting the resemblance between himself and the phoenix, the "augel" who, "di voluntaria morte / rinasce et tutto a viver si rinova" ("after voluntary death, is reborn and all renews itself to life" [7–8]). Specifically, Petrarch's desire ("lo mio voler") enacts the life-cycle of the phoenix, turning to the sun, becoming consumed, and then returning to its former state: "arde et more et riprende i nervi suoi / et vive poi con la fenice a prova" ("it burns and dies and takes again its sinews and lives on, vying with the phoenix" [14–15]). The phoenix proves to be an apt symbol for Petrarch himself because its life-cycle reenacts Petrarch's cycle of desire. Caught between Laura and Christ, Petrarch never progresses towards a unity of self, but instead finds himself trapped in a cyclical pattern of desire, partial repentance, and return to desire.

If indeed, however, Stampa's reference at the beginning of *Rime* 208 is to a phoenix, she makes no allusion to its famous ability to die and to be simultaneously reborn. Instead, she concentrates on its ability to live and breathe in fire, its state of existence. Like the salamander, she has learned to live in the fire of love, and she makes clear that her identity no longer depends on how her beloved treats her, as she has learned "non curar ch'ei che m'induce a tale / abbia di me pietá molto né poco" ("not to care whether he who brought me to this state has either much or little pity for me" [7–8]). In the following poem (which Salza places as poem 215) in the first edition, Stampa continues the analogy to the phoenix. Unlike the preceding poem, however, here she explicitly compares her love for a *new* beloved to the rebirth of the phoenix: "Qual ne le piú felici e calde arene, / nel nido acceso sol di vario odore, / d'una fenice estinta esce poi fore / un verme, che fenice altra diviene" ("in the happiest and hottest sands, in the nest kindled only with a different odor, from a phoenix consumed, comes forth a worm that becomes another phoenix" [5–8]). But whereas Petrarch's allusion to the phoenix is, as we have seen, an allusion to his split self, to his inability to give the narrative of his life a linear force, Stampa here invokes the new birth of a phoenix as a continuation of her state of loving. She thus begins the poem by asking, "Qual darai fine, Amor, a le mie pene" ("How will you put an end, Love, to my sufferings")?

---

[33] Petrarch compares Laura to the phoenix in 185, 321, 323, and 331.

Translating Petrarchan Desire

Here, as in the preceding sonnet, Stampa defines herself as a lover, but not according to how her beloved treats her: "arder per lui m'è sommo, alto diletto" ("burning for him is to me the greatest, highest joy" [14]).[34]

As we move through Stampa's Petrarchan narrative, we increasingly sense that the poet no longer has need of her beloved to provide her with an identity. Furthermore, as she makes clear in several other poems, she identifies this second love as at least partially voluntary, portraying her passion as both willed by her and imposed from without by Love. Poem 213 in the first edition (212 in Salza's ordering) thus recounts an inner debate as to whether she should pursue this second love, and poem 219 (221 in Salza) ends with the following tercet:

> Ma che poss'io, se m'è l'arder fatale,
> se volontariamente andar consento
> d'un foco in altro, e d'un in altro male?
>
> [But what can I do, if burning is my fate, if voluntarily I consent to go from one fire into another, and from one into another grief?]

This love is "fatale," and yet she willingly decides to enter a second fire. Her fate is to love, but she voluntarily embraces it. If we were to look at burning, "arder," as a metonymy for the Petrarchan style of poetry, we can see in Stampa's meditations on her second love a consideration of her use of the language and resources of Petrarchism. She takes the basic conventions of Petrarchan verse as fate, yet she willingly embraces them, and in so doing transforms them into a language that allows her to construct a more autonomous poetic identity. In Stampa's poetry we cease to experience the alternate conceptions of self-formation that we find in Petrarch; nor do we find Colonna's solution to the problem of Petrarchan desire in Neoplatonism. Stampa resolutely avoids in her love poetry a hint that her love could or should lead to something higher; it defines her life here and now, as she writes it on the page. Unlike Colonna, who claims first that her poetry is her husband's — that is,

---

[34] See also Mary B. Moore's chapter on Stampa, "Body of Light, Body of Matter: Self-Reference as Self-Modeling in Gaspara Stampa," in eadem, *Desiring Voices: Women Sonneteers and Petrarchism* (Carbondale: Southern Illinois University Press, 2000), 58–93, arguing that Stampa revises both Petrarchan "ideas of women "and "Petrarchan subjectivity," and seeing the Phoenix poems as key elements of the collection. Unfortunately, this study appeared too late for it more fully to influence my argument here.

her lord's — and then her Lord's, Stampa works within Petrarchan language eventually to push out of it, to use the language of love as a way of constructing a more autonomous self, no longer uniquely dependent on another for self-definition.[35]

If Petrarchan desire can be understood as a yearning for unity of self-definition, then this desire leads Petrarchan poets in the sixteenth century to look for ways of unifying the self. Colonna finds a solution in Neoplatonism, but Stampa looks inward rather than above, finding within her self and in her writing of her own fierce devotion a way of defining herself. While Colonna comes to declare that she and her writing, her instrument of self-definition, are fully her Lord's, Stampa's poetry becomes her own. In poem 152, she compares herself to Echo, the mythical woman who indeed has no words of her own, who can only repeat those of others; Stampa imagines herself following her beloved around, answering him with his last words ("l'estreme sue parole"). Indeed, even if she were to do this, she tells us, she would be unable to force him to stop and listen her tired speech ("s'arresti al suon di mia stanca favella"). But Stampa's involved self-portrayal undercuts the identity that she claims to assume.[36] Her poetry detailing her inner state and grief

---

[35] I have not the space here to treat Stampa's religious poetry, where at times she too seems to yearn for an Augustinian conversion. It is difficult, however, to judge the importance of these poems in Stampa's collection, as it is not clear where she would have placed them. In the first edition of her poetry, they appear as poems 275–282. Salza, however, as noted in notes 25 and 27, altered the arrangement. Starting with poem 275 in the original edition, Salza ordered them in his edition as follows: 304–306, 311, 307–310. He displaced 278 from its place in the sequence of poems in the original edition evidently because it seemed to him the best ending for his view of Stampa's poetry. (It ends with the plea, "dolce Signor, non mi lasciar perire!") Stampa's religious poems, however, seem to me much closer to Petrarch's than to Colonna's; she continuously recounts her desire for change, but she never narrates its realization. Due to the difficulties of determining where these poems belong in the collection, I have limited my discussion to the love poetry, where she never finds herself split between divine and profane love, which is untrue of Petrarch's poetry.

[36] Ann Rosalind Jones has treated the theme of Echo at greater length, arguing that "Women poets [in the Renaissance] interpreted Echo and Philomela through processes of empathetic identification, and they rewrote Ovid's tragic transformations into visions of saving feminine alliance and fantasies of freedom." Instead of merely echoing her beloved, "Stampa's Echo becomes a speaker of her own desires and more, an eloquent accuser of the 'cruelly' self-absorbed male beloved." See "New Songs for the Swallow: Ovid's Philomela in Tullia d'Aragona and Gaspara Stampa," in *Refiguring Women: Perspectives on Gender and the Italian Renaissance*, ed. Marilyn Migiel and Juliana Schiesari (Ithaca: Cornell University Press, 1991), 263–77.

reveals a poet who, far from repeating the words of her beloved, defines herself by writing against them. Although she draws on Petrarchan convention and portrays herself as a helpless woman, it is through her poetry that she is able to construct a narrative teleology that leads away from dependency toward the portrayal of a more autonomous self.

V. Stanley Benfell
BRIGHAM YOUNG UNIVERSITY

"Odious Ballads": Fallen Women's Laments and *All's Well That Ends Well*

In the late sixteenth century, writers on education, public morals, and literary theory were deeply concerned with the problem of literary exemplarity.[1] How do people use the "histories" they read, see, or hear? How does literature change their identities or desires? Philip Sidney argued that literary genres elicit from their audiences distinctions among persons and, in the process, identification with or aversion towards specific types of persons. Comedy offers to include its audience in a judicious public which excludes those who are the subject of comedy. It represents "the common errors of our life" "in the most ridiculous and scornful sort that may be, so as it is impossible that any beholder can be content to be such a one."[2] Tragedy works, more complexly, by both identification and aversion, "stirring the effects of admiration and commiseration" for its ill-fated heroes while also promoting in its audience a desire to escape the tragic fate (*Apology*, 118). Heroic poetry incites the audience to desire to become heroic: "the lofty image of such worthies most inflameth the mind with desire to be worthy" (119). Each genre calls its audience to participate in an affective bonding of a particular kind, one that either decisively includes or excludes the subjects of narrative.[3] Sidney worried, however, about the effect of genre's exclusionary drives. Comedy

---

[1] For examples, see Thomas Elyot and Roger Ascham on the role of poetic forms in moral education: Sir Thomas Elyot, *The Boke Named the Governour* (1531), ed. Foster Watson (London: J. M. Dent and Co., 1907), 34–41; Roger Ascham, *The Schoolmaster* (1570), ed. Lawrence V. Ryan (Charlottesville: for the Folger Shakespeare Library by the University Press of Virginia, 1974), 114–31.

[2] Sir Philip Sidney, *An Apology for Poetry, or, The Defense of Poesy*, ed. Geoffrey Shepherd (London: Thomas Nelson and Sons, 1965), 117.

[3] In describing the relation between audiences and protagonists, the terms "subject" and "object" are easily confused: the subject of a narrative, its hero or anti-hero, is the object of the audience's attention and its drives toward identification or exclusion. Using both terms, "subject" and "object," demonstrates that the claims to subjecthood of these fictional personae are confirmed or rejected by the putative audience the narrative constructs.

asks its audience to enjoy the spectacle of the ridiculous outsider, but "what is it to make folks gape at a wretched beggar and a beggarly clown; or, against law of hospitality, to jest at strangers, because they speak not English so well as we do?" (137). The exclusions and inclusions that genres move their audiences to make produce social distinctions and invest them with affect: admiration or sympathy towards the elevated objects of heroic and tragic poetry, but revulsion towards the foreigner, rustic, or beggar of comedy.[4] Characters' desires are admired and emulated by audiences of tragedy and rejected by audiences of comedy, while in this process the desires of fiction are translated into the desires of social life.

In its depiction of the precipitous social rise of the physician's daughter Helena, Shakespeare's *All's Well That Ends Well* dramatizes the experience of entering public spaces, of becoming the object of an audience's observation and its judgments. In this play, public attention is never neutral; the effects of publicity form a prominent theme in the scenes depicting the discovery of Helena's desire for her mistress's son and her accomplishment of those desires. The process of dissemination, whether through rumor, print, or song, inserts Helena into a fabric of generic expectations — conventional plots and roles which translate her desire for her mistress's son as heroic, tragic, or comic. Becoming the subject of public discourse entails becoming the object of an audience's laughter, emulation, disgust, or admiration. Shakespeare presents Helena as a reluctant subject of public discourse: the Clown sings ballads linking Helena to Helen of Troy, Lafew compares her to Cressida, another fallen woman treated in ballads, and she becomes the subject of a printed broadside. In a telling moment, Helena names her horror of being "traduc'd by odious ballads" (2.1.171).[5] These associations have

---

[4] Sidney condemns the degrading impulse of comedy, which produces laughter by provoking scorn. But he does not offer an alternative vision of comedy, one which might not turn on the delight of distinguishing an abnormal subject. The subject should be merely ridiculous rather than "execrable" or "miserable" (*Apology*, 137). If the distinction between subject and audience is too severe, comedy provokes the laughter that is a "scornful tickling"; less severe, more ethically appropriate distinctions designate the subject as merely foolish, like "a busy loving courtier and a heartless threatening Thraso; a self-wise-seeming schoolmaster; an awry-transformed traveller" (136–37). These subjects induce "delightful laughter."

[5] All Shakespeare quotations are taken from G. K. Hunter's edition in Richard Proudfoot, Ann Thompson, and David Scott Kastan, eds., *The Arden Shakespeare: Complete Works* (Surrey: Thomas Nelson and Sons Ltd., 1998).

in common the figure of the fallen heroine of verse laments, romantic narrative, and popular ballads.

In *All's Well*, fictions construct public roles through various genres, and being translated into the subject of a narrative can either establish or endanger one's social status. The genres of romance and ballad, for example, offer different modes of public action, each with its own social inflection. To take up a role in one of these modes is to enter the privileged space of public action; and to enter the public space of the court, the military parade, or the battlefield entails specific modes of publication: the broadsheet, ceremonial display, the public reading of personal letters, rumor, and ballads. *All's Well* is a play acutely conscious of gradations both in socially constructed private and public spaces and in the punishments allotted to those who too ambitiously presume to "publish" themselves, to become visible in order to deserve great rewards. The various forms of exposure, the roles which these forms offer to public persons, and the status markers of forms of publicity are contested by characters attempting to negotiate the terms of their entrance into public view.

Granting that *All's Well* dramatizes the process of entrance into public view through generic roles, we might still wonder why the play connects Helena to Helen of Troy, Cressida, and ballad literature. Susan Snyder has identified an ironic charge in Shakespeare's identification of Helena, despised by her husband, with Helen, an archetype of sexual desirability.[6] I argue, however, that the play presents Helen of Troy as an example of the infamous ballad heroines with whom observers like the Clown and Lafew link Helena. Helena's passion for her social superior and her journey to the court leave her open to the imposition of unwelcome public roles, particularly the role of the socially ambitious and sexually available woman. The ballad genre is particularly significant in Helena's plot because a prominent group of fallen ballad heroines capture the social dangers of a sexualized public role. In ballads, the dependence of the audience's pleasure on the literary subject's exposure and abjection is especially prominent, as ballads often take as their subjects exposed crimes, social falls, and God's vengeance upon secret sinners. Ballads represent a kind of publicity marked in the sixteenth and seventeenth centuries as degrading, both because of their plots of exposure and punishment and because ballads were sung and sold cheaply in streets, taverns, and

---

[6] Susan Snyder, "Naming Names in *All's Well That Ends Well*," *Shakespeare Quarterly* 43 (1992): 265–79, here 271–72.

fairgrounds.[7] Shakespeare uses ballads to represent social obloquy in *King Henry IV, Part 1* and in *The Rape of Lucrece*.[8]

Ambition and Exposure in Fallen-Women Ballads

The theme of seduction appears frequently in ballads of the late sixteenth and seventeenth centuries, and provides a plot for several ballad sub-genres, including the wooing of a virgin, pastoral courtship, advice to avoid marriage, and the fallen woman's lament. This last ballad category takes its themes from the tradition of female complaint, which has been surveyed by Götz Schmitz and John Kerrigan.[9] The *locus classicus* of elegiac narratives spoken by female lovers is Ovid's *Heroides*, which had, Schmitz argues, a decisive influence in late Elizabethan England, when Samuel Daniel's *Complaint of Rosamond* (1592) and Thomas Middleton's *Ghost of Lucrece* (1600), among others, were published. The female speakers of these verse complaints tell of their sexual misuse by men; through either rape or seduction, they have lost both their honor and their lovers or husbands. The women usually speak from beyond the grave; they plead for sympathy and warn other women to avoid a similarly tragic fate. These mournful speakers became favorite ballad heroines in Elizabeth's reign. During the period in which *All's Well That Ends Well* appeared, we find in the Stationer's Register for 1603 entries for such ballads as "A Lamentable Ballad of the Ladies Fall, declaring how a Gentlewoman through her too much trust came to her end, and how her Lover slew himself," "The Spanish Lady's Love," "The Bryde's Buryall," "Ye fayre Lady Constance of Cleveland and of her Disloyall Knight," and "The Wandering Prince of Troy" (also known as "Queen Dido"); in 1607, "The Life and Death of Fair Rosamond, King Henry the Second's Concubine," and in 1611–1612, "The Lamentable Song of the Lord Wigmoore, Governor of Warwicke Castle, and the Fayre Maid of Dunsmoore: as a Warning to all Maids to have care how

---

[7] On contemporary perceptions of the social milieu of ballad dissemination, see Natascha Würzbach, *The Rise of the English Street Ballad, 1550–1650*, trans. Gayna Walls (Cambridge: Cambridge University Press, 1990), 13–39.

[8] Shakespeare, *The Rape of Lucrece*, 813–819; *King Henry IV, Part 1* (Q 1598), 2.1.43–46.

[9] Götz Schmitz, *The Fall of Women in Early English Narrative Verse* (Cambridge: Cambridge University Press, 1990); John Kerrigan, ed., *Motives of Woe: Shakespeare and 'Female Complaint': A Critical Anthology* (Oxford: Clarendon Press, 1991).

Fallen Women's Laments and All's Well That Ends Well

they yeeld to the wanton Delights of young Gallants." These ballads share common elements: their heroines' youth and lack of status, their seducers' high status, and the shame that often leads to the heroines' death. But most importantly, seeking fame or status leads to each woman's fall, then to her notoriety, which itself becomes a subject of comment and blame.

The relation between the heroine of such a ballad and the audience the ballad constructs — in Walter Ong's phrase, the "fictionalized audience" — is complexly composed of both identification and repulsion.[10] The ballad creates its audience as it specifies the status of its fallen heroine, and either rewards or punishes her by making her the object of sympathy or ridicule. In order to outline this process, I will use as an example "The Hawthorne Tree," an Elizabethan ballad which thematizes women's loss of sexual honor. Like many "merry" ballads, this one initially obscures its true subject in order to provide a surprising and witty conclusion.[11] The narrator describes how "a maide of my countre," happening upon a flowering hawthorn tree, asks the tree "how came this freshness vnto the" (1, 6). Though the tree explains that sweet dew enables it to grow "triumphantly," the maid remains unsatisfied, questioning the tree until finally, it pointedly compares its own uninhibited freedom to flower with her situation:

    And you fair maide canne not do so
    for yf you let youre maidhode goe

---

[10] Walter J. Ong, "The Writer's Audience is Always a Fiction," *PMLA* 90 (1975): 9–21. For convenience, I have modernized all ballad titles in the text, with full titles in the notes. In quotations, I have followed the spelling of the cited editions. All dates are in new style unless otherwise indicated.

[11] Anon., "A mery Ballet of the Hathorne tre," Peter J. Seng., ed., *Tudor Songs and Ballads from MS Cotton Vespasian A-25* (Cambridge, MA: Harvard University Press, 1978), 82-4. Though the reader does not yet know that this is a fallen-woman ballad, the title suggests the topic of love and sexuality; the hawthorn tree was depicted as a symbol of profane love in medieval literature, its thorns representing the pain resulting from lust, as its fragrant blossoms represented its pleasures. Also called the "May tree," the hawthorn flowered in May and its branches were cut for decoration as part of May Day festivities. As we know from Philip Stubbes's *Anatomie of Abuses* (1583) and Robert Herrick's "Corinna's Going A-Maying," the young people's May Day flower-gathering excursions were blamed (or praised, as in Herrick) for encouraging premarital sex. See Susan S. Eberly, "A Thorn Among the Lilies: The Hawthorn in Medieval Love Allegory," *Folklore* 100 (1989): 41–52; and Philip Stubbes, *The Anatomie of Abuses*, ed. M.J. Kidnie, MRTS 245 (Tempe: MRTS, 2002), 209–10.

> then will yt never no more be sene
> as I with my braunches can growe grene (29–32).

The maid blushes and turns away. The moment of revelation for the reader is also the maid's; the maid now suffers "marvelous dowbte" — a doubt based on the intimation that has driven her insistent questions, for she is "suspecting still what she would wene / Her maid heade lost would never be seen" (39–40).

While the hawthorn tree warns the maid that public flourishing is forbidden her, the ballad repeatedly asserts that virginity "shuldbe sene" and should, in fact, display itself as does the hawthorn, "faire and cleane" and "freshe and grene." These contradictory imperatives produce the maid's insistent questioning of her alter ego, the hawthorn tree, whose branches are stripped for May Day festivities shortly after its flowering. The tree's heroic self-publicizing, therefore, courts its destruction, a logic of desire and violence that refers proleptically to the maid's sexual honor, which she must both display and hide from her imagined public's desires. In the final stanza, the narrator resolves this paradox by evoking a community of observers who know the maid's story and speak of her as no longer available for view. Only the publication through rumor of her seclusion and inaccessibility fulfills the ballad's demand that the maid display her sexual honor while hiding herself. In contrast, the tree represents a utopian vision combining public display and fertility: the more it is seen, the more quickly destroyed, and yet "more and more my twedgs growe grene" (20). The tree's wonderful powers of self-renewal provide a foil for the maid's tragic vulnerability to "deflowering."

Just as the maid in the ballad is chastened and reforms once the hawthorn tree has identified her as a woman imperiled, the ballad's female readers, by Sidney's logic, will recognize themselves in the ballad heroine and avoid her fate. This generic convention provides the basis for a witty inversion of expectations in another comic ballad about women's sexual notoriety, William Elderton's "The Pangs of Love and Lovers Fittes" (1559).[12] Elderton's narrator attempts to persuade his mistress to grant him "good will" by citing famous illicit liaisons, including those of Cressida and Helen of Troy, the literary heroines with whom various characters in *All's Well that Ends Well*

---

[12] W[illiam] E[lderton], "The Pangs of Love and Lovers Fittes" (1559), in J. Payne Collier, ed., *Old Ballads, from Early Printed Copies* (London: Printed for The Percy Society, 1840), 25–28.

associate Helena. The narrator of "The Pangs and Fits" repeatedly emphasizes the publication and dissemination of stories about famous love affairs, using phrases such as "I read sometime," "as the stories tell," and "by learned lore"; but these usually cautionary tales are now to inspire his mistress to "fall" herself. As in "The Hawthorne Tree," the narrator invites the audience to share with him the spectacle of a woman (in this case, the ballad's addressee) in danger of imitating sexually truant female archetypes. Here, the endangered woman is explicitly envisioned as a reader or hearer, both of this poem and of the "learned lore" the narrator cites. The ballad parodies the notion of exemplarity by reversing the expected relation between woman-as-reader and woman-as-example: the addressee's sympathy with Cressida, Helen, and the others will lead her to imitate them rather than to avoid their fates. As "The Hawthorne Tree" performs a simultaneous inclusion of the reader and exclusion of the female subject, "The Pangs and Fits" splits the addressee, the mistress, from the audience, who are to recognize Helen and Cressida as tragic figures and cautionary examples and appreciate the narrator's duplicitous wit.

Linked in contemporary works by their common historical context, their sexual availability, and their inconstancy, Helen of Troy and Cressida provide particularly apposite examples for the authors of ballads on fallen women. The later ballad "All in a Green Meadowe" (c. 1620–1650), in which a maiden laments her virginity, turns to Helen of Troy and Cressida to represent sexually satisfied women: "Hellen of greece for bewty was the rarest, / a wonder of the world, & certainly the ffairest; / yet wold she, nor Cold shee, live a maiden still." Women like Cressida, who first accept and then reject their lovers, will find themselves begging for sexual favors: "[If they be li]ke to Cressus to scorne soe true a freind, / [Theyle be] glad to receive poore Charitye in the end."[13] This comic ballad relies on the audience's familiarity with tragic ballads of fallen women, in which famous women mourn the loss of chastity which led to their fall from grace. "All in a Green Meadow" comically reverses the situation by having a lonely virgin complain of missing her sexual chances. The speaker's repeated use of the words "mourn," "complain," and "lament," her warning that "time past is not recalld againe," and her final injunction to "all maids" to be wise and avoid her fate, all remind the audience of more morally orthodox laments.

---

[13] John S. Farmer, ed., *Merry Songs and Ballads* (New York: Cooper Square Publishers, Inc., 1964), 1:82–83.

The fame of their heroines is an explicit subject of fallen-women ballads, for notoriety is both a sign and symptom of their falls. Public exposure, as in "The Hawthorne Tree," puts a woman in danger of losing her honor and reveals the defective virtue which first led her to range abroad. In "A Complaint" (1580), Troilus blames Cressida for the "gadding moode" which led her to wander to the Greek camp, "for wandering women, most men say / Cannot be good and go astray" (1, 6-7). Now Troilus himself has further exposed Cressida by narrating this ballad: "I pleasure not to blaze her blame . . . / But all good women by her shame, / May learn what Catterwauling is" (2–5). Cressida responds that had Troilus married her "the blome of blame had not been spread, / The seede of shame had not bine sowne" (28–29). She accuses Troilus of contributing to her infamy. Both speakers agree in locating two subjects of shame: Cressida's wandering into the Greek camp, and her dissemination through rumor and print. They only debate whether Cressida's "gadding" — into the Greek camp and into print — signals her own volition or her lover's failure to "keep" her.[14]

The theme of sexual publicity is strongly linked with social ambition in the popular ballads on the mistresses of English kings.[15] In these ballads, particularly "Jane Shore" (1603) and "The Fair Maid of London" (1600), women's social and sexual falls result from their desire to become public figures. King Edward speaks the first part of the Fair Maid's ballad, promising her that "In granting your love you will purchase renowne / . . . Great ladies of honour shall 'tend on thy traine" (37, 41).[16] Jane Shore attributes her fall

---

[14] "A Complaint," in *The Paradise of Dainty Devices*, ed. Hyder Edward Rollins (Cambridge, MA: Harvard University Press, 1927), 117–18. Entered as "A proper ballad dialoge wise betwene Troylus and Cressida" in the Stationers Register on 23 June 1581 by Edward White. See also "The history of Troilus whose throtes hath Well bene tried," entered 1565–1566 by Thomas Purfoote: Hyder E. Rollins, *An Analytical Index to the Ballad-Entries (1557–1709)* (Hatboro, PA: Tradition Press, 1967), 57; 99.

[15] On Jane Shore and Rosamond ballads, see James L. Harner, "'The Wofull Lamentation of Mistris Jane Shore': The Popularity of an Elizabethan Ballad," *Papers of the Bibliographical Society of America* 71 (1977): 137–50.

[16] "A Courtly new Ballad of the Princely Wooing of the faire Maid of London by King Edward," in *The Roxburghe Ballads,* ed. W. Chappell (Hertford: Stephen Austin and Sons for The Ballad Society, 1869; repr. New York: AMS Press, 1966), 181–85. An earlier edition appears in the Stationers' Register on 1 March 1600, entered by William White as "A Courtly new songe of the princely wooynge of A fayre mayde of London; also the fayre mayde of Londons Answere to the same"; other editions appear in 1624 and 1675: Rollins, *Analytical Index*, 76; 190-91. On the popularity of this ballad, see Chappell's note in *The Roxburghe Ballads.*

to the vanity which led her to first display herself in her husband's goldsmith shop, spreading word of her beauty abroad until it reached the ears of the king, and then to accede to the king's desires.[17] Shore's move "from City then to Court" brought her private access to the great; "thus advanced on high / Commanding Edward with [her] eye," she "knew the secrets of a King," and became the object of others' gazes: "For when I smil'd, all men were glad, / But when I mourn'd, my Prince grew sad" (43–66). The attention of "all men" becomes her punishment when Richard III forces Shore to do penance in the street, "Where many thousands did me view, / Who late in Court my credit knew"; now she and her husband offer her story as a warning to other women (87–88). Like Cressida's "Complaint," the ballad exhibits little interest in Shore's sexual relationships but a great deal in her public exposure. In the ballads, Cressida's and Shore's crimes are not primarily debauchery or licentiousness, but vanity and the desire for public attention.

To English Renaissance writers, Jane Shore represented a domestic analogue for Helen and Cressida, the fallen women of Troy. In his imitation of Ovid's *Heroides*, *England's Heroicall Epistles* (1597), Michael Drayton replaces the letters of complaint or seduction exchanged by Helen of Troy and Paris, Dido and Aeneas with letters by Edward IV and Jane Shore, and Henry II and his mistress, Rosamond.[18] Cressida, Helen of Troy, Jane Shore, Rosamond, and the Fair Maiden comprise a coherent class of heroines. To mention one is to evoke the others. Drayton drew upon Samuel Daniel's *Complaint of Rosamond* (1592) to write both Jane Shore's and Rosamond's letters.[19] Daniel himself has his Rosamond mention Jane Shore's popularity to defend the publication of her lament; and both the ballad Jane Shore and the Fair Maid defend their self-display by Rosamond's example.[20] By the end

---

[17] [Thomas Deloney], "The Woful Lamentation of Mrs. Jane Shore, a Goldsmith's Wife of London, sometime King Edward the Fourth's Concubine, who for her Wanton Life came to a Miserable End. Set forth for the Example of all wicked Livers" [n.d.], in *The Roxburghe Ballads*, ed. Chappell, 1:483–92. "The Lamentacon of mistres Jane Shore" was entered in the Stationers' Register to William White on 11 June 1603. See E. Arber, *A Transcript of the Registers of the Company of Stationers of London, 1554–1640* (London: privately printed, 1895–1897).

[18] On imitations of *Heroicall Epistles*, see *The Works of Michael Drayton*, ed. J. William Hebel (Oxford: Basil Blackwell, 1941), 5:97–99.

[19] See *Works*, ed. Hebel, 5:102–4, 128.

[20] [Thomas Deloney], "The Life and Death of Fair Rosamond, King Henry the Second's Concubine" [n.d.], in *The Roxburghe Ballads*, ed. Chappell, 6:673-76. The editor's note gives 1607 as the last possible date but suggests that the Rosamond ballad may have been published in 1592/3 in Thomas Deloney's *Garland of Good Will*.

of the seventeenth century, the association of Helen of Troy and Cressida with Jane Shore and Rosamond was utterly formulaic in ballad literature. As the 1707 ballad, "Of King Edward and Jane Shore," proclaims,

> Hellen of Greece she came of Spartan blood,
> Agricola and Cressida they were brave Whores and good . . . .
>
> These were the Ladies that caus'd the Trojan Sack,
> But Jane Shore, Jane Shore she spoil'd King Edward's Back.[21]

The association of Trojan and English fallen women link these heroines together as public figures united by their desire for status, by their shaming, and now by the dissemination of their laments.

As public objects, fallen women continue to tantalize audiences' appetites long after they can no longer transgress with their mortal lovers. Faustus's notorious resurrection of Helen of Troy to satisfy his lust may be taken as paradigmatic of the publicized whore's symbolic sexual availability. Having once, like Cressida, made herself the object of male desire through her "gadding mood," the public whore eternally repeats the sin of accessibility as the subject of ballads and licentious allusion. As narrators of ballads that reveal their sexual history, famous women compound their guilt, even though they offer moral advice and plead for the audience's sympathy. The more they plead in popular song and verse, the greater their fame, and the greater their crime of public accessibility. A sixteenth-century comic poem found by Frederick Moulton riddles on the word "penis," which is a "wand," "sting," "pole," and finally, when wielded by Helen of Troy, a "pen." The author portrays Helen of Troy as author of both her sexual acts and, figuratively, her publication; the penis "is the pen fayre Helen tooke / to wright within her two leavd booke." The agency Helen achieves as the metaphorical holder of the pen suggests that she is the author, not only of her original transgressions, but also of her continuing defamation.[22] Helen takes the pen/phallus herself, as though she sinned not only by adultery but also by authoring the many poems about her — she is blamed, implicitly, even for this bawdy poem itself. Tales of

---

[21] *Merry Songs*, ed. Farmer, 4:100–1.

[22] Quoted in Ian Frederick Moulton, *Before Pornography: Erotic Writing in Early Modern England* (Oxford: Oxford University Press, 2000), 48–49. According to Moulton, the manuscript collection in which this poem appears dates to the early seventeenth century (MS. Rosenbach 1083/15).

fallen women occlude the existence of an author, printers, booksellers, and so on in order to attribute all public agency, and thus blame, to their heroines. They implicitly accuse their heroines of self-commodification, of becoming mere instruments for an audience's pleasure. The heroines' worth is reduced to the very sheet of cheaply printed paper on which their names appear. It is no wonder, then, that when parting from the king Helena asks for "from your thoughts / a modest one to bear me back again" (2.1.126–127).

I have argued that the representation of these women in English ballads focused largely on their status as public objects both before and after death. But the significance of such a status is vexed. Alongside the explicit moral condemnation of women's public exposure in these ballads is a positive view of public women which emphasizes the audience's sympathy for the fallen woman and her power of suasion over other women. Are the audiences who, like Faustus, eagerly revivify Helen and her crimes for their pleasure compounding the public woman's sexual truancy or participating in a reparative social ritual? Does the audience's interest in the heroine generate desire that is morally regenerative or defiling? Christopher Brooke's narrative poem *The Ghost of Richard the Third* (1614) depicts Jane Shore as the object of a voracious feminine sympathy. His Richard III declares that Shore's "fate the women so commisserate / that who (to see my justice on that sinner) / Drinks not her tears: and makes her fact, their dinner?"[23] Richard III's sardonic view of Jane's audience suggests that they take an impious and voyeuristic pleasure in bemoaning her downfall. Throughout these ballads and the commentary on their reception runs the suspicion that the relation between sexualized heroine and sympathetic audience is itself ethically suspect, and perhaps itself eroticized. Accordingly, publication as a sexualized subject can either punish or comfort: Cressida identifies her publication as a source of further shame, while Jane Shore and Rosamond vie for prominence and public sympathy.

Ambition and Exposure in *All's Well That Ends Well*

At first glance, Helena's situation in *All's Well That Ends Well* hardly suggests that that of the pursued woman of ballad literature. If anything, Helena seems to be in danger of never falling, of becoming a "withered pear," in Parolles' phrase

---

[23] Quoted in Harner, "'The Wofull Lamentation',"140.

for "old virginity" (1.1.154–160). Helena is the passionate unrequited lover rather than the seducer's victim; even when he has married her Bertram swears to "never bed her" (2.3.269). Susan Snyder has argued that Helena's name is ironic; while Helen of Troy was a notorious object of lust, Helena must trick her husband into bed.[24] In *All's Well* it is Helena's entry into public view, rather than the familiar seduction plot, which prompts allusions to ballad heroines.

Shakespeare sets each stage of Helena's pursuit of Bertram in a context of public observation and commentary. The Steward overhears Helena's confession of love; Helena must appear before a bawdily bantering audience at court; her cure of the King elicits the publication of a broadside; and she must ceremoniously choose her husband before the court. The atmosphere of lewd commentary which accompanies each of Helena's moments of public exposure gives content to her fear of "Tax of impudence / A strumpet's boldness, a divulged shame / traduc'd by odious ballads" (2.1.169-171). The public role Helena assumes in her pursuit of Bertram also opens her to the charge of social ambition, a charge to which she is highly sensitive from her first appearance in the play. Indeed, the "impudence" and "boldness" she cites apply to both sexual and social presumptions, for the two are closely linked in the cultural archetype of the "strumpet." The fallen women of ballad literature were often depicted as ambitious social risers who, like Jane Shore, sought attention and status through liaisons with men of higher status.

Helena is painfully aware of the ominous social implications of her passion for Bertram; her first soliloquy takes place after the departing Bertram has reminded her of her place: "Be comfortable to my mother, your mistress, and make much of her" (1.1.73-74). Alone, Helena contemplates her position: "Th' ambition in my love thus plagues itself, / The hind that would be mated by the lion / Must die for love" (1.1.88-90). This startling image places sexual desire in a context of physical danger and miscegenation. Helena alters the Petrarchan motif of male hunter and female hunted found, for example, in Thomas Wyatt's "Whoso list to hunt, I know where is an hind." But Helena's version adds another layer of signification — that of social status. "Hind" suggests not only the hunted animal, but the familiar servant.

---

[24] Susan Snyder, "*All's Well That Ends Well* and Shakespeare's Helens: Text and Subtext, Subject and Object," *English Literary Renaissance* 18 (1988): 66–77, here 70–72; eadem, "Naming Names," 271–72.

While the *OED* gives the simple meaning "a servant," Mosby's cutting remarks to Alice Arden in *Arden of Feversham* give the word, with its bestial associations, a contemptuous charge: "Go, get thee gone, a copesmate for thy hinds!"[25] Both Mosby's and Helena's imagery captures the intensity of social transgression inherent in heterosexual servant-master liaisons; but while Mosby's accusation imbues a mistress's sexual interest in her servants with shame, Helena imagines a mating with her master as dangerous rather than shameful. Helena's imagined destruction in the act of sexual union extends the conventional sexual quibble on "dying for love" to a brutally literal extreme. Here Bertram is both lord and master and wild and predatory lion — this despite the fact that Bertram neither pursues Helena nor recognizes her love. For Helena, her difference in status from Bertram alone suggests that he is dangerous to her.

In Helena's image, the gentle hind goes to meet its wild predator, and its death, gladly. Despite her images of complaisance — Helena admits that "In his bright radiance and collateral light / Must I be comforted, not in his sphere" and "my idolatrous fancy / Must sanctify his relics" — she is still "the hind that would be mated by the lion," and Helena will repeatedly assert that she is ready to die for love. Helena elevates her desire by embracing its possibly destructive outcome. The overtones of this speech are not hopelessness and passivity, but intimations of the heroic cast which Helena will give to her quest to win Bertram.

One prominent strain of criticism on *All's Well* reads this first soliloquy as a statement of the virginal passivity that Helena must eschew in order to pursue Bertram; the play thus seeks to overcome both Helena's and Bertram's anxieties about sexuality and marriage. Robert Grams Hunter has provided the most optimistic version of this account, arguing that by surmounting their sexual restraints Helena and Bertram revivify and transform a decrepit and sterile society. Similarly, for John F. Adams the play idealizes procreation in order to redeem sexuality from the taint of lust.[26] But other critics, such as Richard Wheeler, Carol Thomas Neely, and Janet Adelman, have seen less utopian consummation and more deep-seated anxiety in the

---

[25] *OED* 2, s. v. "hind," $n.^2$, 1–2. *Arden of Feversham* (1592), 8.104–105.
[26] Robert Grams Hunter, *Shakespeare and the Comedy of Forgiveness* (New York: Columbia University Press, 1965), 109–12; John F. Adams, "*All's Well That Ends Well*: The Paradox of Procreation," *Shakespeare Quarterly* 12 (1961): 261–70.

sexual thematics of *All's Well*.[27] Views of the play which emphasize the problematic reconciliation of marriage and sexuality make use of Helena's association with two female archetypes: Diana and Helen of Troy. Each figure represents one side of Helena's character: Diana her chastity and restraint, and Helen her intense sexual desire for Bertram.[28] I contend that Helena actively assumes the positive role of "Diana's knight," while the repeated negative associations with famous fallen women are assigned to Helena by others. To take Diana and Helen of Troy as roughly equivalent female archetypes for the two sides of Helena's sexuality erases their social connotation: Helen of Troy is a figure not for feminine desire but for the eroticized object of social opprobrium.

Helena's sexual choices reflect her dependent social position and the play's context of real threats of public shame and infamy. *All's Well's* theme of virginity and sexuality, I argue, is inseparable from the theme of mastery and dependency and its careful depiction of the dangers and rewards that public attention offers Helena. When she admits her feelings to the Countess, Helena first excuses her love for Bertram as "poor, but honest," like her upbringing; she will not dare to claim love from him, but "Indian-like . . . adore / The sun that looks upon his worshipper / But knows of him no more" (1.3.190; 199–202). Here Helena disavows any expectation of Bertram's raising her to his own social level, since their status difference precludes marriage. But she appeals to the Countess' own experience of love —

— O then, give pity
To her whose state is such that cannot choose
But lend and give where she is sure to lose;
That seeks not to find that her search implies,
But riddle-like lives sweetly where she dies! (1.3.209–212)

---

[27] Richard Wheeler, "Imperial Love and the Dark House: *All's Well that Ends Well*," chap. 2 in *Shakespeare's Development and the Problem Comedies* (Berkeley: University of California Press, 1981), 35–91; Carol Thomas Neely, "Power and Virginity in the Problem Comedies: *All's Well That Ends Well*," chap. 2 in *Broken Nuptials in Shakespeare's Plays* (New Haven: Yale UP, 1985), 58–104; Adelman, "Bed Tricks: On Marriage as the End of Comedy in *All's Well That Ends Well* and *Measure for Measure*," in *Shakespeare's Personality*, ed. Norman N. Holland et al. (Berkeley: University of California Press, 1989), 151–74, here 161–62. See also Arthur C. Kirsch, *Shakespeare and the Experience of Love* (Cambridge: Cambridge University Press: 1981), 108–43.

[28] Snyder, "Naming Names," 276–79.

Fallen Women's Laments and All's Well That Ends Well 147

The "riddle" alludes to the symbolic end of the "hind": both the possible "death" of her virginity, and the threatening social implications of her love for Bertram.[29] Helena is not just any woman in love, but one "whose state is such" that finding "that her search implies," Bertram's love, would mean disaster.[30] We see just such a disaster when Diana, claiming Bertram as husband, meets with universal calumny in the final scene.

By the time Helena states her fear of the taint of sexual errancy we have already seen it realized. The public revelation of Helena's love for Bertram unfolds gradually in a scene which opens with the Countess and two of her familiar servants, her steward and clown. The Countess announces that the absent Helena will be the subject of this scene: "I will now hear. What say

---

[29] *All's Well* often dramatizes paradoxes and riddles, and the final scene's structure is that of the setting up and solving of the riddle of Diana, who insists she is both maid and not maid. Incidental riddles multiply: Parolles asserts that Bertram loved "as a gentleman does a woman... He lov'd her, sir, and lov'd her not" (5.3.243–246). These proliferating riddles take love and sexuality as their subject and call attention to the tension between exploitative aspects of sexual desire and the idealization of Helena's love.

[30] The laments of women who lose their honor to socially superior men use similar riddling metaphors, as the "Fair Maid" does:

> Oh, wanton King Edward! thy labour is vaine
> To follow the pleasure thou canst not attaine,
> Which getting, thou losest, and having, dost wast it,
> The which if thou purchase, is spoil'd if thou hast it.
>
> But if thou obtainst it, thou nothing hast won;
> And I, losing nothing, yet quite am undone;
> But if of that Jewell a King doe deceive me,
> No King can restore, though a Kingdom he give me (53–60).

Here, as in Helena's many allusions to "dying for love," the paradox of spoiling by gaining refers to a loss of sexual honor which ends in the woman's death. Likewise, Dido, Phillis, and the "desperate damsel" die of despair; the king's wife Eleanor poisons Rosamond; the gentlewoman of "The Lady's Fall" dies of shame; and Jane Shore "for her Wanton Life came to a Miserable End." Thus Helena connects death with public shame and ballad publication in her strange wager with the king, offering to venture not only "Tax of impudence / traduc'd by odious ballads" but "worse of worst, extended / With vildest torture, let my life be ended" (2.1.169–173). See "A Fayre Mayde of London," "A Lamentable Ballad of the Ladies Fall," "The desperate Damsell's Tragedy," [H. G.], "The Tragedy of Phillis," and "The Wandering Prince of Troy," in *The Roxburghe Ballads*, ed. Chappell, 1:181–85, 6:764–65, 1:265–70, 2:608–10, 6:548–51.

you of this gentlewoman?" (1.3.1).[31] Before the Steward can speak the Clown breaks out into witty denunciations of marriage and women's perfidy. The subject of the scene, we assume, is still Helena, despite the long deferral of the steward's report. When the Countess accuses the Clown of being a "foul-mouth'd and calumnious knave" (1.3.54–55), he defends himself as a singer of ballads and a purveyor of known truths:

Clo. A prophet I, madam, and I speak the truth the next way:

For I the ballad will repeat
Which men full true shall find:
Your marriage comes by destiny,
Your cuckoo sings by kind (1.3.56–61).

Ballads convey "truth the next way," the Clown asserts, for "destiny" and "kind" dictate their subjects. In the role of ballad-singer and seller, the Clown publishes adultery as "full true" history and, by the same token, prophecy, using the logic of exemplarity we have seen in the ballads of fallen women. Moreover, the Clown does offer a "prophecy" of sorts — his scurrilous ballads anticipate the announcement that Helena loves Bertram. The Clown projects a degraded version of events before they are officially disseminated.[32]

---

[31] A series of incongruous digressions follow, and apparently the play only returns to Helena 122 lines later. First the Steward explains that he wishes to avoid speaking of his services to the Countess, for we "make foul the clearness of our deservings, when of ourselves we publish them" (1.3.3–6); then the Countess reminds the Clown of his bad reputation: "the complaints I have heard of you I do not all believe." This sequence captures the general atmosphere of public judgment in the play. *All's Well* is a play insistently concerned with public performances and the audiences which evaluate even ordinary acts, as well as in the dissemination of a person's "credit" through rumor and allegation. Here the steward has offered to report on a gentlewoman under his supervision in light of, as he later delicately remarks, "the loss that may happen" (1.3.115–116). For a discussion of other deferrals in the play, see Susan Snyder, "'The King's Not Here': Displacement and Deferral in *All's Well that Ends Well*," *Shakespeare Quarterly* 43 (1992): 20–32.

[32] When Bertram's letter rejecting Helena reaches Rossillion, the Clown again anticipates the news with a parallel announcement. While the Countess reads the letter, the Clown muses aloud that "I have no mind to Isbel since I was at court" (2.2.11). We then hear that Bertram "has no mind to" Helena. Noticing the Clown's tendency to voice concerns which belong to other characters, Susan Snyder has argued that the Clown is "a voice available to say the unsayable, in his sexual aversion speaking for Bertram but in his obsessive, driving desire speaking for Helen." In my reading, the Clown's

The Clown continues his derisive allusions to Helena's situation by evoking her famous namesake, Helen of Troy:

> Was this fair face the cause, quoth she,
> Why the Grecians sacked Troy?
> Fond done, done fond,
> Was this King Priam's joy? . . .
> Among nine bad if one be good,
> There's yet one good in ten. (1.3.67–70; 74–75)

Here Shakespeare stages the Clown's strategic use of a familiar ballad to demean Helena by association. Even before the discovery of her secret, Helena is publicized in the company of ballad heroines and the context of sexual disorder. As with the maid in "The Hawthorne Tree," the audience recognizes in Helena's story the ballad plot of the fallen woman. Apparently the Clown quotes a well-known ballad, for the Countess recognizes that he has taken liberties with it: "What, one good in ten? You corrupt the song, sirrah" (1.3.76–77). The Clown has not only changed "nine good" to "nine bad," but changed the subject from Paris ("King Priam's joy") to Helen because "And we might have a good woman born but or every blazing star or at an earthquake, 'twould mend the lottery well; a man may draw his heart out ere 'a pluck one" (1.3.83–86).[33] An audience familiar with this ballad would note that the Clown has both redirected a ballad about Paris to attack Helen and changed the words to make Helen of Troy represent all women. The Clown's "corruption" of the song attempts to impose upon Helena a public role as "Example to all Wicked Livers" or "Warning for Women," like Jane Shore and Helen of Troy.

In "The Hawthorne Tree," the audience's recognition of the imperiled-virgin plot unites them with the narrator and an imagined public enjoying the spectacle of the maid's shame. Here, however, Helena herself describes her desires and the danger she faces before we encounter the Clown's mockery.

---

use of conventional genres such as the ballad and its attendant themes and jokes suggests that his publication of other characters' acts through debased allegories is itself at issue: cf. Snyder, "'The King's Not Here'," 23.

[33] Hyder E. Rollins hypothesized that this ballad was "The lamentations of Hecuba and the ladies of Troye," entered in the Stationers' Register in 1586. See G. K. Hunter's note to 1.3.67–76, and Peter J. Seng, *The Vocal Songs in the Plays of Shakespeare: A Critical History* (Cambridge, MA: Harvard University Press, 1967), 177–78.

When the Clown makes Helena a subject of scandal, the audience is distanced from this demeaning reinterpretation of Helena's desires. Here, it is the Clown who is isolated; we are forewarned that he is a "foul-mouth'd and calumnious knave," and the Countess rebukes him and sends him away (1.3.54–55). The Countess points out that the Clown strategically "corrupts" the ballad to slander Helena. *All's Well* is a play deeply suspicious of prophecies; Bertram recognizes that Parolles "has deceiv'd me like a double-meaning prophesier" (4.3.95–97). As in *The Winter's Tale*, in this scene Shakespeare assumes in his audience a skeptical attitude towards the truth of ballads.[34] The audience then can take the Clown's association of Helena with Helen of Troy as the very "tax of impudence" Helena has feared from "odious ballads," and assess the ballad as a revelation not of Helena's sexuality but, instead, of her public reception.

Like the Clown, the nobleman Lafew associates Helena with a famous fallen woman: in this case it is Cressida. Lafew has appeared as the judicious elder statesman and friend of the Countess, but he strikes a merrily salacious pose in presenting Helena to the king. He promises that Helena's "simple touch / Is powerful to raise King Pippen, nay, / To give great Charlemain a pen in's hand / And write to her a love-line" (2.1.74–77). The bawdy joke in Helena's "raising" King Pippin and giving Charlemagne a "pen in's hand" recurs in Bertram's response to hearing that the king's cure has procured him a wife: "But follows it, my lord, to bring me down / Must answer for your raising?" (2.3.112–13). Bertram has cause to resent Helena, but Lafew has none; Lafew apologizes twice for his "light deliverance" on the subject of Helena, but nevertheless the ribald connotations of this event are too compelling for him to resist, for he adds, "I am Cressid's uncle / That dare leave two together. Fare you well" (2.1.96–97). Helena again irresistibly recalls to her audience the famous stories of ambitious, sexually available women. After this, Helena's request for "from your royal thoughts / a modest one to bear me back again" and her fear of being "traduc'd with odious ballads" seem justified (2.1.126–127, 171). The public reaction to the king's cure also appears in Lafew and Parolles' dialogue, in which Lafew places Helena and the king in bawdy contexts and again excuses himself. Furthermore, Helena now has become the subject of a printed broadsheet taking her as a miraculous agent of the divine, "A showing of a heavenly effect in an earthly actor" (2.3.23–24). This positive representation of Helena's actions depends, however, upon the same logic of exemplarity as the sexual associations with Cressida and Helen of Troy.

---

[34] Shakespeare, *The Winter's Tale*, 4.4.

Clearly, such narratives of exposure are strongly shaped by genre. It is the context of ballads that give Helen of Troy's and Cressida's tales their edge of cheap commerce, their whiff of the street stall and the fairgrounds. Each genre of publication offers its own public roles, and Shakespeare allows Helena to choose another genre that makes of the desiring woman an entirely different kind of public subject. The conceptual opposition of Helen of Troy and Diana, to which many critics of the play have pointed, structures Helena's public personae.[35] But while other characters connect her to Helen of Troy, it is Helena herself who invokes Diana, referring to herself as "Diana's knight." More appropriate to the generalized Diana myth would have been "Diana's nymph," or perhaps "Diana's vestal," emphasizing her chastity. Instead, Shakespeare chooses for Helena's self-portraiture the heroic image of the female knight devoted to chastity — as E. M. W. Tillyard pointed out, this description recalls Edmund Spenser's Britomart in Book 3 of *The Faerie Queene*.[36] Spenser treats Helen of Troy as Britomart's opposite number; in Canto 9, Spenser apologizes for the forthcoming "odious argument," which will introduce a "paragone / of evill" in that "wanton Lady" Hellenore, a latter-day Helen of Troy. Still, "white seems fairer, macht with blacke attone," and Hellenore's perfidy demonstrates, by contrast, Britomart's chastity.[37] As Mihoko Suzuki observes, "Britomart's errancy, set against Hellenore's subjugation, emerges as a sign of her independence and freedom."[38] As a knight errant, Britomart makes wandering the foundation for a positive model of desiring femininity that directly contrasts with the meaning of "going astray" for a ballad heroine.

Helena describes the attainment of her love as a quest.[39] The Steward reports Helena's complaint that Diana is no "queen of virgins, that would

---

[35] See, for example, Neely, "Power and Virginity," 65–70; Adelman, "Bed Tricks," 160–61; and Adams, "Paradox of Procreation," 261–70.

[36] E. M. W. Tillyard, *Shakespeare's Problem Plays* (Toronto: University of Toronto Press, 1949), 117.

[37] *The Faerie Queene*, ed. Thomas P. Roche (London: Penguin Books, 1978), 3.9.1-2. Mihoko Suzuki traces in detail Britomart's relation to Hellenore and to Florimell, another Helen of Troy analogue, in *Metamorphoses of Helen: Authority, Difference, and the Epic* (Ithaca: Cornell University Press, 1989), 150–77.

[38] Suzuki, *Metamorphoses of Helen*, 168.

[39] Helena employs the heroic mode to combat the taint of social presumption and waywardness suggested by the Clown and Lafew. But as the play progresses Helena chooses new strategies: upon winning Bertram in marriage she proclaims a change of allegiance from "Diana's altar" to "imperial Love," and upon the failure of her scheme she seems to regret the heroic mode, apologizing for acting as "vengeful Juno" and declaring herself now "Saint Jacques' pilgrim" (2.3.74–75; 3.4.4, 13).

suffer her poor knight surpris'd without rescue in the first assault or ransom afterward" (1.3.110–112). Here Helena's connection to Diana is explicitly martial; Helena is no votary but an adventurer. She offers to "venture / The well-lost life of mine on his grace's cure," and the Countess responds in like spirit: "I'll stay at home and pray God's blessing unto thine attempt" (1.3.248–249). "Attempt" here, like "venture," has the trappings of glory, and Helena also uses the word in this sense:

> Impossible be strange attempts to those
> That weigh their pains in sense, and do suppose
> What hath been cannot be. Who ever strove
> To show her merit that did miss her love? (1.1.220–223)

Helena allies her "strange attempt" with others well known to the audience by alluding to "what hath been," assuming the familiarity of stories of women who won their loves. Helena's references are to feminine heroes who did not merely love faithfully but actively pursued their loves by showing their worthiness. Such women were found in the pages of chivalric romance: in Spenser, but also in Montemayor's *Diana*, Ariosto's *Orlando Furioso*, *The Boke of Huon of Bordeaux*, and the Amadis cycle of romances.[40] The female knight seeks renown, and finds it; but hers is a powerful version of female agency. Her body is shielded by armor, and though she is known for both beauty and martial prowess, she presents an impervious and undifferentiated exterior to the world, retaining the status of private subject behind that

---

[40] Each of these romances was translated into English (most in several editions) during the sixteenth century. Montemayor's *Diana* and Gil Polo's *Enamoured Diana* were published in Bartholomew Yong's translation in 1598; John Bourchier's translation of *Huon of Bordeaux* appeared in two editions by 1515 and again in 1601; John Harington's translation of *Orlando Furioso* appeared in 1591, and books of the *Amadis* were translated by Anthony Munday, Lazarus Pyott, and Thomas Paynell in 1572, 1590, 1595, and 1598. On women warriors in these romances, see Winfried Schleiner, "Le feu cache: Homosocial Bonds Between Women in a Renaissance Romance," *Renaissance Quarterly* 45 (1992): 293–311; Alison Taufer, "The Only Good Amazon Is a Converted Amazon: The Woman Warrior and Christianity in the Amadis Cycle," in *Playing with Gender: A Renaissance Pursuit*, ed. Jean R. Brink, Maryanne C. Horowitz, and Allison P. Coudert (Urbana: University of Illinois Press, 1991), 35-52; Diane Watt, "Read My Lips: Clippyng and Kyssyng in the Early Sixteenth Century," in *Queerly Phrased: Language, Gender, and Sexuality*, ed. Anna Livia and Kira Hall (New York: Oxford University Press, 1997), 167–77. [Ed. note: See also the essay by Ascoli in this volume.]

barrier. She is public without seeking approval, without revealing her body or her femininity, and thus could never be accused of self-commodification: rather than pandering to the crowd, she unhorses and roundly beats almost every knight she encounters. Her cross-dressing and her martial role allow the female knight to be unaffected by the public gaze and to maintain a reserve of privacy and its privileges.

The play reinforces Helena's allusions to fame through adventure by juxtaposing the Countess's and Helena's farewell with the immediately following farewell scene at court (2.1). The scene in which the king sends the French lords off to war replicates the structure of the Countess's scene with Helena: the Countess' final words promise Helena "means and attendants," while the king begins by dividing gifts among the lords. He then admonishes them to

>   see that you come
> Not to woo honour but to wed it, when
> The bravest questant shrinks: find what you seek,
> That fame may cry you loud. (2.1.15–17)

The king's marriage metaphor recalls Helena's situation rather than that of the anonymous French lords. Helena wishes to "show what we alone must think, which never returns us thanks" (1.1.181–182). She conceives of attaining a public role as demonstrating merit, which then should bring her the reward of fulfilling her "ambitious love." Comparing this language to that of "Jane Shore" and "Troilus and Cressida" demonstrates how distinctive is Helena's language of feminine merit. In the ballads I have examined, the urge to show one's merit condemns a woman to wantonness and the stamp of "whore." Helena conceives of a heroic version of the public woman, and cites a body of familiar examples which legitimate her self-publication as quest rather than fall. She embraces the "death" threatened by social obloquy and transforms that threat into proof of her own heroism.

Helena replaces one expression of female heroism — the elegiac voice of the ballad lament — with another: the epic voice of the female knight. But the ballad genre's construction of its heroines is itself split, as we have seen, between sympathy for its heroines' tragic histories and disgust for their sexual transgressions. Helena's fear of "odious ballads" registers the insistent question of the play: whether Helena's ambitious desire for her mistress's son will meet with vilification — as does the ambition of her social peer, Parolles — or admiration from her audience within and without the play.

Thus genre in *All's Well That Ends Well* conflates the social and the literary; Helena's social fate is a question of her generic affiliation, as the genre of the play itself hesitates between tragedy and comedy. David Scott Kastan has argued that the play's deferral of comic closure and dalliance with tragic outcomes suggests a critical view of formal closure itself — of the very notion of "ending well."[41] Shakespeare's use of Helen of Troy and Cressida, who are notorious for their bad ends, examines the notion of "ending well" from another perspective: the dangers and rewards of sexual and social ambition for women such as Helena.

Mary Trull
St. Olaf College

---

[41] David Scott Kastan, "*All's Well That Ends Well* and the Limits of Comedy," ELH 52 (1985): 575–89.

Translating Power
City, Lineage, Ideology

Teaching How to Translate: Love and Citizenship in Brunetto Latini's *Tesoretto*

Brunetto Latini's *Tesoretto* represents a transitional moment in the *translatio* of desire across national and cultural borders. As a poetic rendering of Brunetto's *Tresor* — a longer, encyclopedic French prose work containing arts of love and classical political theory — the *Tesoretto* stages the practice of poetic translation and maps the way love poetry can be used as an educational model for Florentine citizenship. Drawing from the *Roman de la Rose*, the *Tesoretto* allegorizes the journey of an exiled lover who must wander through both wilderness and desert before making his way back to a community of lovers represented by the enclosed garden. This journey's difference from the one to gain the rosebud in the *Rose* is significant for two reasons: it translates the lover's quest for a love object into an overtly homosocial quest for entrance into a *community* of lovers, and it more clearly values desire as a conduit for citizenship rather than as an end in itself. In other words, by removing the love object completely from the narrative, the *Tesoretto* makes clear that the *Rose*, and by extension other love poems, were read within a socio-political, as well as poetic, framework by the Florentine *literati*.

The *Tesoretto* relies upon three separate guides for the exiled lover: the Chartrian figure of Nature, an Aristotelian Queen of Virtue, and Ovid's *magister*. While all three discourses are appropriated at some level from the *Rose*, they are more functionally valued in the *Tesoretto*, which emphasizes how they move desire from the simply personal or procreative, to social virtue and even civic harmony. Common to the *Tesoretto*'s discourses of desire is the need for governance and measure — of the text, lover, citizen, and finally by analogy, of the city. Charting the pilgrim's progress through the various *magistri*, I argue that the *Tesoretto* offers the translator and poet, Brunetto, as a *magister* to his own divided city. As a poet who can control his own desire and who, with art, can translate other men's desire back into the community (and harmony) of Genius's garden, the Brunetto-poet rewrites himself as the *"maestro"* of Florence. This process is reflected (within the poem) by the lover's journey, and mirrors the reader's progress (outside the poem) in a process I call "navigational reading." Thus, Brunetto sets up an extended analogy where reading, writing, loving, and leading a city all require lessons in navigation and translation modeled in the *Tesoretto* itself. The translation of personal desire into poetry and politics is represented by Brunetto's journey as the only path to peace for the divided Florence.

Ser Brunetto and the *Fanti*

To most readers, Brunetto Latini is best remembered by Dante's placement of him in the group of sodomites in *Inferno* 15. In that canto, we learn that Dante considered Brunetto his teacher, addressing him as "ser Brunetto" and "maestro," and that the Dante-pilgrim is surprised to find Brunetto in hell with the company of the sodomites. This brief interaction in *Inferno* has prompted scholars to spend the past five hundred years speculating about Brunetto's sexual preferences and trying — mostly in vain — to prove whether he was guilty of sodomy or whether Dante used the sin of sodomy figuratively to point to an intellectual or political crime. In all this time, no one has been able to produce any evidence that Brunetto Latini engaged in, sympathized with, or had a reputation for any kind of deviant sexual behavior.[1]

Yet suspicion and speculation remain attached to any critical attention paid to Latini's major works; why would Dante place his own teacher in hell — in the circle of sodomites no less — and then acknowledge the influence of the master on his pupil?[2] Surely Dante must have known that to put

---

[1] Brunetto fathered at least three children, and had an excellent reputation as a politician and rhetorician — and there is no historical evidence that he was ever accused of sodomy. In fact, in the *Tesoretto* he firmly condemns sodomy as a sin. In an odd apologia for the poem (called *La Penetenza* and not present in all manuscripts), the Brunetto-pilgrim decides to repent, and his sermon inveighs against a host of sins including sodomy. In a manner reminiscent of Capellanus's third book of the *De Amore*, Brunetto urges the "friend" to whom the *Tesoretto* is dedicated to repent of all sins (just as he has now done), although he does not confess specifically to sodomy or any other cardinal sin.

[2] For an excellent article that explores Dante's relationships to Brunetto, see Peter Armour, "Canto XV," *Lectura Dantis: A Forum for Dante Research and Interpretation* 6 (1990): 189–208; idem, "The Paternal Paterine," *Italian Studies* 38 (1983): 1–38 is also useful. See also Elisabetta Sayiner, "From Brunetto Latini to Dante's Ser Brunetto"

Brunetto (the character) in hell with the sodomites would be to consign the scholar's reputation to its own hell, where his *fama* would always be linked to canto XV rather than derived from the reputation of his own work. Even today, an equal number of critical articles deal with Brunetto as he appears in the *Commedia* to those which address his own corpus of texts.[3] Of the articles that do treat Brunetto Latini as an *auctor* in his own right, most (like this essay) must first acknowledge Brunetto's placement within the circle of sodomites and justify space for Brunetto *outside* of Dante's interpretive frame.

Indeed, there is no more fitting way to discuss the *translatio* of desire than to look at Brunetto Latini: for it is Dante's interpretation of Latini, superimposed upon the author himself, which ends up translating all of Latini's work for the rest of time. Just as we must first go through Dante — objections, suspicions, innuendo and all — to get to Brunetto, Florence went through Brunetto's version of Guillaume de Lorris and Jean de Meun's *Rose* to get to desire. This translation of literary desire is, in practice, the translation of authority and privilege into the vernacular, and it is also the rendering of cultural currency. The *Tesoretto*, as such, becomes a model for navigating metaphorically French hegemony just as its main character metaphorically navigates the mountains between the two regions.

(Ph. D. diss., University of Pennsylvania, 2000); and Michael Camille, "The Pose of the Queer: Dante's Gaze, Brunetto Latini's Body," in *Queering the Middle Ages*, ed. Glenn Burger and Steven Kruger (Minneapolis: University of Minnesota Press, 2001), 57–86. For a somewhat dated overview of the criticism on canto XV, see Deborah Contrada, "Brunetto's Sin: Ten Years of Criticism (1977–1986)," in *Dante: Summa Medievalis*, ed. Charles Franco and Leslie Morgan (Stony Brook, NY: Forum Italicum, 1995), 192–207. Richard Kay is perhaps one of the most persuasive critics arguing that Latini's sin was not sexual: see "The Sin of Brunetto Latini," *Mediaeval Studies* 31 (1969): 262–86, and idem, *Dante's Swift and Strong: Essays on* Inferno *XV* (Lawrence, KS: Regents Press of Kansas, 1978). James Wilhelm, "Dante's Two 'Families': Christian Judgment and the Pagan Past," *Italica* 47 (1970): 28–36 links the sexual sin to Latini's praise of the pagan authors. Andre Pézard, *Dante sous la pluie de feu (Enfer chant XV)* (Paris: Vrin, 1950) was one of the first to argue that Brunetto Latini's sin was to betray his own language by writing the *Tresor* in French.

[3] For example: of the twenty or so most recent articles on Brunetto Latini that appear in the *MLA International Bibliography*, over half are either on "Brunetto's Sin," or compare Brunetto to Dante. Only a handful of articles focus on Brunetto's work on its own merit and not through a Dantean lens. See now the introduction to Spurgeon Baldwin, *Brunetto Latini: Li livres dou tresor* (Tempe: MRTS, forthcoming).

The *Tesoretto* tells us that Brunetto received news of his own exile, and the defeat of the Guelphs at Monteperti, while traveling back from a diplomatic mission to Alfonso the Wise in late 1260:

> Venendo per la valle
> Del piano di roncisvalle,
> Incontrai uno scolaio
> Sour un muletto baio,
> Che venia da bolongnia,
> ◊ ◊ ◊ ◊ ◊ ◊
> Ed e' cortesemente
> Mi disse immantenente
> Che guelfi di fiorença,
> Per mala provedença
> E per força di guerra,
> Eran fuori de la terra. . . . .
>
> [Coming through the valley of the plain of Roncesvalles, I met a scholar upon a mule who was coming from Bologna . . . and he courteously told me immediately that the Guelphs of Florence, through ill fortune and through the force of war, were exiled from that land.][4]

In one of the most enduring moments from the *Tesoretto*, Brunetto receives this news of defeat and exile in the pass of Roncesvalles, itself a path for pilgrims and a site forever linked with Roland's defeat, brought about by the treachery of his own family. By insinuating himself and his own tragedy into this setting, Brunetto begins his narrative by reclaiming a literary moment pregnant with meaning and possibility. He opens textual space for his project by translating the valley filled with dead French bodies (texts) into his own encyclopedic text, and mapping the betrayal of empire and Roland onto his own allegorical body as his betrayal by Florentine factional leaders.

---

[4] Brunetto Latini, *Il Tesoretto*, ll. 143–147, 155–160. All citations of the *Tesoretto* taken from *Brunetto Latini: Il Tesoretto*, ed. and trans., Julia Bolton Holloway (New York: Garland, 1981); hereafter parenthetically cited by line number in the text. I have also consulted Giuseppe Petronio's edition in *Poemetti del duecento* (Torino: Classici italiani, 1951). The Guelphs were defeated by the Ghibellines and King Manfred, acting on the advice of Farinata del Uberti, on 4 September 1260. On 13 September, the Guelph leaders were driven from Florence and into exile.

Brunetto also links his own exile to war, both explicitly and implicitly. Claiming that his exile derives *per força di guerra*, he emphasizes his own absence from the fighting, juxtaposing his role as ambassador and his belief in the power of language to effect change against those Guelphs who made war and adopted a strategy of force to achieve their ends. He seems also to be implicitly responding to Aristotle's claim that exile (and those who are exiled) is linked with violence (and those lovers of war): "And he who by nature and not by mere accident is without a state, is either a bad man or above humanity . . . the outcast is a lover of war."[5] While Brunetto's wording overtly argues that he is an outcast *not* by nature or his own inclination toward warmaking, he does receive his exile while in a pass once filled, most famously, with the dead bodies of the defenders of the Holy Roman Empire and Charlemagne's most powerful defense of imperial sovereignty.[6] By selecting this particular geographical and symbolic locus for the news of his own exile, Brunetto is able to distance himself from the Aristotelian and medieval commonplace that exiles were suspect, potentially dangerous sorts; by mapping the violence onto either the faction that expelled him or onto Roncesvalles in the imaginations of his readers Brunetto removes any agency or responsibility from himself. Translating the moment of great French and imperial loss (inhabiting the physical and literary space of Roncesvalles) to the demise of his own Florentine faction redefines the journey of the Brunetto-pilgrim and situates the author's allegorical poem as both a reaction against his own immediate predicament and a poetic response to the greater cultural significance of exile and *mala provedença*.

Brunetto fashions a personal and political recovery from the defeat handed to him at the outset of the narrative, making an argument that the

---

[5] Aristotle, *Politics* I.ii. Brunetto could easily have had access to William of Moerbeke's very popular Latin translation of this work (1260–1264) while in France.

[6] Holloway points out that the pass was also on the pilgrimage route to Compostela, and that Alfonso the Wise's laws defined pilgrims as those who "exile themselves in order to serve God" (*Tesoretto*, xiii). I disagree with Holloway that Brunetto chooses this fate: at the end of the *Tesoretto*, the pilgrim goes on to Montpellier to repent. But if Brunetto becomes a pilgrim at the end of his text and understands his exile as derived from God, it only occurs *as a product* of the conversion of the textual narrative and the encounters encompassed therein. At the outset, his exile is not self-chosen and his masters are not holy. See also J. B. Holloway, "The Road to Roncesvalles: Alfonsine Formation of Brunetto Latini and Dante," in *Emperor of Culture: Alfonso X the Learned of Castile and his Thirteenth-Century Renaissance*, ed. Robert Burns (Philadelphia: University of Pennsylvania Press, 1990), 109–23.

productive citizen derives from a desiring subject. Throughout the narrative, however, by the very nature of that defeat, he is forced to reside — linguistically, poetically, and spatially — outside of his city. Yet, rather than simply present an encyclopedia or compendium of classical and theological retorts to worldly loss, Brunetto creates an allegory of recuperation wherein he occupies the primary position of both student and teacher, pilgrim and narrator. He finds the materials for his response in many classical texts and, most importantly, in the *Rose*: an extended allegorical narrative of a lover who has lost, and desires to regain, something dear to him — something emblematic of his worldly identity. For Brunetto's pilgrim, what has been lost is citizenship in his community, his beloved Florence.

One of the aspects in particular that Brunetto appears to find useful from the *Rose* is its allegorical structure and its lover /narrator.[7] Allegory offers both the author and the audience a chance to construct and interpret meaning (although there is less difference in these two actions than we might assume) within the same text. The terms upon which meaning hinges are radically different in allegorical narrative from those in the type of rhetorical *compendia* Brunetto helped to develop earlier with the *ars dictaminis*.[8] When he began work on the *Tesoretto* and *Tresor*, Brunetto was already known as the *maestro* of the political letter: not only did he establish a model and manual for it in Florence, but he also continued to put its lessons into practice in his own diplomatic work. While this genre gave way within Brunetto's lifetime to a more openly factional end, its methods remained the same. The *Tesoretto* and *Tresor* might seem to represent a significant departure from Brunetto's rhetorical and political style, but upon a closer look, many of the same tactics — albeit less overtly used — are present in his exile-period works. Brunetto's poetic works, however distanced from the explicitly rhetorical art of letter writing, nonetheless share the technique of using structural elements as the main navigational device for controlling a reader's interpretation.

---

[7] See Elio Costa, "Il Tesoretto di Brunetto Latini e la tradizione allegorica medievale," in *Dante e le forme dell'allegoresi*, ed. Michelangelo Picone (Ravenna: Longo, 1987), 43–58; Julia Bolton Holloway, *Twice Told Tales: Brunetto Latini and Dante Alighieri* (New York: Peter Lang, 1993); Earl Jeffrey Richards, *Dante and the Roman de la Rose: An investigation into the Vernacular Narrative Context of the* Commedia (Tubingen: Niemeyer, 1981).

[8] Brunetto is one of the earliest of the literati who develop this genre in Italy and, especially with his translation of Cicero, Brunetto was established as both a rhetorician and a statesman/philosopher.

The *Tesoretto* also associates controlled and measured rhetoric with citizenship and political critique. Containing plenty of classical authorities and addressing each as "master," it leans heavily on the didacticism found in the *ars dictaminis*, and, I would argue, is concerned with adopting the proper rhetorical connection between author and speaker. But despite such similarities, most scholars and readers have characterized the *Tesoretto* as simply another allegorical dream vision concerned with love. Even Kevin Brownlee's article on the *Tesoretto* reads the poem as a cultural and linguistic challenge to French hegemony and not necessarily as a political response to Brunetto's own exile or loss; and for scholars still trying to determine of which kind of sodomy Brunetto must be guilty, the *Tesoretto* and *Tresor* are interesting only inasmuch as they can illuminate an unnatural practice regarding the use of one vernacular language versus another.[9]

The text itself offers us an answer to why Brunetto chose to use an allegorical narrative poem written from the first-person perspective to address the political factionalism that caused his exile from Florence and the division of his precious city:

> Né che fosse divisa;
> Ma tutti per comune
> Tirassero una fune
> Di pace e di ben fare,
> Ché già non può scampare
> Terra rotta di parte (ll. 174–179)

> [Or that it [Florence] be divided; but all in common should pull together on a rope of peace and of welfare, because a land torn apart cannot survive.]

What the allegory offers Brunetto is a chance to address civic unrest, and his own role as a victim of it, within an extended analogy emphasizing responsibility

---

[9] K. Brownlee, "The Practice of Cultural Authority: Italian Responses to French Cultural Dominance in *Il Tesoretto*, *Il Fiore*, and the *Commedia*," *Forum for Modern Language Studies* 33 (1997): 258–69. See also Pézard, *Dante sous la pluie de feu*, and Earl Jeffrey Richards, "The *Fiore* and the *Rose*," in *Medieval Translators and their Craft*, ed. Jeanette Beer (Kalamazoo: Medieval Institute Publications, 1989), 265–83. Holloway is an exception to the tendency to read the poem simply as a mediocre translation exercise for the *Rose* or a precursor to Brunetto's longer *Tresor*.

and governance. The topos of the lover is the foundation for this structure, but as such, the social and political message of the text is in danger of being overlooked by later critics. Readers who cannot see beyond the apparent focus on love, or readers who cannot read beyond Dante's response to Brunetto's very political pilgrimage, have tended to dismiss the *Tesoretto* as an exercise for "fanti."

Nevertheless, as Duncan Kennedy points out, "'love' is no less (though perhaps less obviously) the focus for contestation" of meaning and cultural signification throughout literature than other, "essential," topics we have readily identified as pertaining to the political.[10] Brunetto's ability to read desire in the *Rose* as a site for cultural contestation is what he attempted to replicate in the *Tesoretto* — imbuing his own allegory with a range of possible, culturally-inflected meanings hinged on the arrangement of figures in the narrative of a lost lover seeking his way through unfamiliar lands. The allegory can be polemic, political and didactic; or it can be read literally as a dream vision. Brunetto may not have been sure his audience would find their way through the *littera* to the *sensus* as clearly as if he had written within the *ars dictaminis* genre; in a preface he complains that he has already seen his work badly copied and made "worthless" by the hands of "boys":

> Poi, con dolor lo dico:
> Le vidi in mano di fanti,
> E rasemprati tanti
> Che si ruppe la bolla
> E rimase per nulla (104–108)

[Then, with sorrow I say this; I saw them in the hands of boys, and so badly copied that the seal was broken and they became worthless.]

Reading like a "boy" instead of a man results in the misreading and destruction of his *treasure*. This is a fitting preface, because *loving* like a boy instead of a man will also render love's treasure worthless. The *Tesoretto* promises to become, then, the treasure map for both reading and loving — and Brunetto promises to become both model and *magister* of that navigational process.

---

[10] Duncan Kennedy, *The Arts of Love* (Cambridge: Cambridge University Press, 1993), 43.

"Parole dite in consilglio o'n aringha": Speaking to the City

The cultural climate of the *Tesoretto* is a complex moment of rapid change and bitter conflict, both politically and intellectually.[11] The work was most likely written while Brunetto was in France, exiled from Florence by the Sienese Ghibelline leaders, and completed at the same time as or slightly after he wrote the *Tesoro*.[12] Italy in the thirteenth century resembled the politics of ancient Greece, with its self-governing city states based loosely upon a republican model of representative rule. In Florence, that ideal had, as Aristotle predicted, degenerated into an oligarchic rule by Dante's time in the early fourteenth century; the lines were no longer drawn simply between the Guelphs, who sought extended self-rule for Florence, and the Ghibellines, who courted favor with Pope and Emperor as a means to establishing order. Instead, the Guelphs had splintered into two distinct factions: one representing the more wealthy merchant interests, and another rejecting the increased oligarchic control of the city. Consensus, and the ideal of rule by consent, was challenged both by Ghibelline moves toward strong central power located outside Florence, and by *bianchi* and *neri* factions who differed on how much authority needed to be positioned in a pope to attain peace in Florence. In place of consent, the idea of virtuous governance by representatives serving limited terms had taken hold. Thus the link between self-governance over one's desire and appetites, on the one hand, and governance over a city ripped apart by factional warfare, on the other, made the metaphor of the lover politically appealing to a writer seeking his own place in Florence's civic future.

---

[11] The best treatment of Brunetto's life and times remains Thor Sundby, *Della Vita e delle opere di Brunetto Latini*, trans. and ed. Rodolfo Renier (Florence: Le Monnier, 1884); also useful is Robert Davidsohn, *Storia di Firenze*, trans. Giovanni Battista Klein (Florence: Sansoni, 1957). See also the introduction to Baldwin, *Li livres dou tresor*.

[12] The dating of either work cannot be independently verified. Giovanni Villani, in his *Chronicle*, was the first to claim that the *Tesoretto* was keyed to the *Tesoro*, "fece il buono ed utile libro detto Tesoro, e il Tesoretto è la chiave del Tesoro" (Villani, *Chronicle*, 8.10; the text can be accessed easily at http://www.fordham.edu/halsall/source/villani.html). This would seem to in-dicate that the works were written in close proximity, but certainly between 1262 and 1266, when Brunetto was in and around Arras. Carmody pointed out that many of the manuscripts for the *Tresor* originate from Arras scriptoria, and, based on manuscript evidence, most scholars have accepted these dates for the *Tesoretto* as well (*Li Livres dou Tresor de Brunetto Latini*, ed. Francis J. Carmody [Berkeley: University of California Press, 1948], xlvi). However, see now the introduction to Baldwin, *Li livres dou tresor*, for a reevaluation.

In addition, Florence had seen, and was going to continue to see, many waves of exile as a means to ending the bloodshed and civil strife that had ravaged its citizens. Brunetto had taken part in the decision to exile the Ghibelline leaders who, with the help of Manfred in 1260, exiled him and his party for the next six years. In 1266, with the defeat of Manfred by Charles of Anjou, the Guelphs were returned to Florentine power and peace was ensured (for a brief time) by the marriages of a younger generation of prominent Guelph and Ghibelline families.[13] This last-ditch effort to use marriage as a harmonizing power fared better on a theoretical level than it did on a practical one, however. Historical records show that Brunetto spent his remaining years in Florence invested in securing civic peace and serving his beloved city with his diplomacy, leadership, and considerable rhetorical skills.[14]

During this time, political and personal acts of vengeance and hatred continued to occur and challenged any hope of establishing continued peace and stability for Florence. The very performance of citizenship in Florence could be dangerous: not just making enemies for oneself, but also embroiling one's family in a cycle of exile and murder that could last generations.[15] In this context, to fashion oneself a citizen is to take enormous personal risk for the sake of the public good. And in such a milieu, both rhetoric and poetry have an extra significance for political life: as the classical rhetoricians Brunetto introduced to the Florentine *literati* show, words become one of the few weapons the efficacy of which continues beyond the borders of exile and the limits of the material. The words of a poet especially can speak directly to the local and particular while generating suitable replies to the potential and universal. Unlike the carefully-crafted political letter, the love poem advocating "proper" loving remains relevant throughout the time when calls for "proper" citizenship are also needed, and particularly when overtly partisan rhetoric is mistrusted.

The *Tesoretto* does just that. More powerfully than the *ars dictaminis*, the *Tesoretto* promises a future peace by responding to a present crisis. The text

---

[13] For example, Guido Cavalcanti, Dante's friend and a fellow student of Brunetto's, was married to Farinata degli Uberti's daughter. Dante has the hostile parents, Cavalcante Cavalcanti and Farinata, housed in the same tomb for all eternity in canto XIII of *Inferno*.

[14] He acted as *protonotario* in 1271, "notarius consiliorum communis Fiorentini" in 1273, Chancellor from 1272 to 1279, President of the League of Florence, Genoa, and Lucca against Pisa in 1284, and *dittatore* in 1289. After 1292, his name no longer appears in public documents. For more on his public tenure, see Sundby, *Della Vita*, 201-7.

[15] For example, in 1288 Ugolino (a Guelph) was imprisoned with his sons and grandson and left to starve by Ruggieri (a Ghibelline archbishop). See Dante's retelling in canto 33 of *Inferno*.

has the ability to influence because it draws on the power of analogy and creates an extended narrative that forces readers to establish meaning by linking themselves and their own cultural, political, and ethical realities to the narrator in the text. Paul Strohm, responding to the *Rose's* use of narrator/lover, points out that such texts represent "a kind of ideal biography which happens to touch on the narrator's own experience at several points."[16] Recognizing the power to be exploited in such slippage, Brunetto constructs his narrator and (evidenced by the section with Ovid as his *magister*) lover in much the same way, supplied with details from Brunetto's own life. Without the directness found in the rhetoric manuals, Brunetto still manages to distill classical ethical lessons and combine them in such a way that the reader learns to distinguish between means and ends, appetite and desire, justice and charity, at both the individual and the communal level. The *Tesoretto* seeks nothing less than the restoration of Florence through the shaping of Florentine citizens and lovers. As a Florentine Ovid, Brunetto educates a generation of young men, inscribing his lessons on their backs just as Ovid's lovers do.[17]

One tool in that arsenal is Brunetto's use of the narrative "I" as his protagonist and narrator in the *Tesoretto*. For example, in his introduction to and dedication of the work, he names himself and his text thus:

> Io, burnetto latino,
> Che vostro in ogni guisa
> Mi son sança divisa,
> A voi mi raccomando.
> Poi vi presento e mando
> Questo riccho tesoro. (ll. 70-75)

[I, Brunetto Latini, who am yours in every way, without reservation, commend myself to you. Then I present and send to you this rich *Treasure*.]

Once inside the fictional journey itself, he frequently interjects narrative commentary as well, reminding readers of his dual role as maker of the text and pilgrim within it. "I tell you," he says,

---

[16] Paul Strohm, "Guillaume as Narrator and Lover in the *Roman de la Rose*," *Romanic Review* 59 (1968): 3-9, here 8.

[17] *Ars Amatoria* 2.743–744: "Sed quicumque meo superarit Amazona ferro, / Inscribat spoliis 'Naso magister erat'" [But whoever overcomes the Amazon with my sword, write on the spoils "Ovid was my master."]

> E sança dir mençongna
> Molt'era savio e prode:
> Ma lascio star le lode
> Che sarebbero assai. (ll. 148–151)

[And without telling lies, he was very wise and brave: but I leave behind the praises that would be great indeed.][18]

Details such as these continually remind the reader that the story is at once "fictional" and "true." The narrator posits a particular teleological moment despite the equally valid allegorical frame that calls attention to larger, universalizing claims being made for the text. Simply put, he is translating his own narrative into a text that can be ventriloquized by the next generation of Florentine men, and transforming his manhood (emblematized by his love and desire for his city) into an object onto which they can be cathected.

The allegory and autobiography work together, encouraging the reader to assume the particular role of the pilgrim by making claims that this man could be an everyman. The pilgrim's education at the hands of Lady Natura and Ovid, and his penance at Montpellier, all aim to recuperate, at some level, the reputation and authority of the pilgrim and author by forcing us to see ourselves cast adrift by fortune or exiled from our own community. Unlike simple allegory, however, we are given particular details for this speaker. The rest of the allegory's referents may be fluid, but the speaker remains centered historically and geographically in our imagination. Thus the meaning of the events that occur *to* him are left for our analogic abilities to translate. Brunetto's poetic strategy shows that, by anchoring the speaker in a reality we identify as historically and ontologically present, the reader is forced to view the causal events (factional politics, forced exile) as deriving from *outside* of the hermeneutics of the narrative — outside the control of the speaker. The narrative, at one level, then exemplifies something like the saying "when bad things happen to someone good," but at another level of abstraction, providence and the poet become conflated. By translating his experience as an exile into the allegory of a lost lover trying to navigate his way back to a community of fellow lovers, Brunetto is able to offer political commentary without appearing to take responsibility for it. Instead, he appears to be

---

[18] Of course there are numerous examples of narrative intrusion throughout the text: see especially ll. 248–271 for one such conventional interruption combined with a modesty topos.

eschewing factional divisiveness by blaming fortune for his personal fate, and by appearing to rise above partisanship.

For example, at the same time that the pilgrim (initially) is the individual against whom events occur, and the narrator recalls or recounts the events from a perspective occurring later teleologically, the poet constructs the narrative and orders the sequence of events to impart meaning and significance from the whole. The poet, even beyond the characters of Natura and Ovid, occupies a still later perspective through which the events are arranged and understood.[19] Yet the reader variously inhabits the different perspectival loci in the narrative as well, and Brunetto's skill in manipulating the reader's response to his personal and political circumstances depends on his ability to enforce particular reading stances at various points in the literal path.

As we have already seen, the opening of the text constructs the pilgrim, narrator, and poet as a more unified composite of an historical person. This Brunetto is still distinct from the real Brunetto Latini who wrote the *Tesoretto* and who was active in Florentine politics in the second half of the thirteenth century, but as an author-function based primarily upon the reputation (*fama*) of Brunetto and the envoi of the poem, it becomes embodied in the imagination of the reader.[20] As the narrative progresses, however, the distinctions between personae increase and avatars for the poet multiply. One

---

[19] The classic example for Brunetto would be Augustine's *Confessions*; its influence can certainly be seen in the decision of the pilgrim to enact his confession and penance as a palinode at the end of the *Tesoretto*. But both Ovid's *Ars Amatoria* and Jean de Meun's continuation of the *Roman de la Rose* would have offered themselves as secular examples of multiple temporal perspectives present within the literal fiction of the text. For more on the first-person perspective as related to an unsuccessful lover, see Zumthor's discussion of troubador and trouvère narrators (P. Zumthor, "Autobiographie au Moyen Age?," in idem, *Langue, Texte, Énigme* [Paris: Seuil, 1975], 165–80).

[20] I am aware of the danger in making claims for any connection between an historical author and the functional author as constructed by the text, and I think that the *Tesoretto* purposely draws attention to the possibility of overlap between these two positions. As Tony Spearing points out, documents exist "precisely because [their] originator cannot be present." "Medieval awareness of this connection between writing and absence is indicated by statements such as John of Salisbury's (quoting Isidore of Seville) that 'Litterae ... absentium dicta sine voce loquuntur' [letters speak without voice the sayings of those absent]": "Prison, Writing, Absence: Representing the Subject in the English Poems of Charles D'Orleans," *MLQ* 53 (1992): 83–99, here 91. The quotation is from Isidore, *Etymologiae* 1.3.1, and is quoted by John of Salisbury, *Metalogicon* 1.13; ed. J. B. Hall and K. Keats-Rohan, CCCM 78 (Turnhout: Brepols, 1991), 32: trans. D. D. McGarry (Berkeley: University of California Press, 1955), 38.

particularly clear example of this can be seen after the pilgrim loses himself in the woods; he becomes a pupil of Lady Natura and receives a lesson in the structure and creation of the cosmos. Besides offering a useful summary of Aristotelian and Boethian representations of man and universe, this section rhetorically accomplishes two goals: it keeps the pilgrim in a position of passivity and effaces the link between him and authorial responsibility, and it sanctions Lady Natura as a surrogate for the poet (distancing the pilgrim from the poet even further). After a conventional description of Natura's beauty and grace, in the manner of a lover to his beloved, the narrator recounts:

> Ma poi ch'ella mi vide,
> La sua cera che ride
> Inver' di me si volse,
> E poi a sé m'accolse
> Molto bonaremente,
> E disse immantenente:
> 'Io sono la natura,
> E sono una factura
> De lo sovran factore.
> Elli è mio creatore:
> Io fui dal lui creata
> E fui incominciata;
> Ma la sua gran possanza
> Fu sanza comincianza.
> El non fina né more;
> Ma tutto mio labore,
> Quanto che io l'allumi,
> Convien che si consumi.' (ll. 283–300)

[And after she saw me, she turned toward me that smiling face, and then she greeted me very graciously, and said immediately: 'I am Nature, and am a creature of the sovereign Creator. He is my maker. I was created by Him and set into motion; but His great power had no beginning. It has no end and never dies. But all my works, however much I give them life, must perish.'][21]

---

[21] This passage and the following thirty lines repeat common Chartrian descriptions of Nature as God's vicar. Though Brunetto certainly could have taken this from Alain of Lille, or possibly Bernardus Silvestris, most likely he is translating from (and

The pilgrim continues, at this stage in the narrative, to be a recipient of fortune and not an active agent for his own actions; he is at the mercy of Natura's grace, just as she serves at the discretion of the Creator. Natura's introduction emphasizes the relationship of power and agency involved in serving another, higher master.

Brunetto also overtly draws attention to the analogic relationship between poet and creator with the end rhymes "factura" and "factore," "creatore," and "creata."[22] Such repetition of word-stems is a method Dante will later use in *Inferno* canto XIII (the suicides) to describe the sound of Pier del Vigne's hissing.[23] Leo Spitzer argues that Dante uses the tradition of word-stem repetition to draw attention to the subtle similarity between language (the act of speech) and the body, and I argue that we see the same impulse in Brunetto's earlier linkage of creation by language and creation by divine impulse.

As God's vicar in the *Tesoretto*, Nature completes His creation process and is limited, in her own ability and range of possibility, by God's desire ("che vuole") and guided by His will ("suo talento"). By analogy, the poet's characters are created and set into motion solely by him; they act at his desire and by his will. Further, the poet's work (the text) remains beyond any constraints of mortality: once created, it exists by the power of the reader and its own circulation.[24] In short, by setting up and drawing attention to the economy of creation, Nature has drawn attention to the economy of the text and has emphasized the active role of both reader and author for establishing meaning beyond the literal reading (represented by the pilgrim).

---

compressing) the *Roman de la Rose*, Nature's confession to Genius (ll. 16,699–17,847). See George D. Economou, *The Goddess Natura in Medieval Literature* (Cambridge, MA: Harvard University Press, 1972), esp. 141–50.

[22] The usual reading of Nature and the poet is that as nature is to God, so the poet is to God through Nature. Both the poet and Nature use *ingenium* or *ars* to make their work: see Winthrop Wetherbee, *Platonism and Poetry in the Twelfth Century: The Literary Influence of the School of Chartres* (Princeton: Princeton University Press, 1972), 256–57; and Peter Allen, *Art of Love: Amatory Fiction from Ovid to the Romance of the Rose* (Philadelphia: University of Pennsylvania Press, 1992), 91.

[23] Leo Spitzer, "Speech and Language in *Inferno* XIII," *Italica* 19 (1942): 81–104, here 96 n. 19. In Spitzer's persuasive reading, the episode is a way for Dante to clear himself by, at some level, clearing Pier del Vigne of charges from an "unjust society." Thus, like the *Tesoretto*, the rhetoricity of the canto is integrally linked to the intention of the author, and character, to recuperate his own political reputation.

[24] As Alan of Lille reminds us, though, God creates, while Natura *recreates* and the poet-lover *procreates*.

At various points throughout Natura's speech, Brunetto links her with an economy of need and emphasizes the relationship between "ongni," "tutto" (all or whole), and "ciascun" (each or single):

> Ed essa c'al podere
> Ad ongnuna rendea
> Ciò ched ella sapea
> Che'l suo stato richiede,
> Così tutto provede.
> E'o, sol per mirare
> Lo suo nobile affare,
> Quasi tutto ismarrìo ... (ll. 514–521)

[And she, according to her power, rendered to each that which she knew each being required, thus [she] provided for all. And I, alone admiring her noble doings, was most confused.]

The plenitude of Natura dispensing to a community of *gente* according to their needs is sharply contrasted with the pilgrim's place outside of that system with the line "E'o, sol per mirare." Its placement directly following "Così tutto provede" juxtaposes her abundance with the pilgrim's lack, as well as reinforcing his solitary existence and exile. A few lines later, the pilgrim will tell us that "such was the desire" he had to know (and I would argue *to experience*)[25] more about the "grande storia" of which she had memory, that he turns and prostrates himself before her: "mi volsi intorno, / Ançi m'inginocchiai." His desire to know is a reinforcement of his lack of community, in that he longs to hear more about the *great history* of which he is a part. The pilgrim searches for a place to belong in the face of his own exile, and Natura offers him a teleological home rather than a geographical *patria*. Her history is the history of humanity and a harmonious ordering of the universe to which he, like the others, can fulfill his need "sua bisongna compiére" (l. 513). Natura's educational lesson establishes the divinely-ordered need for the lover-pilgrim to belong to a larger group, and rhetorically functions to dismiss any oppositional claim that Brunetto does *not* belong to Florence any more. Indeed, the "grande storia" she narrates is one of how desiring subjects come

---

[25] "Ma tanto era il disio" in the original (l. 522).

together to form empire and is based on the *Rose*'s "grande storia" of how lovers come together to create community.[26]

Art, Order, and Harmony: Poetry and the Community

With the aid of "sottile ingegno," the pilgrim is promised he will be able to retain for his entire life all that he has learned from Natura (ll. 539–546). *Ingenium* will allow the pilgrim to understand and order what he has learned at the individual level, but also allows the poet to order his own *grande storia* — and gives us the means to navigate through it. Because Brunetto is offering an educational corrective to the problem of Florence's factional politics and waves of exile, personal history is translated as communal history and *ingenium* informs both processes.

Natura's focus on *ingegno* is important for the education of the lover-citizen in two ways. First, as an overdetermined rhetorical term, *ingegno* emphasizes the problem of hermeneutics between medieval reader and author and lays the groundwork for a discussion of control (*mesura*) within a poetic and procreative frame. For classical rhetoricians like Cicero and Quintilian, *ingenium* was a subset of invention. Quintilian places *ingenium* as a subset of *inventio* but emphasizes the need for *iudicium* (judgment) to guide both (*Institutio Oratoria* 10.2.12). Both Matthew of Vendôme and Geoffrey of Vinsauf use the paradigm of divine creation for their discussion of poetic invention, whereby mental conception (*ingenium*) is the first step in the process of invention; Matthew likens it to the breathing of spirit into creatures (by analogy with Genesis 2:7), a process of individuation and generation.[27] Thus the key element *ingenium* shares with the paradigm of creation is the shaping of potentiality into something useful (and beautiful). In all cases, *ingenium* was a necessary component in the creation and understanding of meaning in a text, and inspired the poet to fashion the text — signifying the natural talent of man to construct meaning and logically order input. Just as the poet

---

[26] Or, more appropriately, to create political parties. Amant's party in the *Rose* works together to defeat a rival party and recapture the rosebud and the castle in which she is imprisoned.

[27] *Ars versificatoria* 3.50; trans. R. P. Parr (Milwaukee: Marguette University Press, 1981), 92. See also Douglas Kelly, *The Art of Medieval French Romance* (Madison: Wisconsin University Press, 1992), esp. chap. 2, "Antecedent Paradigms of Invention: Literary Paradigm," 32–67.

uses *ingegno* to order his *grande storia*, so men must order their community by ordering their social discourse.

But within the poetic tradition, *ingenium* conveys another, less positive, meaning. For Virgil, *ingenium* is deception: the exemplary moment in the *Aeneid* refers to Sinon lying or tricking the Trojans into receiving the horse.[28] Closely allied with powers of speech and the ability to manipulate through speech acts, this Virgilian use is carried over by Dante in the *Inferno*, when we are introduced to Ulysses. In canto XXVI, Dante-poet digresses in order to remind himself, and his reader, that talent or genius must be curbed and controlled to reflect virtue:

> Allor mi dolsi, e ora mi ridoglio
> Quando drizzo la mente a ciò ch'io vidi,
> E più lo 'ngegno affreno ch'i' non soglio,
> Perché non corra che virtù non guidi (26.19–22)

[It grieved me then and now grieves me again when I direct my mind to what I saw; and more than usual, I curb my natural skill, that it doesn't run where virtue does not guide.] (Translation mine.)

The lines occur immediately after Florence has been ironically praised for her engendering of so many citizens in hell, and the passage can be read as a restriction of the poet's own wrath and desire for retribution upon his city.[29] Later, in *Purgatorio* 33, Dante returns to the topic of *ingenium* again, noting that the "curb of art" will make him stop his narrative at the end of this second book (ll. 141–143). Importantly, both occurrences happen while the poet speaks directly to his reader and comments upon his own poetic responsibility and talent, and both contain moments of wrath and prophesied retribution.[30] For Brunetto, like Dante, the emphasis on *ingenium* is also an emphasis upon the relationship between poet and reader, and exhibits an awareness of the poet's role as seducer. Not surprisingly, "inganno" appears at another place in Natura's lecture: in her description of Lucifer's fall, where Eve and Adam are "deceived" by the serpent's *inganno* (ll. 592–602).

---

[28] Virgil, *Aeneid*, 2.76ff.

[29] Note especially "affreno" (bridle or restrain) would thus imply the danger of desire or wrath overtaking the poet.

[30] In *Inferno* 26, the poet prophesies God's eventual retribution against Florence, while in *Purgatorio* 33 Beatrice prophesies God's vengeance against the dragon.

Love and Citizenship in Brunetto Latini's Tesoretto

There is another reason we should look closer at the placement of *ingenium*, and its relationship to poetic creation and translation, in this section of the *Tesoretto*. In the *Roman de la Rose* (and following the *Complaint of Nature*), Nature is paired with Genius in encouraging the lover to have procreative sex as the fulfillment, and enactment, of human potential. But while the *Tesoretto* closely replicates this section, the character of Genius does not appear formally within the narrative. Returning for a moment to the section quoted above, however, we can see Brunetto's pun on *ingegno* as the inclusion of the *Rose*'s allegorized Genius. Natura says to the pilgrim (and, by extension, the reader):

> "Amico, i'ben vorria
> Che ciò che vuoli intendere
> Tu lo potesse apprendere;
> E sì *sottile ingegno*
> E tanto buono ritengno
> Avessi, che certanza
> D'ongnuna sottilgliança
> Chi volesse trattare,
> Tu potessi apparare
> E ritenere a mente
> A tutto'l tuo vivente" (ll. 536–546)

["Friend, I would truly wish that you would be able to understand that which you want to learn; and then such *subtle genius* and such good retention you would have that truly of all subtlety which you would wish to treat, you would be able to learn and retain this in your mind for your entire life."]

As a personification of *ingenium*, Genius shapes the narrative (and the pilgrim's desire) into an exemplary model and useful text for the reader. Genius is a figure who carries a reed pen in one hand and parchment in the other, constantly writes and orders the events he sees into a narrative of life and history.[31] So

---

[31] Alan of Lille, *De planctu naturae* 18.68–74 (ed. / trans. J. J. Sheridan [Toronto: Pontifical Institute of Mediæval Studies, 1980]). Genius:

> vero calamum papiree fragilitatis germanum numquam a sue inscriptionis ministerio feriantem, manu gerebat in dextra: in sinistra vero morticini pellem novacule demorsione pilorum cesarie denudatam, in qua stili obsequentis

while Natura will continue to offer the pilgrim a great history of mankind, including the "divers" parts which make up the elements of the world and of man himself, the pilgrim (and reader) will need Genius to make sense of the text and to translate it into something useful for his life. Brunetto's role as translator of authority for his community — a role previously established in his influential work in the *dictiminis* genre and now reinforced by the very production of his multilingual *Tresor* and *Tesoretto* — is highlighted by Natura's lessons. By analogy, his translation of cultural and intellectual capital is necessary for the smooth working of Nature and community.

Returning to the *Tesoretto*, Natura continues her lecture on universal hierarchy and the taxonomy of the human condition. Most of the episode is a reduced version of the middle section of the *Tresor*, where Brunetto translates Aristotle's *Ethics* for his reader, and thereby attempts to map the different jurisdictions of the body and soul in order to highlight what presupposes human action. Brunetto follows a Thomist reading of will, reason, and desire; what emerges is a constant emphasis upon "measure" as a condition for human happiness. For example, Natura claims that the difference between the baseness of animals and the dignity of man is that animals "son sanza ragione / E sieguon lor volere / Sanza misura avere" (are without reason and follow their will, without having measure) (ll. 686–688). Natura then expounds on reason and why reason ultimately overcomes will and desire to cause action.[32] Unlike the *Rose*, which separates out each theory of individual and communal philosophy into its own persona, Brunetto's translation conflates several discourses into one overarching argument for harmony made by Natura.

Once reason's participation has been established for the working of human happiness, Natura sets up the groundwork for one of the *Tesoretto*'s most

---

subsidio imagines rerum ab umbra picture ad veritatem sue essentie transmigrantes, vita sui generis munerabat. Quibus delectionis morte sopitis, nove nativitatis ortu alias revocabat in vitam.

[... carried in his right hand a reed of frail papyrus, which never rested from its occupation of writing; and in his left he bore an animal's skin from which a knife had cut and bared the shock of hair, and on this by means of his compliant pen, he gave to images, which passed from the shadow of a sketch to the truth of very being, the life of their kind. And when these slumbered in the death of deletion, others were called to life in a new rising and birth.]

[32] Brunetto's position here is unlike that of Dante, which follows the more voluntarist postion of arguing that the will moves the self to action.

important analogies: that harmony should exist between the parts and the whole of any system or organic body. All of the taxonomies and divisions so painstakingly labeled for the reader finally begin to pay off at this point, as links are made between macro- and microcosmic order. Repeatedly emphasizing "divers" segments, and "partute si parte" in nature, the planets, and the humors of the body, Natura underscores her own role in reconciling the divisions into a whole. Speaking of the humors, she says:

> E queste quattro cose,
> Così contrariose
> E tanto disiguali,
> In tutto li animali
> Mi convene accordare
> E in lor temperare
> E rinfrenar ciascuno . . . (ll. 799–805)

[And these four things, thus so opposed and so unequal, in all animals I have to reconcile, and temper in them and bridle each one . . . .]

The idea of bridling and combining art and poetry plays a part in this quotation as well, but even more evident is the way Natura's lecture emphasizes cosmic harmony as a necessary act prevailing over division. The city is included in the hierarchical analogy she sets up, and the factional division of Florence must also be brought under the control of a harmonizing presence, just as the individual must bring the various parts of his own nature (and especially desire) into reconciliation. This is strengthened by her insistence on creating taxonomies and hierarchies that serve to enclose and subsume individual subjectivity and desire within larger social and cosmic structures. Immediately following the above quotation, Natura reverses that ratio by drawing an analogy between the humors (microcosmic) and a macrocosmic level:

> Altressì tutto'l mondo,
> Dal ciel fin lo profondo,
> È di quattro alimenti
> Facto ordinatamente;
> ◊ ◊ ◊ ◊ ◊ ◊
> E tutti per ciascuno
> Sì rinfrenaro a uno,
> Che la lor discordanza
> Ritorni in aquallianza:

> Ché ciascun è contrario
> All'altro ch'è disvario.
> Ciascuno a sua natura
> È diversa factura,
> E son talor dispàri;
> Ma io li faccio iguali;
> Tutta la lor discordia
> Ritorna in tal concordia
> Ch'io per lor ritengno
> Lo mondo e lo sostengo,
> Salva la voluntate
> De la divinitate (ll. 811–814, 822–836)

[In just this way all the world, from the heavens to the depths, out of the four elements is put in order.... And each through each, thus, is controlled by one, which may restore their discordance into balance; for each is contrary to the other that is at variance. Each one by its nature is a different factor, and is sometimes separate; but I make them equal. All of their discord returns to such concord that I, through them, control the world and sustain it, except for the will of the Divinity.]

As Natura makes unavoidably explicit, only through reconciliation and order can the universe function; the pilgrim's exile becomes, then, significant *beyond* the personal level. The reconciliation of Brunetto to his city is as necessary to Florence's ability to function properly as it is for Brunetto to achieve his potential as a citizen. Throughout this entire text, the repeated emphasis on acting in "accordance to nature" or behavior reflecting a specific "kind" highlights and calls into question the very practice of exile. As man is "political" and "social by nature," the expulsion of citizens from a city becomes, therefore, an "unnatural act." It should be no surprise, then, that shortly after Brunetto returns to political power, and during his remaining years, Florence returns to a practice of forced intermarriages between the factions rather than expulsion and exile. The *Tesoretto* becomes one of the strongest arguments against exile as a political method for controlling the city: its analogies can be used in both directions, since individual and cosmic are conflated.

The passage also creates another analogic paradigm for proper political function. The final section of Natura's speech focuses on governance and her role as reconciler of faction, where she becomes the model for proper rule. She emphasizes the need for all of the different parts and different humors to work together in achieving wellness of the body or ordering of the universe, and Natura takes her leave of the pilgrim so that she may "cura / in ongne creatura / ch'è sotto'l mio mestero" ("care for every creature that is beneath my control") (ll. 921–923). She governs by making sure that each creature follows the path she has given it, determining that "sotto mio reggimento è tutta la lor'arte" ("under my rule is all their art") (ll. 848–849). By encouraging all those under her dominion to follow their "nature" and to maintain a proper course of behavior in life, Natura also returns to the idea of *misura*. Order can be kept only so long as each member of a community moderates himself and controls his passion (just as she models this behavior to the lover-pilgrim).[33]

As we saw earlier in the *Inferno*, art is the curb for wrath; but it is also the curb for excessive desire — and the pilgrim of the *Tesoretto* will leave Natura for a new *magister* in Ovid. Literally, Natura encourages the pilgrim to keep to the right, to philosophy rather than love, in his wanderings. However, if we look closer at her phrasing, it becomes evident that Natura is again exposing the power of words and poetry to lead men to their proper course:

> Disse: 'fi di latino,
> Guarda per che'l gran cammino
> Non torni esta semana,
> Ma questa selva piana
> Que tu vedi a sinestra,
> Cavalcherai a destra.' (ll. 1133–1138)

[She said: "Son of Latino, watch that from the high road you do not turn this week, but through this wooded plain that you see on the left, ride to the right."]

Holloway points out that the choice between the left or right path is conventional to pilgrimage allegory, but the passage also reflects a concern over the proper negotiation of words and desire (especially *"semana"*) — and as such, provides the link between the two masters of the *Tesoretto*.[34]

---

[33] Brunetto ironically follows the typical medieval pattern of associating *misura* with the masculine realm of reason. It is no accident that Brunetto's argument for governance (both of the self and the city) excludes the female as anything but an objectified stand-in. This is a poem about male desire and citizenship limited to well-born Florentine men.

[34] *Tesoretto*, ed. Holloway, 59 n. 9. Dante, for example, will veer to the left, through the *Inferno*, and then to the right in *Purgatorio*.

Social Virtue and *Misura*: Controlling Desire and Controlling the City

The Pilgrim sets out with every intention of following Natura's advice, but ends up losing his way in what appears to be a desolate, unrecognizable wasteland:

> Per lo cammino stretto,
> Cercando di vedere
> E toccare e sapere
> Cio ch'elgli è destinato;
> E non fui guari andato
> Ch'i' fui ne la diserta,
> Dov'io non trovai certa
> Né strada né sentero.
> De! Che paese fero
> Trovai in quelle parti;
> Ché, s'io sapese d'arti,
> Quivi mi bisongnava,
> Ché, quanto più mirava,
> Più mi parea salvagio:
>   ◊ ◊ ◊ ◊ ◊ ◊
> Né cosa ch'io conosca (ll. 1184–1197, 1204)

[Along the narrow path, seeking to see and touch and know what is destined for him; and I had not gone for long when I was in a desert, where I could find certainly neither street nor path. Ah, what a savage country I found in those parts! For, if I knew any arts I needed them there, since the more I looked, the more it seemed a wilderness.... Nothing that I could recognize.]

The "cammino stretto" which the pilgrim loses recalls an Ovidian landscape rather than the "narrow way" of the Gospels, and certainly both desert and wilderness are stock allegorical loci representing the lost psyche. This quotation shows more of Brunetto's playful *translatio* of desire, as it derives from the Friend's speech to Amant in the *Rose* — where the *cammino stretto* is the Road to Poverty, itself an Ovidian translation (especially *Ars amatoria* 2.243–246).[35]

---

[35] See also the "dark valley" (*valle scura*) where the pilgrim will find himself for three days before entering the "grande piano giocondo" (ll. 1217–1221), and see also Ovid's

But the savage, comfortless country in which the pilgrim finds himself astray signifies more than the wanderings of a lost soul. Instead, the emphasis on art, knowledge, and signs points to a continuation of the education of the pilgrim and reader. As the pilgrim must negotiate his way through unfamiliar and unpopulated territory, so the reader must negotiate the text, the lover negotiate his desire, and the citizen negotiate the fluid politics of the city. Ovid, as *magister*, more clearly moves desire, and the dangers of translating it, along the analogic continuum from personal or poetic desire to social, and then to political, virtue.

By using the senses (*vedere e toccare*), pilgrim and reader will attempt to discern, and eventually lose, the way — but with art, the pilgrim can see past what *seems* a wilderness to find something recognizable. And what the pilgrim and reader both need is the sign to point them in the proper direction and impose order on what seems a "paese fero." Indeed, it is only after the pilgrim remembers that he has the sign given to him by Natura, now described as "securo sengnale," that he is assured of finding his way through the labyrinth of wilderness (or wilderness of texts). The art that the text emphasizes as necessary for navigating one's way will be repeated as the pilgrim encounters the four Queens who instruct him on becoming a proper citizen and *omo* — so that he may enter Love's court. Thus we are shown that the process of navigation taught by this text and modeled by the lover-pilgrim turns one from a *fante* to an *omo* — from an inexperienced lover to one who can control his desire and moderate his response (*misura*). Just as *ingenium* was important for the pilgrim's education in the first half of the *Tesoretto*, here in the second half *ars* will empower him to negotiate his exile successfully and reconcile his desires with his beloved city. This begins literally with the pilgrim negotiating the wilderness and curbing nature's art with his own "sign."

The excursus with the four Queens (Courtesy, Generosity, Loyalty, and Prowess) provides the gateway into the second half of the *Tesoretto*'s narrative and, as such, replicates the transition between authors in the *Rose*. The other text subsumed into the structure and under the control of the *Tesoretto*, however, is the *Tresor*; so, unlike the *Rose*, Brunetto is rewriting himself.[36]

Tristia 1.3.83 (another work of exile). Thanks to Dr. Leslie MacCoull for bringing this suggestive passage from the *Tristia* to my attention.

[36] Roger Dragonetti's claim, that the Guillaume de Lorris of the *Rose* is really Jean de Meun's creation, provides an interesting link here. If true, then the *Tesoretto* would be, indeed, more like the *Rose* than scholars have presumed. See Dragonetti's seminal text: *Le mirage des sources: l'art du faux dans le roman médiéval* (Paris: Seuil, 1987).

Since we are unsure whether the *Tesoretto* or the *Tresor* was written first, it is unclear whether Brunetto is alluding to a work he has already written, or forecasting it proleptically. Nonetheless, the excursus distills a similar section in the *Tresor*, where the lover will be advised on the importance of virtue and taught how to lead a virtuous life — as Brunetto himself tells us in the *Tesoretto*:

> Di tutte quattro queste
> Lo puro sanza veste
> Dirò'n questo libretto:
> Dell'altre non prometto
> Di dire né di contrare;
> Ma chi'l vorrà trovare,
> Cerchi nel gran tesoro
> Ch'io farò per coloro
> C'anno lo cor più alto (ll. 1345–1353)

[Of all four of these plainly, without adornment, I will speak in this little book: of the others I do not promise to speak of or to describe; but he who wants to find this should look in the great Treasure that I will make for those who have a higher heart.][37]

Here in the *Tesoretto*, the pilgrim must linger with the Queens long enough to learn how to behave virtuously before the art of love will aid him (rather than destroy him); the narrow path, upon which the pilgrim set out and seemed to lose his way, is itself a device leading to the virtuous Queens. As a test of sorts, the pilgrim must read (with the help of signs) his way through the wilderness to find virtue, and only after finding and imitating virtue's *exempla* will the pilgrim be able to progress to love. Again the prevailing metaphor for both loving and citizenship becomes virtuous governance. The lover and citizen both learn to move desire to social virtue (the proper end of all desire), and publicly to practice that virtuous behavior (habit); once a community of virtuous men models those habits, *custom* is established. Thus by teaching an individual lover virtuous habits, one can create and enforce

---

[37] Available to those "who have a higher heart" and who speak or read French, as Brunetto says in the next lines: "Per dirle più distese / Ne la lingua françese" (ll. 1355–1356).

customs of civic virtue for an entire city. Brunetto has translated Ovid for his readers, but through the lens of Jean de Meun and Alan of Lille — and in the process turned desire more exclusively into a homosocial bond while bridling male rivalry.

Likewise, the various other analogic relationships engendered by the narrative respond to this education of the pilgrim. As we have seen in the Natura section, the allegorical construction of the text bears witness to the poet's place both within and outside that same text. While it is the poet who leads us through the wandering route to completion and understanding of the poem, the poet is also the pilgrim, "maestro burnetto," who draws attention to the tension within that narrative space by reminding us he is both the master of the text and subject to it. *Maestro burnetto* emphasizes mastery over a number of other things as well: fortune, Ghibelline self-interest, Florentine politics, rhetoric and its proper use, literary and cultural relations, and even mastery over Brunetto's physical self. At the end of the narrative, it is this sense of mastery that presents itself as most obvious and which most closely aligns him with the pilgrim — and in contrast to the unruly body of Roland buried in Roncesvalles and beneath the allegory of the *Tesoretto*.

The discerning reader sees a more complete recuperation of the exile and excavation of the allegory. For instance, the reader (as the pilgrim) must negotiate the *litera* to find the *sensus* of the text; at one level that reading is certainly aimed at appropriating the exegetical expectations of the allegorical journey. But like the *Rose*, the *Tesoretto* seems to anticipate many different kinds of readers, and it is to the discerning reader that the analogy recuperates as well. For that reader, the pilgrim is a stand-in for the city and the necessity of virtue is a precondition for harmony or love to come to the city; the education of the pilgrim is the education of Florence:

> ... quattro n'a tra lloro
> Cu'io credo e adoro
> Assai più coralmente,
> Perché lor convenente
> Mi par più gratioso
> E a la gente in uso:
> Cortesia e larghezza
> E leanza e prodezza (ll. 1337–1344)

[There are four of them, whom I obey and adore very much with my heart, because their working together seems to me very gracious and useful to the people: Courtesy and Generosity and Loyalty and Prowess.]

The emphasis on *buona usanza* found in the first half of the *Tesoretto* again makes its appearance here, but now it has moved from the concern over individuals following the "proper" use or their appropriate "nature," to showing how individual action affects the entire community.[38]

The Queens offer a series of rules for behavior focusing on the social expectations of virtuous deportment for a lost knight: the pilgrim decides to follow him and learn the rules himself. While the knight seems to fit the allegorical expectations engendered by the *Rose*, he seems out of place in the *Tesoretto*, where the pilgrim, we are told at the beginning, is an aged ambassador, Brunetto, and not a young lover or knight.[39] And as Holloway has noted, the rules for virtuous behavior presented here are bourgeois at best (*Tesoretto*, xxiv), focusing on an honor which is decidedly less exclusive and more economically based than one might expect. In other words, an ideal lover's habits are portrayed as less courtly and more civic in the *Tesoretto*, less Guillaume's idealized discourse of desire than Jean de Meun's pragmatic advice. For a poem about a lover's journey, this text has surprisingly few portrayals of unruly erotic desire, but plenty of discourses of control and discipline. More than anything, Brunetto's rules show one how to construct a social identity based on moderation and measure; they emphasize appearance, custom, and reputation as integral parts of identity, pointing out that "just as with the arts," one must correct bad habits and,

---

[38] Note, for example, how Loyalty talks about betrayal on a communal level:
E chi di te si fida,
Sempre lo guarda e guida,
Né già di tradimento
Non ti vengna talento.
E volglio c'al tuo comune,
Rimossa ongni cagione ... (ll. 1935–1940)
[And whoever gives his word to you, always keep it and guide it, so that no desire of betrayal will ever fall on you. And I hope that to your city, with every other motive removed, you will be true and loyal ...]

[39] Compare Chaucer's and Gower's narrators, who are also inappropriate and aged lovers; Chaucer makes reference to Brunetto and the *Tesoretto* in the *House of Fame*, as does Gower in the *Confessio Amantis*.

> Ti tieni a buona usanza,
> Però ch'ella t'avanza
> In pregio e in onore,
> E fatti esser melglioe
> E dà bella figure ...
> ⋄ ⋄ ⋄ ⋄ ⋄ ⋄
> Ma d'altra ti procaccia
> A cui'l tuo facto piaccia (ll. 1657–1661, 1669–1670)

> [You must hold to good usage, because it advances you in rewards and in honor, and makes you better and gives you a good appearance.... But gain for yourself from others to whom your deeds are pleasing.]

The performativity emphasized by the Queens is perhaps most evident in that last line, which links identity with deeds and reputation, and, even more problematic, hinges on whether one is found "pleasing." Virtue, as defined here, is a garment which can be assumed and altered to fit various occasions, but which (like art) is always projected outward to mediate the relationship between self and community.

If being "piace a la gente" and performing good deeds promises one entrance into a community (of men), it is not without risk. As in the *Rose*, Larghezza confesses that although these things would seem to make men equal, "custom" (*usanza*) still conquers a great part of her teaching.[40] In a divergence from the *Rose*, however, much of Larghezza's guidance tends to return to practical advice on how to handle yourself when violence or misunderstanding threatens the social identity adopted at the Queens' encouragement. For example, the pilgrim is told to "hold onto reason" and get a lawyer,

> Ch'elgli è maggior prodeçça
> Rinfrenar la mateçça
> Con dolçi motti e piani
> Che venire a le mani (ll. 2011–2014)

---

[40] The repeated emphasis on custom and habit reflect Brunetto's Aristotelian subtext as much as it reflects this text's republican, and educational, model for civic reform. Community can be achieved by a group of virtuously *acting* men, even if their desires and beliefs differ greatly. In this, the difference between Dante and Brunetto might be described as the difference between Habermas and Arendt. Brunetto (like Habermas) would argue that the best social model is one where men in dialogue (rather than agreement) with each other, and exhibiting virtuous habits, provide the greatest potential for emancipatory progress.

[For it is the better deed to restrain madness with words sweet and slow than to come to blows.][41]

However, if that does not work, the conclusion of this section on virtue tells us we should be prepared to fight; specifically, we should guard ourselves well and "abbie sempre appresso arme o compangnia a casa e per la via" ("always have at hand arms or companions in the house and on the street") (ll. 2060–2062). And this is why Ovid must be invoked to complete the education of the pilgrim: while nature and virtue make promises for bringing together and reconciling a community of men, it is ultimately only art that can unify them and redirect the violence and war, which began the narrative, into a civilizing authority. Brunetto's (and the *Rose's*) subtext for desire and *civitas* is Ovid's *Ars amatoria* 1.101–132, where the founding of Rome is conflated with the violence and rape of the Sabine women, linking desire, competition and community.[42]

Back in the *Tesoretto*, on May Day, the pilgrim comes to a beautiful meadow described as a garden "sometimes round" and "sometimes four-sided," alternately filled with people and pavilions and then with no one.[43] In this translatable space, he watches people variously happy and sad, engaged in

---

[41] Note that reason is here coded as *misura* and not philosophy: Aristotle has been reduced even more completely to praxis.

[42]   Primus sollicitos fecisti, Romule, ludos,
      Cum iuvit viduos rapta Sabina viros.
            ◊ ◊ ◊ ◊ ◊ ◊
Respiciunt, oculisque notant sibi quisque puellam
      Quam velit et tacito pectore multa movent.
Dumque, rudem praebente modum tibicine Tusco,
      Ludius aequatam ter pede pulsat humum,
In medio plausu (plausus tunc arte carebant)
      Rex populo praedae signa petita dedit.

[You first, Romulus, did disturb the games, when the rape of the Sabine women consoled your wifeless men .... (The warriors) look about them, and each notes with his glance the woman he desires, and they brood much in their secret hearts. And while to the Tuscan flute player's rude strains the dancer struck the leveled floor three times with his foot, in the middle of the applause (the applause then was without art) the king gave to the people the expected sign (of rape).]

Translation adapted from *Ovid II: The Art of Love and Other Poems*, Loeb Classical Library (Cambridge, MA: Harvard University Press, 1979).

[43] Richards, "The *Fiore* and the *Rose*," and Holloway argue that Brunetto must have read Jean de Meun's section of the *Rose* as well as Guillaume de Lorris's because of this emphasis upon shape-shifting and the squaring of the circular garden (*Tesoretto*, ed. Holloway, 109 n. 4).

singing, dancing, and chasing, such that he stands in awe and "maravilgliai," until finally someone points out the god of love and tells the pilgrim he has indeed become a witness to Fortune and Love, "ventura e d'amore." Despite Natura's warning to avoid this place and this path, he has sought it out "intently." Here is a crucial distinction in the economy of the narrative, for, like Dante later, Brunetto rejects Natura's ability to provide an ultimate solution. The lover-pilgrim needs to join a community: he desires to become a citizen of the *Rose*'s garden. The lover of the *Tesoretto*, almost at the completion of the poem, stands at the precise spot where the *Rose* begins its narrative — watching the dancers and other lovers, he longs to join their ranks, to become a part of their community. Thus the *Tesoretto*, while translating the *Rose* and even Ovid's *Ars* beneath that, into a story of longing and community, nonetheless remains a poem about loss and exile as much as it promises to teach men how to become citizens and lovers of Florence.

The pilgrim finds that, in Cupid's court (the *Tesoretto*'s version of the *Rose*'s garden), there reigns a counterpart to the four Queens of virtue:

> Quattro donne valenti
> Tener sopra le genti
> Tutta la sengnoria;
> ◊ ◊ ◊ ◊ ◊ ◊
> E so vi dire lo nome:
> Paura e disiança
> E amore e sperança (ll. 2275–2277, 2280–2282)
>
> [Four valiant ladies holding over the people the total lordship; ... And I know how to speak their names: Fear and Desire, and Love and Hope.]

The four rule over lovers eternally, creating a tension from which one cannot escape without art. Their master, Cupid, is described as "un fresco fante" ("a fresh naked boy") (l. 2262) — recalling the "fanti" Brunetto is afraid will misread his text. Cupid, and all of the lovers in the garden, are dangerous because they love without art (inordinately), just as some *fanti* are dangerous to Brunetto because they will read his text without art (i.e., too literally). The "fino amante," without Ovid's art, is at the mercy of these four rulers, because despite their ability to conjoin (*congiunti*) men and *partes* into a harmonious whole, the lover will be unable to find balance from the volatility of love and fortune. In fact, the pilgrim confesses that he himself has succumbed to the excess of love and reminds us:

> Voi dovete pensare
> Che l'omo che è 'nnamorato
> Sovente muta strato (ll. 2354–2356)

[You should think that a man who is in love often changes his state.]

Ovid, "per arte," is the one able to give the pilgrim mastery over love and fortune — and moves him, finally, to the conclusion of his wandering. But by analogy, Ovid's art also promises to offer the citizen mastery of political mutability; thus we are reminded of the pilgrim's status as outsider, seeking to join a community of *fedeli d'amore* just as the exiled poet seeks to write his way back into Florence.

Ovid, like Natura and the Queens of Virtue, is valued in the *Tesoretto* for the ability to master the text. He not only collects and puts into verse the "acts of love," but he orders and translates the different parts of language into a pleasing text:

> Vidi ovidio maggiore,
> Chelgli atti del amore,
> Che son così diversi,
> Rassempra e mette in versi (ll. 2359–2362)

[I saw great Ovid, who collected and put into verse the acts of love, which are so diverse.]

Symbolically and literally, the *Tesoretto* has Ovid passing on his art to the pilgrim (and poet) *in buona fede* and *in volgare* (l. 2373). The Brunetto-poet here openly advertises his properly-directed desires by using the qualifier "buona fede." He, as the ultimate *magister* and citizen, translates the *grande storia* in good faith for Florence. The poetic power to discern and order various parts, to be impervious to the carnality of the text — in short, the ability to navigate and translate desire — is appropriated for a new vernacular audience and signifies the completion of the poem.[44] All that is left for the

---

[44] See Michael Calabrese, *Chaucer's Ovidian Arts of Love* (Gainesville: University Press of Florida, 1994). For alternate views of how the Middle Ages read Ovid, see Alison Sharrock, *Seduction and Repetition in Ovid's* Ars amatoria 2 (Oxford: Clarendon Press, 1994); Warren Ginsberg, "*Ovidius ethicus*? Ovid and the Medieval Commentary Tradition," in *Desiring Discourse: The Literature of Love, Ovid through Chaucer*, ed. James J. Paxson

narrative to accomplish, once the pilgrim (thanks to Ovid's help) has found the way from which he had strayed, is for the pilgrim to move beyond the allegory begun at Roncesvalles. Pilgrim and poet converge once again and, together, transcend the exile of the text by confessing and renouncing (literally) the "little book":

> E questo mio libretto
> E ongn'altro mi'detto
> Ch'io trovato avesse,
> S'alcun viçio tenesse,
> Commetto ongni stagione
> In lor correctione (ll. 2407–2412)

[And this, my little book, with every other writing that I have invented, if they contain any vice, I commit at all times to [the Friars'] correction.]

The *Tesoretto* (proper) concludes rapidly once Ovid's art has been won by the pilgrim, although many manuscripts include Brunetto's "La Penetenza" as a final, but separate, section of the poem, which breaks off amidst a discussion of planetary harmony by Ptolemy.[45]

The narrative of the poem, it should to be recounted, moves from the generative but localized impulse enforced by Nature to Ptolemy's transcendent cosmic perch, and ends with a vision — not unlike Dante's — of perfect harmony.[46] As the focus of this journey, the lover is taught how to move from being merely procreative and conceptual, to finally mastering and "curbing" his own urges and appetites, and ordering his own history. The *Tesoretto* offers a map for how to accomplish that drive to render meaning from chaos at the individual, poetic, and civic levels by insisting on the ability of

---

and Cynthia A. Gravlee (London: Associated University Presses, 1998), 62–71; Jeremy Dimmick, "Ovid in the Middle Ages: Authority and Poetry," in *The Cambridge Companion to Ovid*, ed. Philip Hardie (Cambridge: Cambridge University Press, 2002), 264–87. Though not necessarily focused on Ovid, a particularly cogent discussion of medieval reading practices and masculinity is Marilyn Desmond, *Reading Dido: Gender, Textuality, and the Medieval Aeneid* (Minneapolis: University of Minnesota Press, 1994).

[45] Some extant manuscripts also contain a Ciceronian-inspired poem on friendship, "The Falvolello," at the end of the manuscript. See Petronio, *Poemetti* and *Tesoretto*, ed. Holloway for manuscript descriptions.

[46] Perhaps this accounts for Dante's placement of Brunetto in hell: he concludes his journey not with a vision of the divine, but of the earth from the celestial spheres.

art to govern desire. As its lover learns how to navigate exile and loss, faction and diversity, its reader learns how to translate these lessons into a model for proper citizenship and community.

Heather Richardson Hayton
GUILFORD COLLEGE

WHAT SILENCE DESIRES: FEMALE INHERITANCE AND THE ROMANCE OF PROPERTY IN THE *ROMAN DE SILENCE*

Silence, the girl raised as a boy who becomes a minstrel of enormous talent and a knight of great prowess in the thirteenth-century romance that modern editors call simply the *Roman de Silence*, has understandably aroused the gender-bending curiosity of modern readers. The author, Heldris of Cornwall, is otherwise unknown, and the question has even been asked whether Heldris — like that other Cornwall native Silence herself — was a "transvestite she."[1] Silence's parents conceal her female body with masculine clothes in order to circumvent a capricious law that prevents women from inheriting property, but in her life as a man Silence turns out to be a bit too successful for her own good. She eventually becomes the favorite knight of King Evan of England, the same king whose law she is dodging, and the plot consists primarily of adventures and misadventures arising from the dramatic possibilities of a cross-dressed hero and the danger of being discovered.

Academic readers of the early twenty-first century have been prepared — perhaps too well prepared — for the delights and frustrations of such a text by everything from Shakespearean comedy to feminist theory.[2] Despite some

---

[1] Sarah Roche-Mahdi, "Introduction," in Heldris of Cornwall, *Silence: A Thirteenth-Century French Romance*, ed. and trans. eadem (East Lansing: Colleagues Press, 1992), ix–xxiv, here xi n. 2.

[2] Regina Psaki, in her edition of the poem, calls it "at least proto-feminist" ("Introduction," in Heldris de Cornuälle, *Le Roman de Silence*, ed. and trans. eadem [New York: Garland, 1991], ix–xxxvii, here xxx), and another recent editor suggests that it deals with "matters that the modern reader might reasonably expect to find expressed so explicitly ... in French feminist criticism of the 1970s rather than in a medieval romance" (ed. Roche-Mahdi, xx). Edward J. Gallagher has remarked that the romance has "an almost uncanny air of modernity about it" ("The Modernity of *Le Roman de Silence*,"

anachronistic excesses, much progress has been made in understanding this recently-discovered text, especially the unusually large scope it gives to exploring the construction of gender. A growing body of work also now recognizes the centrality of the "feudal politics of lineage" to Silence's story.[3] For Heldris's contemporary audience, property and gender were inextricably linked as determiners of identity, and the gender games in which the text engages are at least partly a fictionalized space in which to explore other questions of social identity.[4] The law of inheritance that provides the central plot

---

University of Dayton Review 21.3 [1992]: 31–42, here 39). This is a story, the critics tell us, about the "politics of gender" (Roberta L. Krueger, *Women Readers and the Ideology of Gender in the Old French Verse Romance* [Cambridge: Cambridge University Press, 1993] chap. 4); "the role of performance in gender identification" (Peggy McCracken, "'The Boy Who Was a Girl': Reading Gender in the *Roman de Silence*," *Romanic Review* 85 [1995]: 517–36, here 517); "deconstructed masculinity" (Lorraine K. Stock, "The Importance of Being Gender 'Stable': Masculinity and Feminine Empowerment in *Le Roman de Silence*," *Arthuriana* 7.2 [1997]: 7–34, here 9); "sexualized textuality," (Kate Mason Cooper, "Elle and L: Sexualized Textuality in the *Roman de Silence*," *Romance Notes* 25 [1985]: 341–60); "gender neutrality" (Erin F. Labbie, "The Specular Image of the Gender-Neutral Name: Naming Silence in *Le Roman de Silence*," *Arthuriana* 7.2 [1997]: 63–77); "queer identities" (Elizabeth A. Waters, "The Third Path: Alternative Sex, Alternative Gender in *Le Roman de Silence*," *Arthuriana* 7.2 [1997]: 35–46, here 38); and "lesbian desire" (Kathleen M. Blumreich, "Lesbian Desire in the Old French *Le Roman de Silence*," *Arthuriana* 7.2 [1997]: 47–62). It is a *"texte de jouissance"* (Peter L. Allen, "The Ambiguity of Silence: Gender, Writing, and *Le Roman de Silence*," in *Sign, Sentence, Discourse: Language in Medieval Thought and Literature*, ed. Julian N. Wasserman and Lois Roney [Syracuse: Syracuse University Press, 1989]: 98–112, here 98) in which the intertwined ambiguities of gender and language make it a "map of its own misreadings" (R. Howard Bloch, "Silence and Holes: The *Roman de Silence* and the Art of the Trouvère," *Yale French Studies* 70 [1986]: 81–99, here 98).

[3] The phrase belongs to Sharon Kinoshita, who wisely observes, "any attempt to gauge the political significance of *Silence* without taking into consideration the social institutions and practices by which feudal society reproduced itself is at best partial and at worst misleading": "Heldris de Cornuälle's *Roman de Silence* and the Feudal Politics of Lineage," *PMLA* 110 (1995): 397-409, here 397). Kinoshita has recently extended this work in "Male-Order Brides: Marriage, Patriarchy, and Monarchy in the *Roman de Silence*," *Arthuriana* 12.1 (2002): 64–75.

[4] Until recently the social dimension of the poem was seldom viewed as centrally important to its meaning, noteworthy exceptions being Simon Gaunt, "The Significance of Silence," *Paragraph* 13 (1990): 202–16, who suggests, "Heldris's praise of Silence reinforces class hierarchies rather than breaking down gender stereotypes" (212); and Kinoshita, "Feudal Politics." Recent work emphasizing the importance of genealogy, property, and class includes: Kinoshita, "Male-Order Brides"; Peggy McCracken, *The*

motivation to *Silence* is no mere plot device, but rather speaks to fears and desires with deep roots in the realities of thirteenth-century inheritance practices. Silence's story, written during a century in which the rapid evolution of those practices reflects well-known power struggles between kings and nobles — and driven as it is by a desire to preserve landholdings — may aptly be called a romance of property rights.

Reading the romance in terms of the desire for property resolves two impediments to interpretation. First, it helps explain the status of the *Roman de Silence* as a chivalric verse romance at a time when prose romance and vernacular historiography were in the ascendant.[5] Though Heldris does not avail himself of the legitimating effects of prose or of historical subject matter, the *Roman de Silence* does give voice to many of the same preoccupations that were spurring the rise of prose romance and prose histories at the time of its composition. Much contemporaneous writing addresses such topics as dynastic succession and the proper relations of princes and nobles by referring to an authoritative past that has been idealized into a model for the present, a transcendent model that tends to subsume the actions of individuals into narratives with long (and often tragic) trajectories.[6] Heldris, on the other hand, by translating the secure transmission of landholdings into the object of a traditional romance quest, orients his narrative around the identity formation of an individual. The practical difficulties faced by thirteenth-centry nobles in acquiring and holding onto the landed wealth that defined their identity resonate deeply with the sudden reversals and random interruptions of *Silence's* romance narrative, yielding a relationship to contemporary concerns

---

Romance of Adultery: Queenship and Sexual Transgression in Old French Literature (Philadelphia: University of Pennsylvania Press, 1998), who notes that Silence is "a figure who seems to subordinate erotic desire to a desire for property and proper succession" (148); and Robert S. Sturges, "The Crossdresser and the *Juventus*: Category Crisis in *Silence*," *Arthuriana* 12.1 (2002): 37–49.

[5] On the tendency of thirteenth-century historical writing to fashion itself after romance, see Gabrielle M. Spiegel, *Romancing the Past: The Rise of Vernacular Prose Historiography in Thirteenth-Century France* (Berkeley and Los Angeles: University of California Press, 1993); and eadem, *The Past as Text: The Theory and Practice of Medieval Historiography* (Baltimore: Johns Hopkins University Press, 1997), esp. chaps. 10–11.

[6] Spiegel, in both of the works already cited, addresses in detail the purposes and forms of thirteenth-century writing about the past. On the adoption of historiographical concerns into romance, see Lee Patterson, "The Romance of History and the Alliterative *Mort Arthure*," in idem, *Negotiating the Past: The Historical Understanding of Medieval Literature* (Madison: University of Wisconsin Press, 1987), 197–230.

every bit as tangible as the idealized and linear patterns of contemporaneous prose narratives. The poem's heroine makes her way in the world as a disinherited heiress whose male disguise is constantly in danger of being discovered, and her struggle to keep her inheritance, like any other romance quest, has obstacles that must be overcome. Silence's quest thus shares the characteristic pitfalls and shifting fortunes common to romance, but it also dramatizes — from the perspective of an individual heiress — the real-world complications of the quest for property.

The second benefit of a reading that foregrounds the inheritance of property is that it allows at least a tentative answer to the question, "What does Silence desire?" Others have noted that Silence, although she is desired by many, has no perceptible desires of her own.[7] Or, more precisely, her only explicit statements of desire take a negative form, as in these remarks at the age of twelve (the threshold of medieval adulthood): "'Ne voel perdre ma grant honor, / Ne la voel cangier a menor. / Ne voel mon pere desmentir'" ("'I don't want to lose my high position; / I don't want to exchange it for a lesser, / and I don't want to prove my father a liar'" [2651–2653]).[8] The narrator, who goes along with Silence's self-negation by using masculine pronouns to describe her, confirms that her renunciation of desire is habitual: "Et tols jors ert pres a contraire / A Cho que ses cuers voloit faire" ("He was always ready to go against / what his heart wanted him to do" [2677–2678]). It is easier to construe Silence's negatively-framed statement of desire if we remember Northrop Frye's definition of desire's function in romance: "the quest-romance is the search of the libido or desiring self for a fulfillment that will deliver it from the anxieties of reality but will still contain that reality."[9] As a cross-dressed female who aspires to inherit her father's patrimony, Silence *is* one sort of desiring subject in this romance of property, one who has her choice of identity crises: she can be a disinherited heiress or a female knight. Both alternatives are feudal unthinkables that reflect, in Frye's terms, a cultural desire to be delivered from the uncertainties of noble inheritance but

---

[7] McCracken, "'The Boy Who Was a Girl'," 530; Barbara Newman, *From Virile Woman to WomanChrist: Studies in Medieval Religion and Literature* (Philadelphia: University of Pennsylvania Press, 1995), 165; and eadem, *God and the Goddesses: Vision, Poetry, and Belief in the Middle Ages* (Philadelphia: University of Pennsylvania Press, 2003), 122–34.

[8] Quotations are from *Silence*, ed. and trans. Roche-Mahdi. Subsequent citations appear in the text.

[9] Northrop Frye, *Anatomy of Criticism* (New York: Atheneum, 1967), 192.

simultaneously to engage and overcome those anxieties in a romantic fantasy that contains a recognizable feudal reality. And the desire of Silence and her parents to preserve her inheritance operates in tandem with another version of the desire to be delivered from feudal uncertainty: since marrying an heiress was one of the few methods by which a medieval nobleman could add to his patrimonial holdings and increase his status, Silence also functions as the desired object of the quest.[10]

Silence gives voice to feudal anxieties via the atmosphere of uncertain outcomes and shifting procedures that the poem shares with the aristocratic culture that produced it. The feudal hierarchy was in its application a highly varied network of practices, with the laws governing inheritance often becoming in actual use a game of find-the-loophole. And who got to inherit what depended at least as much on custom and local patronage as it did on law. Both customs and laws were in rapid transformation at the time of the poem's composition in the second half of the thirteenth century. At this time, relatively few noble inheritances would have been governed strictly by primogeniture (even fewer in France than in England), and in fact medieval noblemen — with the help of a growing legal profession — went to great lengths to provide for their daughters, younger sons, and widows. Silence's father Cador, whose idea it is to cross-dress his daughter, is in one sense doing what every medieval nobleman did: maneuvering to protect his property and to take care of his family interests. Cador's maneuvering, however, must operate within strict limits because he and his wife Eufemie hold their land directly from the king of England, making them tenants-in-chief subject to stringent royal controls in matters of property succession. They would not have available to them the legal instruments for designing a custom inheritance package that were becoming increasingly popular with those of lower aristocratic rank, and the royal decree they circumvent stands as a reminder that inheritance rights were a major bone of contention between medieval kings and their greatest vassals.

The application of feudal history to *Silence* would admittedly be easier if we knew more details about its author and its first audience, but while it is impossible to know the provenance of the poem with certainty, the contest

---

[10] See Georges Duby, "Women and Power," in *Cultures of Power: Lordship, Status, and Process in Twelfth-Century Europe*, ed. Thomas N. Bisson (Philadelphia, University of Pennsylvania Press, 1995), 69–85. Duby notes that when a woman stood to inherit a lordship, "if she chanced to be an orphan without a brother, then the husband gathered up with her the power of which she was the legitimate holder" (71).

between royal control and baronial privilege was of equal concern in both France and England during the thirteenth century. In favor of English influence on the poem, Heldris does claim to be from Cornwall, the setting is in England, and English law and custom are strikingly relevant to the property considerations in the text. Lynne Dahmen has convincingly related *Silence's* themes of lineage and feudal legitimacy to other insular romances of the period.[11] The poem's heroine, however, does a good deal of cross-Channel shuttling as a minstrel and a knight, and there is no reason to think the poem's author stayed in one place either. The only extant manuscript of the poem is written in Picard dialect (not Anglo-Norman), and French inheritance practices, though exhibiting considerable regional variation as well as differences from those of England, also show substantial resonance with the situation in the poem. The process of centralization that Norbert Elias has called the "monopoly mechanism" peaked somewhat earlier in England than in France, but on both sides of the English Channel the thirteenth century was characterized by royal aggrandizement and noble attempts to contain it.[12] French nobles would certainly have been aware of the more restrictive controls under which their English counterparts had traditionally lived, but also of Magna Carta and its attempt to limit royal power. So the dramatization of inheritance and royal control might play differently on opposite sides of the English Channel, but it would still play.

In *Silence*, the heavy royal hand in matters of noble inheritance comes to the fore when King Evan institutes the law that prevents women from inheriting in response to an inheritance dispute involving twin sisters:

---

[11] Lynne Dahmen, "Heldris' Use of Insular Materials in the *Roman de Silence*," paper at the International Congress on Medieval Studies, Kalamazoo, MI, 5 May 2000. I am indebted to Professor Dahmen for providing me with a copy of this unpublished paper. As Dahmen notes, much of Susan Crane's work on insular romances is helpful in articulating the intersection of history and romance in *Silence*; see esp. chap. 2, "Land, Lineage, and Nation," in S. Crane, *Insular Romance: Politics, Faith and Culture in Anglo-Norman and Middle English Literature* (Berkeley: University of California Press, 1986), 53–91.

[12] Norbert Elias, *The Civilizing Process: Sociogenetic and Psychogenetic Investigations*, trans. Edmund Jephcott (Oxford: Blackwell, 2000), 263–64, 266–67, 268 ff. On the rapid increase of the royal monopoly in France under Philip Augustus, see Jean Dunbabin, *France in the Making 843–1180* (Oxford: Oxford University Press, 1985), 371–73; John W. Baldwin, *The Government of Philip Augustus: Foundations of French Royal Power in the Middle Ages* (Berkeley: University of California Press, 1986).

> .jj. conte esposent les puchieles.
> Cho dist cascuns qu'il a l'ainsnee;
> Por quant li uns a la mainsnee. /
> Mellee i ot por son avoir,
> Car cascuns [violt] la terre avoir.
> Li uns le violt par mi partir;
> Li altres dist qu'il iert martyr
> Et vis recreäns en batalle
> Ançois qu'il a plain pié i falle. (280–288)
>
> [Two counts married the girls.
> Each one claimed to have the older,
> but one of the two must have had the younger.
> There was a quarrel over the inheritance,
> for both of them wanted to have the land.
> One wanted to share it equally;
> the other said he would be a martyr
> and vile coward in battle
> before he would yield an inch of it.]

The counts attempt to settle the dispute through trial by combat, but both are killed in the process. It is as though feudal culture threatens to self-destruct when confronted with perfect equality, either in the disposition of property or on the field of judicial combat. King Evan is so outraged by the deaths of the two counts that he declares, "no woman shall ever inherit again / in the kingdom of England / as long as I reign over the land" ("Ja feme n'iert mais iretere / Ens el roiame s'Engletiere, / Por tant com j'aie a tenir tiere" [314–316]).

In something like a twisted version of *conjointure*, that familiar romance technique whereby multiple story lines are woven into one harmonious whole, the case of the two sisters, their count husbands, and King Evan functions as a *disjointure* in which several dissonant social realities collide in one romance situation. All the participants have differing interests going into the dispute; all experience significant losses as a result of it; and the new law damages the interests of heiresses — such as the poem's heroine — who are not yet born at the time of its inception. With some modification, Fredric Jameson's comments on the cultural underpinnings of romance shed light on the social discord of this episode in *Silence*:

> As for romance, it would seem that its ultimate condition of figuration... is to be found in a transitional moment in which two distinct modes of production, or moments of socioeconomic development, coexist. Their antagonism is not yet articulated in terms of the struggle of social classes, so that its resolution can be projected in the form of a nostalgic (or less often, a Utopian) harmony.[13]

If we substitute mode of inheritance for mode of production and remember that the struggle is not a latent one between classes but an overt one within the aristocratic class, Jameson's formulation suggests the power of romance to address the anxieties surrounding a moment of transition. New regulations and shifting practices regarding the division of land among sisters, the status of heiresses in relation to their husbands and male relatives, and the role of the king in the inheritances of his greatest vassals were sources of considerable disquiet for thirteenth-century nobles. Silence's struggle to resolve her inheritance problems is indeed a utopian quest to work out such anxieties. In the poem's dramatic denouement, Silence, after maintaining her masculine disguise through many narrow scrapes and high adventures, is finally revealed by Merlin's magic to be female. In this idealized romantic outcome, the king restores Silence's land to her, repeals the law forbidding female inheritance, and marries her himself, thus bringing psychological resolution to an unresolved social problem.

But before I say more about the poem's idealized ending, the situation of the twin sisters and their judicially killed husbands needs further contextualization. Heldris's episode of sisterly discord was not the first romantic treatment of such inheritance difficulties; it is essentially an inside-out version of a similar story found a century earlier in the *Yvain* of Chrétien de Troyes (4704 ff., 5820–6446), and the differences between the two versions illustrate the shifting status of female heirs during the thirteenth century. In Chrétien's story, it is the sisters rather than their husbands who quarrel over the inheritance, and there is no dispute about which sister is older, only about whether the elder should divide the inheritance with the younger. In *Yvain*, the equally matched combat between Yvain and Gawain (the champions the sisters have chosen) ends when the two friends recognize each other and — with a courtesy contrasting sharply with the grim determination of

---

[13] Fredric Jameson, *The Political Unconscious: Narrative as Socially Symbolic Act* (Ithaca: Cornell University Press, 1981), 148.

the counts in *Silence* — each proclaims he has been defeated by the other. And King Arthur's intervention could hardly be more opposite to King Evan's: Arthur proclaims that the younger sister shall have her share. In Chrétien's time, the division of land between sisters could still have been seen as an innovative resolution and the king's intervention as a noble gesture that settled a matter in which he had no personal stake. But by Heldris's time, as we shall see, kings took a much more direct interest in the division of land and were acutely conscious that dividing it among heirs could remove some of it from royal control.

Silence thus conflates together several issues that would have been at stake when sisters stood to inherit property. If it were really just a dispute about which child was the elder, it would have been a problem for twin sons as much as for twin daughters. Inheritance by daughters, however, was often considered more partible than inheritance by sons; girls were expected to share. Not, however, in any straightforward or universally attested fashion, and especially not in any way that remained constant during the course of the thirteenth century or on both sides of the English Channel. At the beginning of the century in England there was usually a mix of feudal law and family obligation in which one daughter inherited the property and did homage for it, but was in turn expected to provide for her sisters. Normally the heiress would have been chosen by the overlord, and which daughter the lord chose depended as much on her husband's relationship with that lord as it did on the heiress's seniority.[14] Both the choice of which daughter would inherit and how that daughter would provide for her sisters became increasingly regularized during the course of the thirteenth century, although that regularization proceeded more slowly than did corresponding customs regarding male inheritance, and a higher degree of uncertainty would have accompanied any devolution of land in which the heir or heirs were female. The expectation that the lord would choose the eldest daughter gradually became more fixed, but so did the expectation that the eldest daughter would divide the inheritance equally with her sisters. In France, the partition of estates among both male and female heirs had long been more common than in England, but there were considerable regional variations, and discontinuities between

---

[14] S. F. C. Milsom, "Inheritance by Women in the Twelfth and Early Thirteenth Centuries," in *On the Laws and Customs of England: Essays in Honor of Samuel E. Thorne*, ed. Morris S. Arnold et al. (Chapel Hill: University of North Carolina Press, 1981), 60–89, here 66.

customary law and practice could easily lead to conflict.[15] Despite more varied practices, the makers of French law, like their English counterparts, also attempted to codify female inheritance customs in a way that kept the main residence and its associated feudal service with the eldest sister but divided the land equally. In Champagne, for example, a baronial council of 1212 legislated that when land was divided among sisters, "the eldest daughter would inherit the castle, but her sisters would share all other assets of the inheritance equally."[16]

The increasingly standardized partitioning of land between sisters may have been a welcome innovation to most thirteenth-century aristocrats, but from the point of view of the overlord or king, the practice brought with it the same problems as the older system of *parage* upon which it was based. *Parage* was a partition of land among male heirs wherein the younger brothers did homage to the eldest for their portions and only the eldest did direct homage for his portion to the original lord. The practice had been brought to England by the Normans but abolished in the mid-twelfth century; in France it was a common practice until expressly forbidden in 1209 by Philip Augustus.[17] The reason for its demise during the tenure of strong central rulers seems clear: only the eldest brother's portion was under the direct control of the overlord, and the revival of the practice as a model for dividing inheritances among female heirs also reintroduced the diminishment of central control. Depending on whether one was a lord or a vassal, an elder sister or a younger sister, born early in the thirteenth century or later, the changes in how land was partitioned among heiresses would have been variously welcome or unwelcome, and the transitions were neither smooth nor uncontested.

---

[15] Malcom Vale, *The Angevin Legacy and the Hundred Years War 1250–1340* (Oxford: Blackwell, 1990), 82, 101–2.

[16] Theodore Evergates, ed. and trans., *Feudal Society in Medieval France: Documents from the County of Champagne* (Philadelphia: University of Pennsylvania Press, 1993), 51.

[17] On *parage* and its abolition see Baldwin, *The Government of Philip Augustus*, 262–63; Marc Bloch, *Feudal Society*, trans. L. A. Manyon (1961; repr. London: Routledge, 1989), 205, 208; Ch. Petit-Dutaillis, *The Feudal Monarchy in France and England*, trans. E. D. Hunt (London: Routledge & Kegan Paul, 1936), 303. On later female inheritance practices derived from *parage*, see Evergates, *Documents from the County of Champagne*, 49–54; J. C. Holt, "Politics and Property in Early Medieval England," in *Landlords, Peasants, and Politics in Medieval England*, ed. T. H. Aston (Cambridge: Cambridge University Press, 1987), 65–114, here 107; Scott L. Waugh, "Women's Inheritance and the Growth of Bureaucratic Monarchy in Twelfth- and Thirteenth-Century England," *Nottingham Medieval Studies* 34 (1990): 71–92, here 74–75.

The overdetermined situation of the two counts and the twin sisters in the *Roman de Silence* sets a match to this volatile mix. The indistinguishability of the counts as much as the exact parity of the daughters ensures that there would be a conflict regardless of whether older customs or newer customs are applied, but the particular nature of the dispute highlights the emerging inheritance practices of the thirteenth century. One of the counts claims that the inheritance should be divided equally, suggesting that newer rules favoring partition apply, but then it makes little sense for him to claim that his wife is the elder daughter and the sole heir. The other count insists that his wife is the elder sister, a fact that would automatically favor him only if the newer rules are in effect. In that case, however, there would also be a formal expectation to divide the property equally, an option he finds less attractive than dying as a recreant in battle (at least he gets his second choice). The king finds no reason to favor one count's claim over the other's, and his extreme reaction to the disastrous duel calls into question the narrator's earlier claim that he was known to be a king who "upheld justice in his realm" ("ot justice en sa ballie" [119]). All of the participants in the dispute seem to find the challenges posed by female inheritance insurmountable, and the contest over the sisters' land dramatizes the dynamics — and the anxieties — of a period of transition.

While twin sisters whose husbands kill each other constitutes a romantic exaggeration, sisterly disputes over inheritance certainly happened, and may even have been relatively frequent.[18] On the British side of the English Channel, the question of dividing land among sisters figured in such prominent cases as the disposition of the earldom of Chester in mid-century and of the kingdom of Scotland at the end of the thirteenth century.[19] In at least two humbler cases from earlier in the century, a younger sister was placed in a

---

[18] Milsom, "Inheritance by Women," 80. Nor does the environment on the Continent appear to have been less litigious. Baldwin, in a survey of exchequer cases heard at Falaise and Caen between 1207 and 1223, sums up, "in matters of inheritance and land possession, over half of the litigants were disadvantaged women and minors" (*The Government of Philip Augustus*, 229).

[19] R. Stewart-Brown, "The End of the Norman Earldom of Chester," *English Historical Review* 35 (1920): 26–53, here 46–47. In *Silence*, Chester is the location of the fateful trial between the two counts married to the twin sisters (293), and also the location of the rebellion in which Silence turns the tide in favor of King Evan (5287 ff.). On the fates of the real and fictional counties of Chester as exemplars of increasing royal control, see Kinoshita, "Male-Order Brides," 67–69.

nunnery by the elder sister and her husband. This might have been considered an appropriate fulfillment of the family obligation to provide for the non-inheriting sister by the sister doing the placing, but in neither case was it considered so by the sister who was placed. The younger sister in one case managed to get married surreptitiously, escaped from the nunnery with her new husband, and claimed the right to inherit property along with her sister. After the new husband cleared himself from abduction charges, the younger couple began a lengthy litigation with the older couple. In the other case the younger sister had been placed in the nunnery as a young child and claimed that "she properly returned to the world when she reached the age of discretion." She was excommunicated and had to pursue her right to leave the nunnery in ecclesiastical courts before taking up her property case in secular courts. She finally reached an agreement with her elder sister about twenty-five years after her first claim.[20] Given the alternative of such protracted litigation, settling a property contest by judicial combat seems almost merciful, but suffice it to say that the sisterly quarrel in the *Roman de Silence*, sensationalized though it is, strays little from the pattern of real thirteenth-century disputes.

King Evan's abolition of female inheritance in reaction to the deaths of the two counts pushes royal sovereignty somewhat further than any medieval king could have been confident in achieving. It does, however, dramatize the difficulties of a time when inheritance customs were in flux and when the king of England maintained older, more stringent forms of control over his chief tenants than those lords could maintain over their tenants, while the king of France was enjoying the fruits of steadily increasing centralization. Of the many forms of royal control, perhaps the most relevant to *Silence* were the restrictions on alienation, especially as it relates to the division of land between female heirs. Alienation simply means a transfer of ownership, but came into use as a conditional gift whereby the grantor could circumvent primogeniture by deeding land to someone on the condition that the grantee deed it back to someone the grantor specified, usually a younger son or daughter.[21] There are two important points about alienation in the second half of the thirteenth century: first, it was rapidly growing in use during this period, and second, it was available to the greatest fief-holders

---

[20] Milsom, "Inheritance by Women," 80.

[21] For a clear introduction to such forms of alienation as entail, use, and enjointure, see Chris Given-Wilson, *The English Nobility in the Late Middle Ages* (London: Routledge, 1987), 137 ff.

only via an expensive license from the king. In England, Henry III expressly forbid unlicensed alienation by tenants-in-chief in 1256.[22] In France, a royal ordinance of 1275 established higher tariff rates for alienation of land held from the king than for alienation of land held from lesser lords.[23] Lords who held land directly from the king thus had the least flexibility of any freeborn persons in how they could dispose of their property.

The actions of real thirteenth-century kings make clear why, in the *Roman de Silence*, King Evan does not attempt to choose one daughter as heir. If he were to partition the land equally as Chrétien's King Arthur does, Evan would lose direct control over the younger sister's portion since she (or her husband) would owe feudal service not to the king but to the older sister. On the other hand, allowing the dispute to proceed to judicial combat also has risks; a general outbreak of violence after the two counts are killed is only narrowly avoided (307-308). By entirely doing away with women's ability to inherit, King Evan appears to be dodging alternatives that are from his point of view equally unattractive, and his decree would have bothered some members of Heldris's audience less than others. There were longstanding complaints in medieval society that female inheritance damaged the social structure by fragmenting great estates,[24] and the variety of opinion is clearly represented in the poem in the words of those who swear to uphold the king's decree: "Alquant le font ireëment / Et li plusor moult liëment, / Qui n'en donroiënt une tille" ("Some did it in anger, / but most did it quite gladly — / the ones who had nothing to lose" [321–326]). But in the real England, unlike King Evan's, no one did anything to stop women's ability to inherit, and for good reason: abolishing female inheritance would have seriously disrupted the functioning of aristocratic society. Between 1200 and 1327, 57.3% of English baronies were inherited by women at least once and 19.5% of all baronial inheritances during the period went to women.[25] The importance

---

[22] Susan Reynolds, *Fiefs and Vassals: The Medieval Evidence Reinterpreted* (Oxford: Clarendon Press, 1994), 382; Scott L. Waugh, "Non-Alienation Clauses in Thirteenth-Century English Charters," *Albion* 17 (1985): 1–14, here 12.

[23] Reynolds, *Fiefs*, 303.

[24] On problems associated with dividing fiefs, see Bloch, *Feudal Society*, 203; Theodore Evergates, *Feudal Society in the Bailliage of Troyes under the Counts of Champagne, 1152–1284* (Baltimore: Johns Hopkins University Press, 1975), 126; Scott L. Waugh, *The Lordship of England: Royal Wardships and Marriages in English Society and Politics 1217–1327* (Princeton: Princeton University Press, 1988), 52.

[25] Waugh, *Lordship*, 19.

of female inheritance pertained to the situation in France as well as England and at various levels of the feudal hierarchy. In the County of Champagne, for example, "women represented over 20 percent of the ordinary fief holders" during the third quarter of the thirteenth century.[26] If over half the barons in the land owe their holdings to a female ancestor and lesser aristocratic inheritances owe a similar debt to the maternal line, a huge sector of the economy would simply disappear into the king's coffers if that king did away with women's ability to inherit.

The emphasis on female inheritance seems to be a conscious choice on Heldris's part, since, in his literary source from the Arthurian *Vulgate*, it is not the cross-dressed maiden but rather her father and brother whose inheritance is lost and then restored.[27] It is not simply, though, the fact of widespread female inheritance in actual thirteenth-century practice that makes Evan's law seem so outrageous, but also the particular function of women's inheritance in noble society. We have seen that there was not much freedom in the way the tenants-in-chief could dispose of their property, and if it was difficult for one noble to grant land to another, then that meant it was also difficult to become the recipient of someone else's grant. What little wiggle room there was derived largely from female inheritance. The loss involved in the fragmentation of an estate when women inherited was someone else's gain, and even when an estate fell to a single heiress it was still someone else's gain. Unlike a dowry, which usually reverted to a woman's family if she had no heirs, and if she did have heirs was likely to be used to provide for daughters and younger sons, the land an heiress brought with her — fragmented or not — was permanently added to her husband's patrimony. By preventing his female subjects from inheriting property, Evan is also depriving his male subjects of an important and rare means of acquiring land and status.[28]

Silence turns out to be an only child, thus underscoring the crude arbitrariness of a law designed to avoid the problems of partible inheritance. There is, however, the precedent of Silence's mother Eufemie, who had also been the only child of the Count of Cornwall. Under ordinary circumstances Eufemie's father could not make a match for her without the king's approval,

---

[26] Evergates, *Feudal Society in the Bailliage of Troyes*, 130.

[27] For the story of Avenable/Grisandole, see Rupert T. Pickens, trans., *The Story of Merlin*, in *Lancelot-Grail: The Arthurian Vulgate and Post-Vulgate in Translation*, ed. Norris J. Lacy, 5 vols. (New York: Garland, 1993), 1:323–29.

[28] See Waugh, *Lordship*, 21–24 on the redistribution of wealth among the aristocracy through the combined effects of marriage and inheritance.

Female Inheritance and the Romance of Property 205

and if he died before his daughter married, the king would have the right of wardship, which means he would collect the profits from her land until such time as he arranged a marriage for her to a man of his choosing. Giving the daughter and the land with her to a man of his own choosing is exactly what King Evan does in arranging the marriage of Silence's parents Cador and Eufemie, except he does so while the Count is still alive and without even consulting him. The king's adviser who explains the situation to Cador reminds him of the inheritance law saying, "the land should have been this lady's, / but she no longer has a right to it" ("Cesti devroit estre la terre, / Mais n'i a droit qu'ele puist estre" [1453–1454]), and the loss of the woman's rights is also a loss of her father's.[29]

The abolition of female inheritance in *Silence* thus exaggerates the already stringent control a thirteenth-century king had over his barons, especially over their female children, and Eufemie's situation also resonates with another royal practice. Upon the death of one of his tenants-in-chief, the king automatically took formal possession of the land, granting it back to the heir only when the heir had paid the relief, a kind of inheritance tax. By enforcing this rule the king preserved for himself another right that lesser lords had long since been forced to give up.[30] King Evan's freedom to dispose as he pleases with the Count of Cornwall's land and daughter while the Count is still alive is simply a nightmare version of the prerogatives thirteenth-century kings actually had over their chief tenants. For the greatest fief-holders of thirteenth-century kings, the ability to reprogram the sex of a child must have seemed almost as attractive — and almost as likely — as any other mechanism for evading royal control. The fluidity of Silence's gender mirrors the social reality in which the laws and customs governing female inheritance were less fixed than their masculine counterparts and where heiresses of great estates offered noblemen the rare opportunity to join the king's monopoly instead of being excluded from it.

The risk of partitioning estates and the hope of acquiring them were both possibilities, we have seen, when women stood to inherit property in late thirteenth-century France and England. King Evan has it both ways:

---

[29] As Kinoshita observes, "the king usurps the father's familial authority" ("Feudal Politics," 401), but I would like to emphasize that such usurpation is already implicit in the abolition of female inheritance.

[30] S. F. C. Milsom, *The Legal Framework of English Feudalism* (Cambridge: Cambridge University Press, 1976), 163.

he forbids female inheritance when the division of an estate between sisters threatens the loss of royal control over the younger sister's portion, but he reinstates it when a single heiress — Silence herself — would bring a great estate on the market. Then he marries that heiress himself, thus asserting direct and undisputed lordship over her land. This action would extinguish the county of Cornwall as a separate barony upon the death of Cador, further centralizing and aggrandizing the king's authority. Our temptation to read this final scene of the romance in terms of Silence's personal success or failure in resisting the patriarchy may cause us to forget that Heldris's first audience was more interested in ascending the patriarchy than resisting it. Aristocratic anxiety in the face of royal strictures is merely the flip side of the nobility's romantic longings for land and status. On the most literal level Silence overcomes the uncertainties of her upbringing and environment to attain the highest status possible for a woman of her birth. She does not, of course, become queen through any ordinary means, and the fact that the best knight in the land marries the king functions as a fantasy of upward mobility for those nobles who could not beat the king at the game of property politics, but also could not join him as Silence does.

Craig A. Berry
Independent Scholar

Resisting Translation: Britomart in Book 3 of Spenser's *Faerie Queene*

Old Archimago, the archi-mage and the arch-image, the enchanter with "mightie science" (1.2.10) and the feckless Old Man, the strongest of the strong and the weakest of the weak, is a figure of male fantasy dominated by the logic of the castration principle.[1] In his role as arch-villain in Book 1 of *The Faerie Queene*, his primary target is not Redcross, the book's hero, but Redcross's lady Una: "For her he hated as the hissing snake, / And in her many troubles did most pleasure take" (1.2.9). That the hissing snake in the ambiguous construction can denote either Una as characterized by Archimago or Archimago as characterized by the narrator draws the two image-makers, Archimago and the narrator, together in a common project of demonization. In this blending of antipapism with misogyny the *pharmakos* of evil illusion becomes the *pharmakon* of poetic truth, the remedial scapegoat that "refuses to be bound or limited: he continually escapes the fictional role of a simple antagonist, and his duplicitous creations threaten

---

[1] I build here on my previous use of this principle to describe the tendency of a narrative to offer anxious and equivocal resistance to patriarchal values that it can never entirely deny. On Archimago as exemplar of the castration principle, see Harry Berger Jr., "Archimago: Between Text and Countertext," *SEL*, 43 (2003): 19–64, where I note that, "The logic of castration may be most concisely understood by conceiving it as the inversion of the logic of Pinocchio's nose: in the latter, the more he lies the bigger it grows; in the former, the bigger it grows the more it lies." On the principle in Book 1 more generally, see idem, "Displacing Autophobia in *Faerie Queene* I: Ethics, Gender, and Oppositional Reading in the Spenserian Text," *English Literary Renaissance* 28 (1998): 163–82. For a general anthropological account of the structural pressures the Pinocchio principle responds to, see idem, "From Body to Cosmos: The Dynamics of Representation in Pre-capitalist Society," *South Atlantic Quarterly* 91 (1992): 557-602, here 585, and passim.

I'm very grateful to Craig Berry for several constructive suggestions that improved this essay.

constantly to contaminate the poet's."[2] Hence his anomalous reappearance in Book 3 (4.45), just when Florimell is about to reenact Una's flight through the woods, brings to the surface the originary power of the castration principle behind the gynephobic discourses disseminated among his surrogates in Book 3. In this essay I examine its manifestations in the legend of Britomart. Its power is explicitly invested not only in the allegorical and magical violence of antipoetic scapegoats — the witch, Proteus, and Busirane — but also in the apparently benign patrons of patriarchal order and continuity. Britomart's violent awakening to love, her induction into the heterosexual regime of the *translatio imperii*, is presided over by an agent whose motives and career are shown to be dominated by the fantasy of castration.

This agent is Merlin, and he is introduced in 3.3 as a figure of folklore by a narrator who reports what "men say" and who addresses the reader like a tour guide promoting the thrills and chills of a weekend in old Wales. He begins, however, with a backward glance at Archimago and Mammon: Britomart and Glauce, disguised "in straunge / And base attyre, that none might them bewray," travel

> To *Maridunum*, that is now by chaunge
> Of name *Cayr-Merdin* cald....
> There the wise *Merlin* whylome wont (they say)
> To make his wonne, low underneath the ground,
> In a deepe delve, farre from the vew of day,
> That of no living wight he mote be found,
> When so he counseld with his sprights encompast round.
>
> And if thou ever happen that same way
> To travell, goe to see that dreadfull place:
> It is an hideous hollow cave (they say)
> Under a rocke that lyes a little space
> From the swift *Barry*, tombling downe apace,
> Emongst the woodie hilles of *Dynevowre*:
> But dare thou not, I charge, in any cace,
> To enter into that same balefull Bowre,
> For fear the cruell Feends should thee unwares devowre.

---

[2] A. Leigh DeNeef, *Spenser and the Motives of Metaphor* (Durham, NC: Duke University Press, 1982), 95.

> But standing high aloft, low lay thine eare,
>   And there such ghastly noise of yron chaines,
>   And brasen Caudrons thou shalt rombling heare,
>   Which thousand sprights with long enduring paines
>   Doe tosse, that it will stonne thy feeble braines,
>   And oftentimes great grones, and grievous stounds,
>   When too huge toile and labour them constraines.... (3.3.7–9)

"The cause some say is this": Merlin commanded his sprights to build a brazen wall around his house of care and to stay at it until they brought it "to perfect end."[3] When his beloved Lady of the Lake suddenly called him away, he bound them to their labor "till his returne," which failed to materialize because, "through that false Ladies traine," he was "buried under beare" (3.10–11). As if to counter this fatal vulnerability, the narrator goes on to exalt his magical powers, especially those enabling him single-handedly to "dismay" huge "hostes of men" and, when he wished, "his enimies to fray" (3.12).

The Merlin Spenser constructs as a folklore fantasy surrounds himself with walls, terrorizes his slaves, and is undone by a Bad Lady. His career profile is depicted in terms that emphasize insecurity, distrust of others, the desire to be invisible, the self-protective aspiration to a level of power that only magic or clairvoyance can guarantee, and the sexual vulnerability that renders all precautions futile. A dextrous reading by Kenneth Gross throws light on this sinister figure: "This agent of truth ... was 'wondrously begotten, and begonne / By false illusion of a guilefull Spright / On a faire Ladie Nonne' (3.3.13) — born, that is, out of demonic violation, or out of [the] meeting of illusion with nothing or 'none'".[4] The pun — begotten on no fair lady; of no woman born — lights up for only a moment, since the next four lines give the mother a name and pedigree, and suggest a demonic form of virgin birth in which the body of a Christian virgin, and of a Christian myth, are appropriated and inseminated by an Archimagian illusion. But what flashes forth from the pun leaves luminous traces after it fades: the fantasy

---

[3] The "chaunge / Of name" underscores the revisionary construction while the new name, Cayr-Merdin, chimes out a conflation of Merlin, his care, and the "ghastly noise" of the forced labor that testifies to his anxiety. All quotations of *The Faerie Queene* are from *Faerie Queene*, Books I–III, ed. J.C. Smith in *The Poetical Works of Edmund Spenser*, 3 vols. (Oxford: Clarendon Press, 1909; repr. Oxford: Clarendon Press, 1961), vol. 2. I have modernized u's to v's and i's to j's.

[4] Kenneth Gross, *Spenserian Poetics* (Ithaca: Cornell University Press, 1985), 153.

of androgenesis as the hyperbolic expression of the male desire of impregnability. Its very impossibility measures the apprehensiveness with which males regard the necessary but less secure practices of heterosexual reproduction. Myths of immaculate conception and divine or demonic rape are attempts to maintain ideological control over female sexuality. We will see that although Merlin's control of Britomart's desire is given political legitimacy, it participates in a similar structure of illusion, anxiety, appropriation or rape, and ideological cooptation.

If the tone of high-spirited disenchantment with which the narrator reports what "they say" makes light of regional superstitions and antiquities, with their apprehensive rocky-horror fantasies, it is to place in the foreground his own creative transformation of Merlin from this menacing and capricious figure to the benign mouthpiece of Clio, the narrator's "dearest sacred Dame" (3.4). But as a product of the intercourse of false illusion with nothing, the Welsh Merlin is by no means canceled out. His effort to bind fiends will be displaced to the effort to use prophecy to bind Britomart to her fate, and the Lady of the Lake's interruption of his wall-building will be replicated by the secret "spectacle" that cuts the prophecy short and leaves him "dismayd" (3.50).[5] Whatever else Merlin was dismayed by, the immediate cause is the specter of the phallic virgin's destruction of a male fortress:

> Then shall a royall virgin raine, which shall
> Stretch her white rod over the *Belgicke* shore,
> And the great Castle smite so sore with all,
> That it shall make him shake, and shortly learne to fall. (3.49)

Even the positive reference to Elizabeth's defeat of the Spanish forces in the Netherlands ("Castle" suggests Castilian) produces a gesture of recoil after the broken ending:

> But yet the end is not. There *Merlin* stayd,
> As overcomen of the spirites powre,
> Or other ghastly spectacle dismayd,
> That secretly he saw, yet note discoure.... (3.50)

Such coyness is a trap for the curious interpreter. For just when Britomart is being conscripted into the discourse of Tudor dynasticism, just when she

---

[5] Replicated in discourse time, but anticipated in story time.

is being shown why she should arc up through the martial then down to the marital and maternal stages of her "fated" trajectory, the very speech aimed at persuading her to submit to the male plot falters over an image of resistance to that trajectory, the glorious descendant who retains the rod of power and refuses motherhood. The unfinished history and wall converging thematically in the motif of endless work; the spirit-binding enchanter now, as prophet, overcome by the spirit's power: these figures of analogy and reversal suggest another ghastly spectacle in which the royal virgin modulates into the Lady of the Lake who will make Merlin "shake, and shortly learne to fall." Thus although the historical agenda of the renovated Tudor Merlin is rhetorically distinguished from the abortive and frenetic activities ascribed to the folk Merlin, their continuity is textually affirmed in a manner that subverts the distinction. Like Pinocchio's nose, the Tudor discourse stretches out the "Soveraines goodly auncestrie, / . . . by dew degrees and long protense" (3.4) — or, as in the 1596 and later editions, "long pretence." The outcome of Merlin's chronicle is informed by the same anxiety that motivates his fiend-binding and wall-building.

This anxiety had been foreshadowed in canto 2 when the narrator described the "vertues" of Merlin's "looking glasse." At first it is depicted in innocuous terms as a useful addition to any royal household: it could show

> . . . in perfect sight
> What ever thing was in the world contaynd,
> So that it to the looker appertaynd . . . .

But from this point on, what appertains to the looker reflects and objectifies the maker's apprehensiveness, and is limited to two kinds of disclosure:

> What ever foe had wrought, or frend had faynd,
> Therein discovered was, ne ought mote pas,
> Ne ought in secret from the same remaynd;
> For thy it round and hollow shaped was,
> Like to the world it selfe, and seem'd a world of glas. (2.19)

The analogy is reversible: the world constructed by phobic fantasy is a world the hollow truth of which has been made transparent when its "concealing continents" have been stripped away. It is the truth of a frangible reality dominated by the secret machinations of foes and false friends. The looker to whom this appertains is constructed in the mirror's image. He or she —

especially she — must discover/disclose the secret desire that will be interpreted and policed according to the necessities of state, and the security of princes, fathers, and lovers.

The next stanza relocates this paranoid construction in the self-shattering folly of sexual jealousy:

> Who wonders not, that reades so wonderous worke?
>   But who does wonder, that has red the Towre,
>   Wherein th'Ægyptian *Phao* long did lurke
>   From all mens vew, that none might her discoure,
>   Yet she might all men vew out of her bowre?
>   Great *Ptolomæe* it for his lemans sake
>   Ybuilded all of glasse, by Magicke powre,
>   And also it impregnable did make:
> Yet when his love was false, he with a peaze it brake.
>
> Such was the glassie globe that *Merlin* made,
>   And gave unto king *Ryence* for his gard,
>   That never foes his kingdome might invade,
>   But it he knew at home before he hard
>   Tydings thereof, and so them still debar'd.
>   It was a famous Present for a Prince,
>   And worthy worke of infinite reward,
>   That treasons could bewray, and foes convince
> Happie this Realme, had it remained ever since (2.20–21)

Since "Ægyptian *Phao*" touches off a thought of Pharaoh the analogue implies that the imperial magician yields his power to the beloved he wants to conceal from potential competitors and that in acceding to her scopic desire he produces the very outcome he most fears.[6] The self-fulfilling fear of

---

[6] Otherwise, it is implied, he would have made the tower of brick. The possible source of this anecdote is obscure. Thomas Roche flatly states that "Spenser's source for this myth ... has not been found" (Edmund Spenser, *The Faerie Queene*, ed. Thomas B. Roche, Jr. with the assistance of C. Patrick O'Donnell, Jr. [New York: Penguin Books, 1979], 1144). In a gloss of the second edition of his text, A.C. Hamilton speculates that Phao is "[p]resumably, the lover of Ptolomæe, the second-century Alexandrian astronomer ... who built her the glass tower" (Edmund Spenser, *The Faerie Queene*, 2nd edition, ed. A. C. Hamilton, text edited by Hiroshi Yamashita and Toshiyuki Suzuki, [Harlow & London: Longman, 2001], 305, hereafter cited as Hamilton, FQ). Hamilton maddeningly

treason and betrayal then marches across the bridge of "Such was the glassie globe" to plant its banner in the counterfactual — and rueful — wish expressed in the alexandrine of stanza 21.[7]

Against this uneasy background I want to glance briefly at the relation between Britomart's awakening to love and the two major subtexts that not only inform Spenser's construction of Britomart but are also persistently and conspicuously echoed during the first three cantos: the stories of Scylla and Myrrha in the *Ciris* and *Metamorphoses* 10. Myrrha wants to sleep with her father, while Scylla's passion for her father's enemy Minos leads her in the opposite direction: she wants to betray her father and put his kingdom in the enemy's hands. When Glauce consolingly distinguishes the confused and distraught Britomart's desire from that of Myrrha (2.41) she echoes the words of Scylla's nurse, Carme (*Ciris* 237–240), mother of the original Britomartis. The two perversions ironically conflated by this intersection and focused on Britomart project a range of threats to the patriarchal organization of family and state, and since so much of Glauce's language echoes Carme's, that alternative to Myrrha's incest looms with special force behind the dialogue in canto 2.[8] By the end of the canto one would think that Merlin had read the *Ciris* and *Metamorphoses* 10 and had designed for Ryence, Britomart's father, a glass that "treasons could bewray and foes convince" specifically with the predicaments of Nisus and Cinyras in mind.

---

gives no source for this reference to the astronomer. But since (as he notes) *Phao* means "light," the name may be a syncopated reminder not only of Pharaoh, but also of Pharos, the site of the lighthouse that is the seventh wonder of the world. According to some sources, the lighthouse was built partly of glass and partly of polished reflecting metal. Different ancient authors assign the lighthouse to the regimes and patronage of different Pharaohs — Suidas to Ptolemy Soter, Eusebius to Ptolemy II Philadephus — and some (Pliny, Strabo) claim it was built for King Ptolemy by Sosastrus of Cnidus, but nobody assigns it to Claudius Ptolemaeus. [The author thanks the Press Reader for suggesting this line of inquiry.]

[7] "Who wonders not that reads so wonderous worke?" The spelling of "wonderous" suggests the force of a verbal adjective: this is a work that makes one wonder, a work about which one wonders, a work that fills one not only with amazement but also with doubt and uncertainty. What crosses across the bridge of analogy and into Ryence's kingdom is the doubt and suspicion of uneasy kings, fathers, mages; the anxiety of men of power about the women they feel they must lock up or subject to total surveillance in order to keep control of them. This characterizes Ryence and Merlin. Merlin's anxieties, discussed above, leave their mark on the next canto.

[8] *The Works of Edmund Spenser: A Variorum Edition*, ed. Edwin Greenlaw, Charles G. Osgood, and Frederick M. Padelford, vol. 3 (Baltimore: Johns Hopkins University Press, 1934), 334–36 (hereafter cited as Var.3).

But Merlin does more. He is allowed to collaborate with the poet who rescues Britomart from her shadowy shelf life in *Ciris*. When the poet reinvents her along Ariostan lines as a woman warrior and dynastic progenitor, he also reinvents Ariosto's Merlin so as to augment his prophetic power with poetic and rhetorical power — the power of shaping, interpreting, and directing the heroine's desire. Yet in restoring Merlin to life the poet not only gives him the power of the mirror but also motivates and contextualizes its defensive virtues by making them reflect the politico-sexual diffidence of a failed career. The genesis of Britomart's passion is represented as the effect and the target of anxieties inscribed in a network of male discourses that can only interpret woman's desire as politically threatening. The same network interprets and promotes the major allegorical themes of each book — holiness, temperance, chastity — in ways congenial to culturally dominant ideals of behavior and thought, ideals of spiritual, ethical, and sexual integrity. It is a network that opposes Eumnestes to Phantastes, the "matter of just memory" to "th'aboundance of an idle braine" (2.Pr.l), the Muses to the Sirens, Contemplation to Archimago, Alma to Acrasia.

This table of opposites adumbrates the problematic of imagination picked out by John Guillory in arguing that what Spenser most fears is "the prospect of the imagination as beginning, displacing some other and more valued origin." Guillory shows that Spenser responds to the danger by reducing the power of imagination "to failed representations," as in the "easy derogation" of Phantastes (2.9.49–52), "to whom any power of origination is being denied," and by praising "Eumnestes ('good memory')', who might also be called 'true re-presentation'":

> The digression through the Castle of Alma in Book II provides Spenser with a needed defense against Phantastes the Poet — his double. Spenser is thoroughly conventional in tracing his poetry to the more authoritative quarters of Reason, who is ... a censor, a "magistrate," ruling and overruling the false productions of the magus, his unauthorized double. The legal analogue fits into the general scheme of repressed imagination.[9]

Guillory's valuable formulation can be protected against an obvious criticism by rewriting "Spenser" as the ideology that is privileged by the narrative and

---

[9] John Guillory, *Poetic Authority: Spenser, Milton, and Literary History* (New York: Columbia University Press, 1983), 37.

narrator but interrogated by the text, which represents the former as a repressive agency. The conflation of Reason with the magus, Merlin, in Book 3 conspicuously stages the problematic described by Guillory because it shows, first, how the originary power of male fantasy is a compensatory response to politico-sexual anxiety of impotence, and second, how this power authenticates its repressive inventions by embedding them in "matter of just memory" and "the more authoritative quarters of Reason" of state. Both the genesis of Merlin and the folkloristic "re-presentation" of his birth, career, and powers conform suspiciously with some of the fantasies buzzing about in Phantastes's chamber: "Shewes, visions, sooth-sayes, and prophesies; / And all that fained is, as leasings, tales, and lies" (2.9.51).

Because this activity is both ideological and repressive, I shall designate it as a function of the poem's ideological police. In the most definitive treatment of the activity to date, these are depicted as the forces within the poem that arrest interpretation, handcuff textuality, and submit all meanings to judgment in the politico-judicial court of allegory:

> The interplay of the text's self-conscious self-interrogation on the one hand and its unacknowledged and partially submerged discursive self-positioning on the other allows us to recognize a critique inscribed within its discursive mediations and juxtapositions, and to trace, to some extent, the analogies between that critique and the kinds of criticism generated by our own ideological position. An important determinant of the analogy that the critic thus constructs is precisely the text's characterization of the workings of "allegory," since this is the mode it identifies with the court and with its political necessity to harmonize any more disruptive picture of literary power with its celebrations of Elizabeth.
>
> In this particular characterization, allegory is deeply implicated in political schemes ... not simply because it is thematically concerned with systems of government, but because it proposes to provide a government for the country of meanings. Allegory — to elaborate the personification — promises to sort out all the competing meanings and to provide a hierarchy [a monarchy rather than a commonwealth] by which one can distinguish which is the most important, and which the least.[10]

---

[10] Susanne Wofford, *The Choice of Achilles: The Ideology of Figure in the Epic* (Stanford: Stanford University Press, 1992), 233–34.

> "Fate"... is one name for the fully authorized explanation that becomes associated with the allegorical (and ... political) claims to assign meaning to the chivalric fiction. (Wofford, *Choice*, 275)

In Book 1 the policing function is relegated to Protestant iconography, the narrator, and the House of Holiness; its function, as Wofford shows, is figured and analyzed in the powers of Arthur's shield "to strip away appearances" and produce the equivalent of epistemological closure, the closure that "destroys, petrifies, or transforms the human gazer, re-ducing what 'seems' to what 'is', and in doing so, suggesting that what 'is' ... can be found only in eternity" (*Choice*, 262–63). In Book 2 the police include Guyon, the Palmer, and Alma's castle.[11] In Book 3 the text's "self-conscious self-interrogation" is even more pointed when the policing function is assigned to a Merlin whose demonic magic conspicuously links him to Archimago and is later evoked by Busirane.

Merlin "tells Britomart that she loves Artegall because with him she will produce a fine lineage — thus he authorizes her love by identifying a future event as its cause," and this authorization "takes the form of compulsion" by fate, which "can be read as a metaphor not only for the constraints of plot but for both familial and cultural constraints imposed on women" (Wofford, *Choice*, 274). She is bound to this fate "by the tree of genealogy" (274) but also by the very ruse of the mirror itself, for in spite of Britomart's fear that the image is a self-created illusion (2.44) the image was "planted" by the police. If, as Wofford states elsewhere, "Britomart imagines an ideal husband whose image is drawn from her own self-reflection within her father's closet," it does not follow that she has withdrawn "into a secluded world of self-contemplation."[12] For it is her father's closet, and Wofford herself notes that what Britomart sees in the mirror is "a literary vision. The image of Artegall is constituted of fragments taken from the epic and romance traditions, his motto appropriately enough being 'written ... with cyphers old'" ("Gendering Allegory," 8). Thus the heroine's complaint that she was snagged by "a hidden hooke with baite" floating within the "hollow" globe of "my fathers wondrous mirrhour" (2.37–38) is truer than she knows. The hook "infixed" fast in her "bleeding bowels" (2.39) turns out, in Merlin's re-description, to be her initial contact with the huge tree "enrooted deepe" in

---

[11] See Wofford, *Choice*, 252, on the Palmer.
[12] Susanne Wofford, "Gendering Allegory: Spenser's Bold Reader and the Emergence of Character in *The Faerie Queene* III," *Criticism* 30 (1988): 1–21, here 7–8.

her womb, which is appropriated in the name of the father and the *translatio imperii* (3.22).

This appropriation is represented as a kind of rape. Since the mirror discloses threats and dangers that "to the looker appertaynd," the prospect of false friends and potential invaders of the kingdom is insidiously displaced to the image that answers Britomart's idle curiosity about the future husband she knows she will have to accept (2.19, 21, 22–25). As Hamilton concisely puts it, "This feature explains why Britomart sees Artegall in the mirror: he invades her kingdom."[13] The invasion is preemptive, and the conspicuously canceled scenarios of the Scylla and Myrrha stories index the anxieties that motivate it. But cancellation is repression. What is being repressed is not simply the potential waywardness of Britomart's desire, which is not even activated until she sees the image. What is being repressed is the waywardness of desire in general as it is depicted throughout Book 3 — the polymorphous carnival of desire that transgresses gender and generation and therefore motivates the effort of the ideological police to enforce the heterosexual contract by writing it on woman's body.[14] Or, to reverse the emphasis and produce an equally probable scenario, Book 3 represents polymorphous desire as a fantasy constructed by the ideological police to justify their inscription of the (otherwise arbitrary) heterosexual contact.

With respect to Britomart, their project is to give her the training and experience that will qualify her for dynastic motherhood by:

> Making her seeke an unknowne Paramoure,
> From the worlds end, through many a bitter stowre:
> From whose two loynes thou afterwards did rayse
> Most famous fruits of matrimoniall bowre . . . . (3.3)

Here the ideological police speak through the narrator. A little later this message will be unpacked by Merlin in a more rigorous account of her responsibility to God, Artegall, and the British future. Having displaced this weighty burden on to Merlin, the narrative briskly sends her forth on her martial exploits, creating opportunities for the display of transvestite puissance and

---

[13] Hamilton, *FQ*, 305. See also Linda Gregerson, "Protestant Erotics: Idolatry and Interpretation in Spenser's *Faerie Queene*," *ELH* 58 (1991): 1–34, here 18.

[14] Not heterosexuality *tout court* but reproductive heterosexuality under patriarchal auspices in the context of domestic partnership.

even, as Wofford observes, allowing her to collaborate with Glauce in writing "her own story" and designing "the plot of knightly disguise" (*Choice*, 275). But brisk and blithe as it may initially seem, this project is beset with crosscurrents of doubt and fear that betray the ambivalence, the sense of uncertain control, marking the narrative's construction of Britomart.

My view of the relations among text, narrative, and character springs directly from formulations Wofford first aired in "Gendering Allegory" and developed in *Choice*. The strength of her approach lies in its compelling integration of structural and ethical insights. On the one hand she argues that because Britomart is "one of Spenser's most fictionalized characters, imagined as quite distinct from the allegory of chastity that is also told in her book," she seems autonomous and possessed of a will of her own (*Choice*, 328). "In the episodes that introduce her story" she "is given a psychological history unusually specific for the characters of *The Faerie Queene*," and she displays in general "an openness of character that leads her into unexpected adventures and makes her respond in unpredictable ways" ("Gendering Allegory," 9, 15). On the other hand Wofford argues that even though the narrative sustains Britomart in her "illusion of 'liberty' by permanently deferring" the subjection to matrimony and motherhood that will write her "out of the action altogether" (*Choice*, 328, 275), it attempts, in the interest of that fate, "to attach specific allegorical meanings to Britomart's quest" and to maintain her as the personification of the ideal of chaste love the fate prescribes ("Gendering Allegory," 13–14, 15).

This disjunctive formulation picks out elements of strain between the character's autonomy and the narrative reaction to it: "the principal characters of Spenser's poem, particularly Britomart, resist the controlling force of the figures that organize the story and give it meaning," and this conflict "limits the poet's claims to allegorical clarity" ("Gendering Allegory," 1). Finally, and most importantly, Wofford reads the conflict in terms of gender and insists that the "voice" of the Spenserian text is not identical with but critical of the voice, stance, and authority of the male narrator it represents:

> The comedy of the narrator's erotic involvement [with Belphoebe] allows Spenser to imply that there may be a separate perspective on events, one that judges the male version of the story. This more expansive authorial perspective makes room for Spenser's female readers; it allows the poem to make use of a male narrator while revealing the

> dangers of the male point of view. The kind of double reading Book III calls for, then, is an androgynous one, but the story of Britomart nonetheless is told from an explicitly male perspective.
>
> In Book III . . . the sexual tension which animates the narrative . . . undermines the absoluteness of the authority of the narrative voice.
>
> Spenser dramatizes . . . the disjunction between the male meanings imposed by narrator or magician and the female understandings represented and acted upon within the story as story . . . .
> ("Gendering Allegory," 6–7, 15, 16)

In the powerful, tough-minded, and self-aware development of her theoretical framework in *Choice*, Wofford maintains this distinction but defines her terms more carefully and is more skeptical about the extent to which "Spenser" may be in full control of the distinction. "The name 'Spenser,'" she argues, "seems to attach itself to the morals provided by the not-always-helpful narrator of *The Faerie Queene*, though there is clearly another 'Spenser' at work throughout, a 'Spenser' who at moments cagily identifies that narrator with such evil geniuses as Busyrane and Archimago while laughing at the poem's own formal need to round out its action in often moralizing alexandrines" (*Choice*, 11). "Spenser" is "a metonym for the discursive . . . practices employed by his text" (296). But, she insists, neither "'Spenser' nor 'the text' is therefore in full control of all the ideological displacements, suppressions, or denials that may be at work, nor is the critical counternarrative that I have found to be a feature of the epic inscribed 'within' each poem in the sense of being located only 'within' its own self-conscious critique of its processes of generating meaning" (11). The counternarrative, a notion Wofford develops by means of a brilliant analysis of the structure of epic simile, functions "as alternative politics or cultural critique" (510), or as a "narrative of resistance" that "figures in the poem as Spenser's own self-interrogation" and makes "space for a challenge to the narrative celebration of power" (228). She maintains that the text "does not disclose a fully satisfactory answer" to the question "whether 'Spenser' participates in the testing and complicating of the discourses his poem employs," but concludes from her analysis that the counternarrative critique is more than a projection from the latterday commentator's "critical discourse"; "it is also crucial to Spenser's own method" (296–97).

So far, my project fits comfortably within this theoretical conspectus. The "figures of compulsion" that dominate the action, that "develop into a systematic poetics of compulsion" (Wofford, *Choice*, 298) and threaten characters with "allegorical bondage," do the work of the ideological police, while the counternarrative voice of the text performs a cultural critique of the mainstream discourses it represents. Yet at one point, in maintaining this complex view of the negotiation between allegorical compulsion and counternarrative resistance, Wofford makes a statement I find confusing. She has been arguing that although such freedom and resistance as that most fully embodied in the portrayal of Britomart "may be deeply desired and even fought for by the characters in the action, the constraints and 'bonds' are consistently reimposed — even in Britomart's case — by the allegorical mode of the text" (320). And she goes on to remark that this containment "makes any escape" from allegorical compulsion "difficult, though this fact is disguised by Spenser's use of the epic fiction to challenge precisely the text's thoroughgoing coercion of its characters" (330). Here it is the action, the epic fiction, that seems to provide the counternarrative site of freedom and resistance, as illustrated by Wofford's remark that Britomart attains "her freedom in part . . . by remaining one of Spenser's most fictionalized characters, imagined as quite distinct from the allegory of chastity" (328). And it is the "text" that provides the site of allegorical compulsion, working, so to speak, behind the back of a character who does not know that she is only a fictional character in a poem.

The problem is that to direct attention to what is "behind the back" of the fictional character produces a structure of interpretive relations different from the structure produced by directing attention to what is "behind the back" of the allegorical narrator. In the former case, the character is the target or object of narrative and figural ironies generated by the allegorical mode and the "poetics of compulsion," which have their own quasi-autonomous logic, their tendencies toward absolutist control of meaning, their "potentially tyrannical powers" (353). But in the latter case the allegorical narrator/narrative is the target or object of devices of impersonation and diegetic construction that are conspicuously parodic and that disclose the target's motivated efforts to misdirect or foreclose interpretation.

Wofford moves back and forth between these options. On the one hand, there is a systematic tendency for "the order of allegory" to reestablish itself and "the structure of compulsion by figures" to reassert itself, so that the forms of escape from this tyranny are "severely limited" (330). On the other hand, allegory can neither contain nor fully control its many antitheses and contradictions. Since it works by positing a system of opposites and arrogates to itself the hyperbolic power to legislate and to move from one to the other, it finds its monarchy always threatened by rebellious underlings, who call attention to themselves by exposing a different significance to events.... When the text finds allegory to have potentially tyrannical powers... it is... forced to disclose that the good government it reveres resembles allegory more closely than its politic plots will allow. Spenser's allegorical narrator may feel that this is a price worth paying for order.... But his poem is less comfortable with this choice.... (353).

These two alternatives are not strictly opposed, and activating either or both when the interpretive situation calls for it gives Wofford the flexibility she needs to do justice to her complex multiperspectival theory and method of reading.[15] But for my purposes, conferring primacy on the second alternative produces a sharper and simpler model of the relation between narrative and counternarrative agencies. It may be arbitrarily restrictive, it may even be simplistic, but the method of reading it underwrites consistently marks out, and travels along, the seam that both divides and correlates the counternarrative site and the narrative/allegorical target of impersonation. In particular, it enables me to show how Wofford's various descriptions of the allegorical drive toward containment convey precisely the sense of diegetic anxiety that, in the earlier essay, "Gendering Allegory," she associates with "the male point of view" dramatized and judged by the "more expansive authorial perspective" she calls "Spenser." In that essay Wofford discusses "Spenser's" revelation of "the dangers *of* the male point of view" (my italics). But her characterization in *Choice* of allegory as a fearful and therefore tyrannical and compulsive force orients us toward the other side of that revelation: the dangers *to* the male point of view.

---

[15] In the former case the epic fiction is an imitation of chivalric exploits that may express the protagonist's freedom and power as well as her/his freedom to abuse the power, authority, or responsibility delegated for the quest. In the latter case the chivalric mode of representation expresses the goal-directed agenda of the ideological police. By moving back and forth between these alternatives, Wofford is able to bring out the ambivalence of chivalric discourse as a site in which — and for control of which — these opposed meanings struggle. And while I find that interpretive benefit attractive, my own agenda calls for a somewhat different explanation of the ambivalence, one that centers on the divided motivation of the narrative agency parodied and impersonated by "Spenser."

It is thus by combining different if not incompatible emphases in Wofford's essay and book that I come up with a revision in which the two concepts introduced above, the ideological police and the counternarrative, may be paired as opposed "voices" we pretend to "hear" in our imaginary audition of the text we read. By "voice" I mean "tone" in the old New-Critical sense but — as we say nowadays — tone with Attitude. There is a narratorial or storytelling voice and there is a textual or counternarrative voice.[16] The two voices are distinguishable but not distinct. On the one hand, the narratorial voice includes and integrates narrator, narrative, and allegory in a single tonal register, and this is the register of the ideological police. It encourages us to read as if listening and visualizing, and to accept what we "hear" and "see" in the spirit of childlike wonder. On the other hand, the counternarrative voice mediates and mimicks the narratorial voice. Its identifying mark is an ebullient and self-delighting spirit of citational parody. Ebullient and self-delighting, but also skeptical and disenchanted: it invites us not only to "hear" and "see" but also to read, to peruse, against the recitational grain. It questions the high seriousness that both the story and the storyteller tonally confer on themselves. It represents fictional episodes and characters as objectifications of the desire, anxiety, interests, values, and aims of the ideological police. But at the same time counternarrative mimicry acknowledges the seductive force of the old stories precipitated out of these objectifications. If it asks us to interrogate our childlike wonder it never lets us lose it. For the voice of suspicion often turns the parody back on itself and mocks its own stubborn childlike attachment to the very discourses it subjects to mimicry and critique. "Who wonders not that reads so wonderous worke?": as I observe above (see note 7), "wonderous" can suggest doubt and uncertainty as well as wonder, "mazement" as well as "amazement." In *The Faerie Queene*, the narratorial voice of wonder is crossed by continuous counternarrative wondering.

I consider this portrayal to be the metanarrative plot of *The Faerie Queene*: the poem is not "about" Britomart or Guyon, chastity or temperance, Elizabeth or Protestantism. It is "about" the way it tells the story of all those things and "about" why it tells it that way. The way includes not only rhetoric but also the whole range of fictive constructions (episodes, plots, characters,

---

[16] For previous versions of this distinction, see my "Narrative as Rhetoric in *The Faerie Queen*," *English Literary Renaissance* 21 (1991): 3–48, and "The Origins of Bucolic Representation: Disenchantment and Revision in Theocritus' Seventh Idyll," *Classical Antiquity* 3 (1984): 1–39.

places). The *why* is diegetic motivation. In order to make this formulation work, one has to premise that narrative agency extends beyond the telling of the story to its invention — invention in its older sense of "finding" (selective appropriation) as well as its newer sense of "creating." Why, for example, invent Guyon as the hero of the book of temperance or Britomart as the heroine of the book of chastity? Why invent the particular episodes, and the sequences of episodes, that make up the book? What do the design and the detail of narrative construction tell us about the motives informing narrative agency? Taking this a step further, I assume that if narrative decisions are to display and objectify diegetic motives they must be assigned the same value one ordinarily assigns to the events and characters of the story — the value of fictions that fall within the purview of interpretation. For if invention produces events and characters that objectify narrative desire and anxiety, it must be a strategy by which the ideological police strive to control the empire of meaning, and this should make it a prime target of textual impersonation. The pages and sections that follow unpack the consequences of this approach in a series of readings centered on the representation of Britomart and Glauce in the first four cantos.

If we think of the narrative as an arm of the ideological police, then we cannot avoid being amused by its persistent habit of making trouble for itself. It tries very hard to be liberal, to rein in the absoluteness of its authority, to give Britomart and Glauce some say in the means by which they will reach the fated end of the quest. So, as Wofford notes, they are allowed to design "the plot of knightly disguise." Wouldn't Merlin have been a more logical choice to inaugurate this chivalric enterprise, and legitimize it by giving it his blessing? Instead, the narrative assigns the major share of the invention to the figure least able to stamp it with the imprimatur it needs: Glauce. She, however, rises to the occasion with admirable chivalric form by suggesting the woman-warrior caper. One would have thought she should be congratulated on her good taste. Why, then, does the narrator not only fail to commend her but add insult to injury by responding to the moment in which she conceives the scheme with a touch of testiness?: "At last the Nourse in her foolhardy wit / Conceiv'd a bold devise" (3.52). Why the epithet "foolhardy"?

The reason she offers for the plan seems eminently sensible. It is preemptive self-defense: "all Britanie doth burne in armes bright," therefore, lest anyone "our passage may empeach," they should disguise themselves as the male enemy and put arms in their "weake hands" (3.52-53). But after this she thinks more aggressive thoughts. She observes that Britomart is "tall, /

And large of limbe," and that a little practice will "shortly make you a mayd Martiall" (3.53), and she reels off an impressive list of steroidal precedents for Britomart to emulate:

> Bards tell of many women valorous
> Which have full many feats adventurous
> Performd, in paragone of proudest men:
> The bold *Bunduca*, whose victorious
> Exploits made Rome to quake, stout *Guendolen*,
> Renowmed *Martia*, and redoubted *Emmilen*. (3.54)[17]

Granted that some of these figures were known as ferocious or unreliable viragos, the narrator himself had made a similar move at the beginning of canto 2 and would do so again at the beginning of canto 4 (see below). Why should this exhortation to Britomart seem foolhardy to the same narrator? Perhaps it is because Glauce's rhetoric and examples urge Britomart not only to behave like but also to compete with "proudest men" in aggression. Even more dubious is her next suggestion, which indicates that she gives gender competition precedence over political alliances: as a model for Britomart, and also as a source of war-gear, she nominates the Saxon Angela, the enemy of the Britons and of Britomart's father, King Ryence (3.55–60) — who presumably could have received intelligence of Angela's whereabouts from his magic mirror.[18] Glauce leads Britomart to the armor and with her own hands "her therein appareled" (3.59). Thus her foolhardy wit is responsible for introducing a subversive signifier of the political enemy into the iconography of Britomart's quest. At least emblematically, this implies that the interests of politics and gender fuse while those of Britomart and her father (which includes the interests of Merlin and the ideological police) divide: women unite against men, virgins against fathers. If this is a purely emblematic figure of betrayal, it nevertheless stirs up subtextual residues of Scylla and the complicit Carme. Donning the armor of resistance and potential rebellion in order to fulfill the political destiny predicted (i.e. imposed) by Merlin, Britomart becomes at least symbolically a threat to her father and

---

[17] The first three are mentioned in Book 2 canto 10 at stanzas 54–56, 18–20, and 42, respectively. The figure named Martia here was called Mertia in 2.10.42. The change emphasizes her warlike character.

[18] See the excellent comments by Gregerson in "Protestant Erotics," 18–19.

the patriarchal order — as Scylla and Myrrha were, in their different ways, to theirs. As an even stranger product of the taint of the subtext, Artegall is placed in the position of Minos, the royal father's enemy.

What to make of all this? Glauce's "bold devise" and its implementation take up the last twelve stanzas — almost a fifth — of the canto, and five of these are devoted to Angela and her armor. This production of an emblem of betrayal seems carefully wrought, and yet it is conspicuously irrelevant to the story. The emblem receives no narrative development and nothing in the story motivates it, therefore it hovers mysteriously and unfixedly over the episode like a "secret cloud of silent night" (3.61). There have of course been attempts to dispel the cloud, attempts to resolve the tension and reconcile the conflicting claims of Glauce's and Merlin's agendas, by finding patterns of resolution and reconciliation in the poem. A. C. Hamilton's note on the following passage concisely epitomizes such attempts: after dressing Britomart in Angela's armor Glauce adds:

> ... a mighty speare,
> Which *Bladud* made by Magick art of yore,
> And usd the same in battell aye to beare;
> Sith which it had bin here preserv'd in store,
> For his great vertues proved long afore:
> For never wight so fast in sell could sit,
> But him perforce unto the ground it bore.... (3.60)

Bladud: a Briton king whose magical powers are told at II x 25–26. The powers of the Saxons and the Britons are brought together in Britomart's armour. (Hamilton, *FQ*, 321)

The coalescence of unfriendly powers, the reconciliation of opposites into a more complex and stable structure, on the model, say, of the ancient theory of the cycle of simple constitutions and the mixed constitution: this is one way to defuse the subversive aspects of the episode.[19] But consider how much it sweeps under the rug. 2.10.25–26 describes more than Bladud's magic powers. It describes his contribution to society, the baths at "Cairbadon" (Bath), in diabolistic imagery echoed in the account of Merlin's subterranean project,

---

[19] This is an approach I tried out many years ago in Harry Berger Jr., "The Spenserian Dynamics," *SEL* 8 (1968): 1–18. A much more interesting and sophisticated version appears in Gregerson's "Protestant Erotics."

and it depicts him as an overreacher whose Icarian folly killed him; the spear protects him from external enemies but not from the enemy within. A male weapon to be used against other men, "his great vertues" give its owner an unfair advantage in single encounters, and these virtues now confer invincibility on the woman who steals it from her father, the current owner, and uses it, or "him," to bear Guyon, Marinell, and Paridell "unto the ground." Thus if the little parable of Bladud's spear is unpacked, it does not speak so much of a resolved *discordia concors* as of a parable of phallic pride and self-protectiveness and of their consequences, i.e. the nocturnal theft of the spear/phallus by the daughter who "resolv'd, unweeting to her Sire, / Advent'rous knighthood on her selfe to don" (3.57).

The theft of Angela's armor plays on the same register. Because her arms were taken by "Britons riding on forray" King Ryence had them put on display "for endlesse moniments / Of his successe and gladfull victory" (3.58–59). But so far as one can tell from reading the text, the victory is over the armor, not its owner; no mention is made of Angela's having been taken or defeated. "Endlesse" carries its characteristic Spenserian ambiguity: what will be celebrated forever will be an unfinished monument/admonition — the armor without its wearer — of an unfinished victory. This irony is now compounded by the quiet rebellion in the king's household, the daughter and nurse who steal first the armor and then themselves away from Ryence, riding "through back wayes, that none might them espy, / Covered with secret cloud of silent night" (3.61).

What disappears into the cloudy night along with Britomart and Glauce is the narrative rationale that might explain the bearing those subversive implications have on the remainder of the segment of Britomart's story that ends in canto 4. They seem, as I said, conspicuously irrelevant to her seaside lament and encounter with Marinell, though perhaps her ferocious spearwork in that episode touches off a jangly echo of Bladud along with its more obvious echo of 1.7, in which the narrator mentions the "secret powre unseene" of the enchanted spear that unhorses Guyon. Yet I think the conspicuousness of their irrelevance to the story, combined with the equally conspicuous manner in which they insist on the reader's attention, is itself significant. Lacking any evident influence on the story proper, they can only reflect the attitude inscribed in the agency responsible for the story. To revert to my alteration of Wofford's formula, they display a nervous awareness of dangers to the male point of view on the story.

Inconsistencies in the portrayal of Britomart have often been noted. Wofford and others have ascribed them to the diverse claims of the allegorical agenda and psychological characterization. The argument goes that Spenser's failure to reconcile these claims resulted in a split between the heroic exemplar and the passion-driven young woman.[20] Richard Lanham attributes "Spenser's problem" to another source, the paradoxes informing the dual gender identities of Britomart's literary forebears: the ancient conflation of Venus and Mars in the figure of the Amazon, and the combination of "sweetness and strength" in Ariosto's woman warrior. Lanham reasons that "the more realistically he characterized her, the more contradictory would her two identities appear. She would be demure maiden one minute, bossy woman the next," and — Lanham adds later — a maiden diseased with passion. These "three ingredients of Britomart's character . . . hardly blend into a credible personality, a consistent literal Britomart," and Spenser fails to integrate them, but if she "does in fact re-enact a dominant image, it is the irritable, domineering virago, the woman who threatens a man's masculinity."[21]

Predictably, my strategy in responding to this view is to get "Spenser" out of the picture and preserve Lanham's astute analysis by shifting its mode from criticism of what the poet failed to do to description of what the poem does. Lanham picks out all the right ingredients and is in my opinion correct in judging them inconsistent, but I conceive of the flawed blend as itself one ingredient in another blend composed, in Wofford's terms, of "the male version of the story" and the "more expansive authorial perspective" that judges the version. This conception can be made more active by changing metaphors: from an authorial perspective that judges the (male version of the) story to a textual voice that performs it in such a way as to mark the performance as mimicry and the story as the target of parody. It is a mimetic parody, by which I mean that the text represents the narrative as an imitation of traditional discourse networks that authorize (give authority to, make an author of) male fantasy.

---

[20] See, for examaple, Roger Sale, *Reading Spenser: An Introduction to "The Faerie Queene"* (New York: Random House, 1968), 77–80; Maureen Quilligan, *The Language of Allegory: Defining the Genre* (Ithaca: Cornell University Press, 1979), 80–81; Georgia Ronan Crampton, *The Condition of Creatures: Suffering and Action in Chaucer and Spenser* (New Haven: Yale University Press, 1974), 172–75.
[21] Richard Lanham, "The Literal Britomart," *Modern Language Quarterly* 28 (1967): 426–45, here 428–29, 436–37.

On the basis of this account, I hypothesize that the varied and often inconsistent inventions by which a "portrait" of Britomart is placed before the reader reflect and objectify the uncertainties of the narrative agency — its anxiety, desire, hopes, plans, and interests. To read the portrayal of Britomart as a continuous construction that continuously objectifies the motives of portrayal is to read the poem as the portrayal of its narrative, the story of its storytelling. So, for example, when we read about the appropriation of Angela's armor we interpret it as a motivated invention. What it expresses and objectifies is the sense of shaky control unsettling a male discourse that aims both to construct a heroine worthy of conscription into its patriarchal service and to do so by committing itself to a profeminist agenda. The conscription is itself problematic since it entails the temporary alienation of phallic power to a militant and passionate virgin; this problem is only exacerbated by a narrative spokesman who proclaims himself a friend of the Ladies and offers the portrait of Britomart as partial redress for the wrongs done them by the dominant male traditions of discourse. Both parts of the narrative project — allegorical conscription and the profeminist enhancement of the independence and interiority that make the heroine a subject, not merely an object, of desire — come into clear focus in cantos 2 and 3; but so also does the uneasiness troubling the flow of episodic inventions that objectify the strains in the project.

This interpretive framework, finally, supplies a context for the reconsideration of the question with which the present discussion began: why does the narrative displace to Glauce its brilliant Ariostan invention of the woman warrior and then accuse "her foolhardy wit"? To catch the tonal valence of "foolhardy" we might recall the description of Redcross rushing "full of fire and greedy hardiment... unto the darksome hole" of the dragon lady named Error (1.1.14), or of Arthur "prickt forth with jollitie / Of looser life, and heat of hardiment" (1.9.12). Condensing "foolish hardiment," "foolhardy wit" pricks out the nurse in similar chivalric pricklings and blames her for the "bold devise" conceived by narrative wit to regale the reader with Britomart's chivalric exploits. It is another of the moves by which the narrative reveals itself to be torn between the desire to imagine a world in which women have freedom and power equal to men and the gynephobic reaction of the ideological police to such a subversive fantasy. The narrative agency that creates, alienates, and empowers Britomart gives her enough autonomy to resist its control and at the same time nervously tries to control her resistance. In cantos 2, 3, and 4 this conflict is given dramatic emphasis in the notable disparity between the narrator's prefatory enunciations and the material they introduce, and it is also discernible in what amounts to a dialogical negotiation between the narrator and Glauce.

Canto 2 begins with an outburst of profeminist ardor:

> Here have I cause, in men just blame to find,
>   That in their proper prayse too partiall bee,
>   And not indifferent to woman kind,
>   To whom no share in armes and chevalrie
>   They do impart, ne maken memorie
>   Of their brave gestes and prowesse martiall;
>   Scarse do they spare to one or two or three,
>   Rowme in their writs; yet the same writing small
> Does all their deeds deface, and dims their glories all.
>
> But by record of antique times I find,
>   That women wont in warres to beare most sway,
>   And to all great exploits them selves inclind:
>   Of which they still the girlond bore away,
>   Till envious Men fearing their rules decay,
>   Gan coyne streight lawes to curb their liberty;
>   Yet sith they warlike armes have layd away,
>   They have exceld in artes and pollicy,
> That now we foolish men that prayse gin eke t'envy.
>
> Of warlike puissaunce in ages spent,
>   Be thou faire *Britomart*, whose prayse I write,
>   But of all wisedome be thou precedent,
>   O soveraigne Queene, whose prayse I would endite,
>   Endite I would as dewtie doth excite;
>   But ah my rimes too rude and rugged arre,
>   When in so high an object they do lite,
>   And striving, fit to make, I feare do marre:
> Thy selfe thy prayses tell, and make them knowen farre. (2.1–3)

In her careful reading of this passage Pamela Benson notes that the first stanza adopts a traditional profeminist view "consonant with Anglican and humanist accounts of women's abilities" though exceptional "in its exclusive attention to military prowess."²² But, she argues, this is only a feint in the direction of a synoptic praise of women throughout history. Midway through the second stanza the narrator begins to back away from that position: from the pivot line on, the stanza "accepts the rule of men over women as a fact of life and although it expresses regret for the state of things, it does not urge rebellion" but maintains the "traditional sexual hierarchy" in which "men make the laws and write the histories and therefore can restrict the liberty of women and create their image for posterity" ("Rule, Virginia," 283). Benson's thesis is that Spenser ultimately articulates the Calvinist viewpoint that women as a group are inferior to men and "unsuited to rule" (277).

Although my reading of the situation differs radically from hers, Benson's subtle parsing of the ideological moves helps me defend "Spenser" from her criticism in the (by now) expected way. For it shows that even as the narrator dissociates himself from fearful "envious Men," his fear of the fantasy of the woman warrior leads him to keep that fantasy penned in the past — in the alternative tradition of the "record of antique times." And he goes on, as Benson notes, to respond to the resilience of latter-day women with relatively mild praise that "may even hold a threat of repression" (285). The split between ancient and modern is repeated in that between Britomart and Elizabeth, with added emphasis on the sharpness of the disjunction: he does write the praise of the paradigm of the *virtù* possessed by women in ages not merely past but "spent"; he would "endite" the praise of the Queen but he lacks the skill. Since, on the analogy of the preceding stanza, her wisdom must be manifested in arts and policy, is there some link or analogy between "we foolish men" who "envy" the praise of modern women and the narrator who refuses to praise Elizabeth on grounds of inability?

I do not agree with Benson that the burden of the lines praising Elizabeth is to exempt her from the process of historical decline "by asserting that she, unlike other women, is not threatened by the power of male envy to tarnish reputation or restrict action," nor do I agree that the alexandrine in stanza 3 "puts the male poet in the background" and emphasizes his "superfluousness as recorder of her fame" ("Rule, Virginia," 286, 287). Rather the

---

[22] Pamela Joseph Benson, "Rule, Virginia: Protestant Theories of Female Regiment in *The Faerie Queene*," ELR 15 (1985): 277–92, here 282. The same argument appears in revised form in eadem, *The Invention of Renaissance Woman: The Challenge of Female Independence in the Literature and Thought of Italy and England* (University Park, PA: Pennsylvania State University Press, 1992), 280–305.

effect of 2.8–9 on 3.4–9 is to inject into the narrator's fear of marring his praise something more than courtly deference or aesthetic diffidence: she threatens the power of male envy to tarnish her reputation, and since "foolish men" have suffered for indicting rather than inditing her praise, he is not going to take any risks. If this histrionic flinch proclaims his "superfluousness," the social and artistic inability of the humble subject, it expresses a legitimate fear — the same fear as that expressed in more copious and courtly terms in the second stanza of the Proem to Book 3. Wofford's gloss on the central couplet of that stanza — "His daedale hand would faile, and greatly faint, / And her perfections with his error taint" — is that the narrator fears he may, like Daedalus, release "the child of his imagination for a doomed flight." His portrait of the Queen "would become an Icarus which would 'faile and greatly faint'," and "marre" her excellence ("Gendering Allegory," 4–5). Wofford reads this set of tactful displacements as expressing a concern for the Queen's image; they also imply apprehension about her power and the poet's safety:

> The female ruler in all her power and danger is represented by Spenser as his ideal and as his most difficult audience. Elizabeth as a political power and Elizabeth as a figurative ideal are two versions of the same emblem which do not always fit easily together.
> ("Gendering Allegory," 3)

> [T]he woman to whom all Elizabethan men were vulnerable was Queen Elizabeth herself. Within legal and fiscal limits, she held the power of life and death over every Englishman, the power to advance or frustrate the worldly desires of all her subjects.[23]

In the face of such extratextual constraints, expressions of inability manifest a politic appreciation of the monarch's power and inexpressible value. But the display of apprehensiveness takes on an altogether different tonal quality when viewed through the lenses provided by commentators who, following Louis Montrose's lead, observe that the display may respond

---

[23] Louis Adrian Montrose, "*A Midsummer Night's Dream* and the Shaping Fantasies of Elizabethan Culture: Gender, Power, Form," in *Rewriting the Renaissance: The Discourse of Sexual Difference in Early Modern Europe*, ed. Margaret W. Ferguson, Maureen Quilligan, and Nancy J. Vickers (Chicago: University of Chicago Press, 1986), 65–87, here 77.

not only to extratextual constraints but also to possible intratextual indiscretions:

> Thus, in the movement of the proem to Book 3 from the queen to her representations, from referentiality to intertextuality, the male subject/poet puts into question the female monarch's claim to shape herself and her subjects, to personify the principle and power of form. What the poet conventionally deprecates as his inability to produce an adequate reflection of the glorious royal image is the methodical process of fragmentation and refraction by which the text appropriates that image, imposing upon it its own specificity.[24]

We know that Elizabeth's regime was very careful about pictorial representations of her physical person — and that if she disliked what an author published about her marriage program, for example, she could have his hand cut off.... Spenser has to tread very delicately in his portrayal of Belphoebe.... Feminist criticism has recently taught us to see in the genre of the blazon ... a subversive movement against female erotic power as well as a celebration of it.... Spenser's blazon [in 2.3] functions as a further movement against Diana/Belphoebe's (and Elizabeth's) power to dismember those mortal males who would look upon her; such a display therefore reinforces the qualification of female power by exposing the female body to an anatomizing gaze.[25]

When, in the proem to the second book of *The Faerie Queene*, Spenser conjoins "the Amazons huge river" and "fruitfullest Virginia"..., he is invoking not only two regions of the New World but two archetypes of Elizabethan culture: the engulfing Amazon and the nurturing Virgin.[26]

---

[24] Louis Adrian Montrose, "The Elizabethan Subject and the Spenserian Text," in *Literary Theory / Renaissance Texts*, ed. Patricia Parker and David Quint (Baltimore: Johns Hopkins University Press, 1986), 303–40, here 324–25.

[25] Maureen Quilligan, "The Comedy of Female Authority in *The Faerie Queene*," ELR 17 (1987): 156–71, here 156–57, 164–65.

[26] Montrose, "Shaping Fantasies," 79. On Amazons, see the whole of Montrose's illuminating discussion in "Shaping Fantasies," 77–80; also Winfried Schleiner, "Divine Virago: Queene Elizabeth as an Amazon," *Studies in Philology* 75 (1978): 163–80, and Mary R. Bowman, "'she there as Princess rained': Spenser's Figure of Elizabeth," *Renaissance Quarterly* 43 (1990): 509–28.

> Britomart ... has the paradoxical advantage of being both virginal and fruitful. Thus she may be chaste in all senses of the word, and thus Merlin may reveal to her the specific fleshly, genealogical connection between her and the woman of whom she is a distant mirror. It is the sole project of Merlin's long prophetic passage to demonstrate and manifest that connection.... "But yet the end is not," Merlin ends (50), and in so doing he confronts — and denies — the very dynastic tension that generates his (and Spenser's) narrative. For ... the queen's own person, ... chaste and barren, subverts the very representation that is the enchanter's, and the poet's text. It is this uniqueness..., the barren integrity of the queen's person, that is at once unspoken and ubiquitous in book 3....[27]

Given this network of innuendoes, I can imagine — can "hear" — the inflections of another voice crossing that of the prudent subject who dutifully proclaims his inability. Even as this second, counternarrative, voice, bumptious and playfully hubristic, mimics the trepidations of the prudent narrator, it implies that no writing but the Queen's could satisfy the Queen, and it gives the poor narrator plenty to worry about. For the repertory of subtly shaded icons of the Queen's two bodies that it assigns to the narrative authority of the "Poet" includes not only Gloriana, Belphoebe, and Diana, not only Britomart, not only Alma, Mercilla, and Isis/Venus, but also Lucifera, Philotime, and Radegund.[28]

Claiming to write Britomart's praises but not Elizabeth's, the narrator restricts the former to her role as the "precedent" of "warlike puissaunce"; her "specific fleshly, genealogical connection" to Elizabeth is suppressed and

---

[27] Bruce Thomas Boehrer, "'Careless Modestee': Chastity as Politics in Book 3 of *The Faerie Queene*," ELH 55 (1988): 555–73, here 561.

[28] See Richard Helgerson, *Forms of Nationhood: The Elizabethan Writing of England* (Chicago: University of Chicago Press, 1992), 312 n. 61.

While refuting Stephen Greenblatt's thesis that "Spenser's art questions its own status" and enhances the Queen's when it "calls attention to its own processes," Montrose claims "that it is precisely when the poet offers to make such referential and deferential gestures explicit — in his encomia to the sovereign — that the text most obstinately refers the reader back into itself" and "calls into question the status of the authority it represents" ("Elizabethan Subject," 331). Most obstinately and — as I have been suggesting — most mischievously, throwing a scare not into the Queen but into the dutiful and pious encomiast.

her distance from Elizabeth rhetorically enhanced by the finality of the phrase "in ages spent." The restriction and suppression are odd, given the subject matter of the canto these stanzas introduce, and by the end of the long discussion of Britomart's love-sickness, they have become conspicuous. When the textual "voice" that performs the narrative function personifies it by impersonating the narrator, its parody raises the figure of a self-professed but not very persuasive profeminist, courtly and a little blustery, whose view of the story he tells is blindered, straitened, stringently policed. Nothing he says registers any allusion to Malecasta or prepares the reader for what is to come. His little speech is in fact a misdirection, as if there is material in the story he does not (care to) notice or will not deal with. The excluded material consists not only of the erotic passages but also of the account of the mirror with all the subversive implications (of gynephobia, specular rape, the conflation of political with sexual anxiety) textually embedded in it. Only one phrase in the first three stanzas glances briefly — furtively, one might say — at those themes, and it falls exactly in the center of the passage, the pivot line of stanza 2: "envious Men fearing their rules decay" gestures broadly in the direction of all the material the narrator keeps at arm's length.

This pattern continues in the stanzas that introduce canto 3. The suspicion that the narrator may be troubled by the story he unfolded in canto 2 is indicated, first, by his attempt to make a distinction between love and lust that puts Britomart on the wrong side of the moral divide, and second, by his recourse to the rhetoric of an uncompromisingly anti-heterosexual tradition:

> Most sacred fire, that burnest mightily
>   In living brests, ykindled first above,
>   Emongst th'eternall spheres and lamping sky,
>   And thence pourd into men, which men call Love;
>   Not that same, which doth base affections move
>   In brutish minds, and filthy lust inflame,
>   But that sweet fit, that doth true beautie love,
>   And choseth vertue for his dearest Dame,
> Whence spring all noble deeds and never dying fame:
>
> Well did Antiquitie a God thee deeme,
>   That over mortal minds hast so great might,
>   To order them, as best to thee doth seeme,

And all their actions to direct aright;
The fatall purpose of divine foresight,
Thou doest effect in destined descents,
Through deepe impression of thy secret might,
And stirredst up th'Heroes high intents,
Which the late world admyres for wondrous moniments. (3.1–2)

The genealogy of this discourse — from the *Symposium* through Christian Neoplatonism to Bembo's speech in *The Book of the Courtier* — is clearly marked, as are its homosocial, homoerotic, and insidiously misogynist implications. By modulating into a vaguely matrimonial figure — "that sweet fit" becomes the husband who chooses virtue to be the mother of his noble deeds — the first stanza expressly displaces woman from the reproductive role, for this ideal of male parthenogenesis is set over against heterosexual reproduction. That the lover of true beauty chooses virtue implies rejection of the love of woman's beauty as if it were less true, or untrue (the lust of brutish minds?), implies also rejection of the reproductive agency that must resort to woman's body and sexuality. But since in the fallen world of dynastic politics such impediments to the marriage of a true mind (with itself) must be admitted, they must be rigorously policed. In the words of a latter-day Pygmalion, "why can't a woman be more like a man?" The narrator has done his best to defeminize Britomart. In the stanzas that open canto 2 he praises her as a woman warrior while engaging in a profeminist critique of "envious Men" who, as chroniclers, refused to record the martial exploits of ancient women and, as legislators "fearing their rules decay," began to "coyne streight lawes to curb their liberty" (1.1–2). But his story compels him to preside over the sexual awakening that takes up so much of the first two cantos, and in canto 3, as if he fears his rule's decay, he participates with Merlin in imposing on Britomart the "streight lawes" of destiny that will eventually curb her liberty.

The effects of this imposition had been graphically represented from Britomart's standpoint in canto 2 in images of mental suffering and bodily pain, images of violation that convey her sense of having lost control over her body and sexuality. The standpoint of the ideological police responsible for such violence is revealed in 3.1–3. The "base affections" and "filthy lust" from which the speaker recoils in the first stanza seem as applicable to the intensity and messiness of Britomart's experience as to Malecasta. In sharp contrast, the Neoplatonic fantasy of the asexual and homosocial reproduction of virtuous deeds is securely determined from above and depicted as smooth and painless: love is "pourd into men." As the next stanza moves from this impossible ideal to the fantasy of dynastic reproduction, and as the narrator edges cautiously toward the heterosexual imperative, his rhetoric stiffens: instead of a sweet fit poured into receptive minds, he describes a power that orders, directs, and effects its fatal purpose through deep impression of its secret might. Though "destined descents" anticipates historical genealogies and "secret might" glances at the covert warfare of "the false Archer" (2.26), the stanza swerves away from the unavoidable contact with woman's body and, if it refers to Britomart, does so only as one of the "Heroes" whose "high intents" are stirred up by heavenly love. When the narrator finally turns to consider her in stanza 3, it is in aggressive and even punitive terms that well accord with the sense of violation she expressed in canto 2:

> But thy dread darts in none doe triumph more,
>   Ne braver proofe in any, of thy power
>   Shew'dst thou, then in this royall Maid of yore,
>   Making her seeke an unknowne Paramoure,
>   From the worlds end, through many a bitter stowre:
>   From whose two loynes thou afterwards did rayse
>   Most famous fruits of matrimoniall bowre,
>   Which through the earth have spred their living prayse,
> That fame in trompe of gold eternally displayes. (3.3)

The sacred power apotheosized by the pagans in stanza 2 now emerges as a figure similar to the Cupid who will materialize in Busirane's house, and the narrator's praise is not so much for the heroine whom the god subjected and tormented but for the god's "maisterie" in driving her to her fate. The narrator seals her fate by moving it back into the remote past and then assigning its disclosure in 3.4 to "my dearest sacred Dame," Clio. In the figure of an asexual but gendered female the muse is transparently an allegory of self-authentication by which the male poet pretends to guarantee the accuracy or truth of "information" gleaned from mortal, fallible, interested, and often unreliable sources. The narrator seeks to control his story, Britomart's sexuality, and his readers by coupling himself to the muse of history. But Clio's history will soon become Merlin's prophecy. When the fantasy of a securely closed past is reimagined as the fantasy of an open and incomplete future, when the medium of disclosure shifts from the muse to the mage who chose as his dearest Dame the Lady of the Lake, then, as we saw, the conditions of disclosure are such as to inscribe the launching of Elizabeth's "glorious auncestry" in an atmosphere of sexual and political diffidence that seems to motivate the stringent and occasionally vindictive rhetoric of the ideological police.

The generic tradition represented and cited in Book 3 — the tradition of epic and romance culminating in Ariosto — establishes a limited behavioral pattern for the figure of the passionate woman warrior. After she falls in love and hears the prophecy only one response is possible, the response predicted by the narrator's praise in 2.3: to transform her passion into "warlike puissaunce." That precedent is too restricted for the new dispensation of British history, and it will cause problems for a narrative that has one foot in the old Mediterranean tradition and the other in the new myth of Tudor England. The old generic model based on the binary opposition and interchangeability of love and war will have to give way to a more complex libidinal economy subjecting desire to the detours and obstacles of the politics of government and reproduction. In the context of this larger framework, the initial move Glauce and Britomart make in response to the prophecy is described in terms that make it seem almost frivolous:

> They both conceiving hope of comfort glad,
> With lighter hearts unto their home retird;
> Where they in secret counsell close conspird,
> How to effect so hard an enterprize,
> And to possess the purpose they desird:
> Now this, now that twixt them they did devise,
> And diverse plots did frame, to maske in strange disguise.
>
> At last the Nourse in her foolhardy wit
> Conceiv'd a bold devise.... (3.51–52)

The rhetoric coolly distances the narrative perspective from the fun and games of the euphoric plotters. Two stanzas later, the narrative assigns Glauce the task of citing examples from the "record of antique times," displacing to her — and thereby placing in question — the praise of "warlike puissaunce in ages spent." The potential subversiveness of this fantasy is actualized in the assimilation of Angela to Britomart.

The reaction of the ideological police to these developments occurs at the beginning of canto 4. There, the narrator first echoes and extends, and then coopts, the brief catalogue of women warriors Glauce gave at 3.54. At first he parades his male feminism in a stanza of *ubi sunts* calling for a revival of women's "Antique glory" that "matter made for famous Poets verse, / And boastfull men so oft abasht to heare" (4.1). The trumpet-tones of the next stanza peak in two self-descriptions that protest the virile manliness of one who, far from being abashed by the prospect, shows himself impatient, excited, even aroused: "I burne with envy sore" and "I swell with great disdaine." It turns out, however, that what he longs for is not the feminist revival itself: he burns to hear "the warlike feates, which Homer spake / Of bold Penthesilee," and he swells when he reads about the mankillers Deborah and Camilla (4.2).

The antique glory is to be resurrected not by women but by poets, i.e. himself. And his specific reason for resurrecting it is to keep it where it belongs — in the fabled past, with other onesided and foolhardy if pleasantly spine-tingling tales of ferocious women — and to reaffirm both his commitment and women's submission to the more civilized, politic virtue of which he writes:

> Yet these, and all that else had puissaunce,
>   Cannot with noble *Britomart* compare,
>   Aswell for glory of great valiaunce,
>   As for pure chastitie and vertue rare....

Britomart will surpass her antique models when she is domesticated, wedded and bedded so as to bear "so faire a blossome ... / As thee, O Queene, the matter of my song" (4.3), matter that enables him to castigate and rewrite the antique "matter made for famous Poets verse." But this noble project is no sooner announced than it is foiled and deferred by the heroine's resistance. The narrator uses her departure from Redcross to symbolize her backsliding:

> Then he forth on his journey did proceede,
>   To seeke adventures, which mote him befall,
>   And win him worship through his warlike deed,
> Which alwayes of his paines he made the chiefest meed.
>
> But *Britomart* kept on her former course,
>   Ne ever doft her armes, but all the way
>   Grew pensive through that amorous discourse,

> By which the *Redcrosse* knight did earst display
> Her lovers shape, and chevalrous aray;
> A thousand thoughts she fashioned in her mind,
> And in her feigning fancie did pourtray
> Him such, as fittest she for love could find,
> Wise, warlike, personable, courteous, and kind.
>
> With such selfe-pleasing thoughts her wound she fed,
> And thought so to beguile her grievous smart;
> But so her smart was much more grievous bred,
> And the deepe wound more deepe engord her hart,
> That nought but death her dolour mote depart. (4.4–6)

Redcross does what every good knight should do: he moves on, motivated by the same chivalric desire he ascribed to Artegall just a moment earlier in story time but two cantos earlier (2.14) in discourse time. Britomart, however, is being bad: "as the rhyme indicates, her former course was an amorous discourse, and it will continue to be one. The lament this pensiveness evokes and the ensuing battle with Marinell illustrate the difficulty of making an amorous discourse, necessarily a deviation from the course, work as allegory or succeed as quest."[29] The sense of deceleration, regression, and deviation is intensified by the two-canto flashback that immobilizes the discussion about Artegall, and leaves the impression that Britomart has continued "To feede her humour" with Redcross's praise of Artegall for a very long time (2.12).

Two stanzas before the flashback the narrator had used the mimicry of free indirect discourse to put the mark of rationalization on the bromides with which she justifies her little experiment in Malecastan self-titillation: Redcross's spirited defense of Artegall

> ... her feeble sence much pleased,
> And softly sunck into her molten hart;
> Hart that is inly hurt, is greatly eased
> With hope of thing, that may allegge his smart;

---

[29] Susanne Wofford, "Britomart's Petrarchan Lament: Allegory and Narrative in *The Faerie Queene* III.iv," *Comparative Literature* 39 (1987): 28–57, here 28. In the final line of canto 3 the narrator writes "The Redcrosse knight diverst, but forth rode Britomart" (3.62). This renders more striking the reversal of direction in 4.4–5: he "forth ... did proceede" while she "kept on her former course."

> For pleasing words are like to Magick art,
> That doth the charmed Snake in slomber lay:
> Such secret ease felt gentle *Britomart,*
> Yet list the same efforce with faind gainsay:
> So dischord oft in Musick makes the sweeter lay. (2.15)

The description that resumes Britomart's pensive dalliance in 4.6 displays the growing impatience and petulance of the describer: she is still fooling herself with these "selfe-pleasing thoughts" two cantos later, and if she continues wilfully to aggravate her condition it is unlikely that she will ever fulfill either her allegorical obligations as the exemplar of "chaste affection" or her historical task as Elizabeth's progenitor. Since her "grievous smart" is self-inflicted she deserves what she gets, and the story punishes her self-indulgence by temporarily installing her, as Wofford shows, in a position the poem discredits, "the position of a Petrarchan lover, with all the dangers for her quest and her poem which that stance entails."[30] The most telling phrase in 4.5 is the middle clause in the statement that Britomart "kept on her former course, / Ne ever dofte her armes, but all the way / Grew pensive." That she never doffed her arms seems initially a puzzling non sequitur, but if we think of the arms as the symbol of Britomart's historical mission the phrase glances at their diversion and subordination to the erotic furor that is nominally the mere instrument of the mission. And perhaps it is also relevant that she wears and bears Angela's arms, which symbolize not only Britomart's mission but also the virgin's internal resistance to it. The narrative thus discloses a mild propensity for Britomart-bashing. The reader who has just heard in canto 3 what Britomart has known for some time must appreciate its impatience with her perverse tendency to prolong the "hard begin" in spite of Merlin's sage and prudent counsel. But she is also prolonging what the narrative clearly marks as a Malecastan hangover, and its impatience can be traced back to its account of her behavior in the Castle Joyeous.

Britomart foregoes the chance to save Florimell in canto 1 because her "constant mind, / Would not so lightly follow beauties chace, / Ne reckt of Ladies love" (1.14). The narrator praises her as if she were the man she is pretending to be. But since he knows better and he knows we know better, the combined earnestness and gratuitousness of his little kudos continues the transvestite funfest that began when the upright Guyon was bounced off his

---

[30] Wofford, "Britomart's Petrarchan Lament," 34.

high horse and received the narrator's heartfelt apologies. The gender joke, however, is about to get serious. In Malecasta's house Britomart will reck of "Ladies love" and receive Malecasta's advances as if she were the man she is pretending to be. But since she knows better, readers are entitled to wonder how this will go down with the narrator who had in effect praised her commitment to heterosexual values in refusing to chase Florimell. Our curiosity crinkles up into perplexity when, during the uproar that concludes the Malecasta episode, Britomart receives a glancing wound in "her side" from a figure named Gardante.

Gardante was introduced at 1.44–45 as the first of the master-mistress's six "liegemen." Since their names denote the stages of ritualized courtly foreplay, Hamilton adds, after translating Gardante as "gazing," that it "denotes loving glances upon beauty" (*FQ*, 297). The scopic nuances of the term range from the voyeuristic to the self-protective, and include gazing, glancing, looking, ogling, viewing, and watching. Which nuance applies to the wound inflicted by Gardante? Is Britomart the object or subject of the scopic activity that wounds her? Does Gardante's action symbolize the effect on Britomart of only the immediately preceding events or does it, as Hamilton suggests, symbolize "her inner wound... by the sight of Artegall" (*FQ*, 316), whose image, we have already been told, "she had seene in Venus looking glass" (1.8)? Hamilton adds that the "gored side is a sexual wound," and this connects it to the narrator's subsequent simile of gestation in the "closet of her painefull side" (2.11). Though obviously allegorical and therefore conspicuously meaningful, the wound is just as conspicuously underdetermined in its meaning. This arouses suspicion and solicits interpretation. To read suspiciously is to wonder what is being withheld, by what agency (narrator? narrative? text?), and why. It becomes difficult to scrutinize the object of representation without scrutinizing the motives informing the act of representation.

The widening network of associations adduced by Hamilton clearly indicates that Britomart can be the subject of the (self-)inflicted wound of Looking only because she is the object of the mirror that "looks" at her, since "Venus looking glas" constructed by Merlin for the security of Britomart's father is a glass that looks. It "sees" her gazing curiously into it and is magically rigged to activate "the false Archer, which that arrow shot / So slyly, that she did not feele the wound" (2.26) until it is reopened by Gardante's arrow. She is selected to embody the mirror's gaze, which is the gaze of the ideological police recruiting her to fulfill its designs. But the tone of the narrator's reference to Cupid at 2.26 is troubling: his statement that the false archer, having furtively wounded her, "Did smyle full smoothly at her weet-lesse wofull stound" is more in the nature of a gloat than a criticism; he sides and smiles with Cupid, admires his efficiency; the statement is a touch vindictive, the smile sardonic; it is the smile of Busirane.[31] Why should this be? The only way to answer this question is to return to the Malecasta episode and examine not only Britomart's response to Malecasta's advances but also the narrative response to her response.

The focus of this double response is the most peculiar and unexpected feature of the episode: the voyeuristic curiosity aroused in Britomart by her ability to arouse Malecasta's desire. The curiosity is suggested first by the narrator's subtly critical characterization of her reaction — she "dissembled it with ignoraunce" (2.50) — and later by his overscrupulous explanation of her reason for entertaining Malecasta's advances: unfamiliarity with "such malengine," and "self-feeling of her feeble sex," produce misplaced sympathy for one who expresses feelings for her/him that match her own feelings for Artegall; the chivalric courtesy appropriate to the role she performs keeps her from "rudely" scorning Malecasta's "faire offer of good will profest" even though "she inly deemd / Her love too light, to wooe a wandring guest" (1.53-55). This makes the narrator's explanation seem disingenuous because it implies that her misconstrual is in bad faith: in his interpretation, she dissembles ignorance of what "she inly deemd" in order to focus on the illusory analogy to her own predicament.

Richard Lanham finds this scene confusing because "Britomart is never tempted" and none of the justifications for Britomart's behavior seems compelling. He concludes that Spenser is "working hard to motivate a scene that had little real motivation" and that "[w]hat the scene really does is further fix the male attributes of Britomart" ("Literal Britomart," 432–33). We can realize the cash value of the final insight by dropping the idea that she is not tempted, for stanza 55 suggests that she is tempted by the chance to imagine herself in Artegall's place and Malecasta in hers:

---

[31] DeNeef argues that here "the narrator is made to adopt Britomart's own view" of Cupid as false archer, and that this strategy "forces the reader to give momentary assent" to the view "simply by voicing them through the detached and observing narrator" (*Spenser and the Motives of Metaphor*, 162). But if we posit the representation of an engaged narrative/narrator, then we also posit a reader who won't give assent to the view but will question the narrator's aggressiveness of tone. For a different interpretation see Sale, *Reading Spenser*, 71; also Alastair Fowler, "Britomart at the House of Busyrane," in idem, *Renaissance Realism* (Oxford: Oxford University Press, 2003), 85–99.

> For thy she would not in discourteise wise,
> Scorne the faire offer of good will profest;
> For great rebuke it is, love to despise,
> Or rudely deigne a gentle harts request;
> But with faire countenaunce, as beseemed best,
> Her entertaynd; nath'lesse she inly deemd
> Her love too light, to wooe a wandring guest:
> Which she misconstruing, thereby esteemd
> That from like inward fire that outward smoke had steemd.

The narrator gives the impression that Britomart enjoys watching Malecasta act out the passion she herself feels and that she enjoys pretending she is the male cause of the outburst, but that if she were Artegall she would not like Malecasta's style. Sympathetic identification with Malecasta thus modulates into sympathetic identification with the "maisterie" of the male source of "imperious love" that Britomart's "hart did vexe" (1.54).[32]

The illusion of psychological complexity in the heroine's response is produced by a shift into free indirect discourse at stanzas 54–55, the effect of which is to transform the narrator's disingenuous emphasis on Britomart's ingenuousness into her rationalization. His gesture of sympathetic identification with Britomart is, however, rendered suspect by other features of the episode. When he interrupts the explanation at 1.54.6–9 with a slightly tart comment on her ingenuous misconstrual ("The bird that knowes not the false fowlers call, / Into his hidden net full easily doth fall"), the "Faire Ladies" in his readership would understand the cause of his impatience. For she fudges precisely the distinction he had consoled them with at 1.49:

> Faire Ladies, that to love captived arre,
>   And chaste desires do nourish in your mind,
>   Let not her fault your sweet affections marre,
>   Ne blot the bounty of all womankind;
>   'Mongst thousands good one wanton Dame to find:

---

[32] This produces a subtler story of gender confusion than does the Bradamante-Fiordispina episode it alludes to (*Orlando Furioso* 25.26–70). Ariosto resolves the dilemma by having Bradamante disabuse Fiordispina and send her twin brother to Fiordispina's bed in her place. This intertextual context highlights both Britomart's interest in keeping Malecasta in the dark and her desire to experience the male role herself.

> Emongst the Roses grow some wicked weeds;
> For this was not to love, but lust inclind;
> For love does alwayes bring forth bounteous deeds,
> And in each gentle hart desire of honour breeds.[33]

They shouldn't feel tarnished by this exception to their rule nor inhibited from pursuing their desires. The rhetoric of the closing couplet suavely negotiates the transfer of bounty and honor from the Ladies to their Men: "bring forth bounteous deeds" both suggests and displaces the "multitude of babes" (1.10.31) the Ladies will breed as they, withdrawing into honorable motherhood, cheer on their Men from the sidelines. Like the "imperious love" that vexes and tyrannizes Britomart's "gentle heart" (1.54, 2.23), the love to which the Ladies "captived arre" is the male-identified force that sometimes materializes as Cupid, to contain whose unruly, tyrannical, and promiscuous desire male subjects rely on the "chaste desires" of those humans they socialize to be Ladies.

Britomart's reaction and behavior in Malecasta's house thus illustrates a transgressive threat both to the instituted gender hierarchy and to the sexual morality it mandates. The misprision produced by crossdressing simultaneously deflates the threat to the level of a sitcom episode and preserves in symbolic form the traces of the anxiety about female transgression that structures the episode. This anxiety is rhetorically focused in the narrator's occasionally mordant comments about Britomart. In an unpublished essay to which my reading is heavily indebted, Sarah Murphy brilliantly analyzes the meaning of Britomart's disruptive influence in this and other episodes:

> Britomart clearly presents a threat to the established chivalric order, evoking a strong conservative... reaction. But from whom? The ambiguity of Britomart's position is mirrored by the ambiguity of the narrative's treatment of her. A straightforward narrator... endorses the chivalric order and... struggles to integrate Britomart into established categories and neutralize her threat. This is the voice that would like

---

[33] Once again the comedy of mistaken gender identity is broached. In the preceding stanzas Malecasta's lust is first branded foolish because she is "ignoraunt of her [Britomart's] contrary sex," and then branded vicious because of her abandon. The implication is that chaste desire will keep one not only from lust but also from making an inappropriate object choice. Cf. also Kathryn Schwartz, "Dressed to Kill: Looking for Love in *The Faerie Queen*," in eadem, *Tough Love: Amazon Encounters in the English Renaissance* (Durham, NC: Duke University Press, 2000), 137–74.

us to believe that Britomart is lovely as the moon and that her victories stem from a magic spear [the symbol of chastity made by a male magician]. Yet this narrator's dilemma regarding Britomart is constantly undermined by a more playful voice . . . that delights in the disorder Britomart brings, viewing a male tradition's floundering attempts to accommodate a female knight. The poem simultaneously represents and mocks the chivalric order, throwing in Britomart, a disrupting presence whose beauty pales in comparison to her penchant for causing chaos, as a way to highlight the rigid biases, assumptions, and limitations on which the tradition is based.[34]

Murphy argues that the conservative reaction is homophobic because the episode "contains the subversive possibility of lesbian relations that could give women autonomy and free them from male domination," and that although Gardante's wound "can be viewed as a punishment for her transgression and a means of propelling Britomart safely back into the category of heterosexual woman, an object of male desire and amorous glances," this attempt at control fails when Britomart responds to the wound by furiously laying about with her sword (Murphy, 6–7).

In the light provided by Murphy's strong reading, not only the narrator's performance but also the very design of the narrative in the next two cantos appear as motivated reactions to the meaning of Gardante's wound. The deferred account of her prior awakening to love melodramatically "propels" Britomart into the position of the subject of female heterosexual desire in canto 2, and in effect intensifies the "punishment" represented by the wound. The link between Gardante's arrow and the reference to Cupid at 2.26 confirms this continuity, as does the aggressiveness that edges the tone in which that reference is voiced. The Myrrha/Scylla subtext justifies the narratorial anxiety and need for control, both of which are displaced on to Merlin in canto 3. At the same time, what Murphy calls the "more playful narrative voice," a voice that delights in deflationary mimicry, is very much in evidence; it asserts itself not only in performing the interlocutory exchanges between Britomart and Glauce but also in its spirited representations of anxiety-ridden male ruses, as in the stanzas on the mirror and

---

[34] Sarah Murphy, unpublished undergraduate essay written for a Spenser seminar at UCSC during the early 1990's. It is the insistence of the "playful voice" and comic effects that serve to distance and parody the disingenuousness and disapproval of the "straightforward narrator," or narrative.

Phao's tower (2.18–20), and of narratorial vindictiveness, as in the alliterative overkill with which the narrator crows over the humbling of Britomart by "the false Archer":

> Thenceforth the feather in her loftie crest,
>   Ruffed of love, gan lowly to availe,
>   And her proud portance, and her princely gest,
>   With which she earst tryumphed, now did quaile:
> Sad, solemne, sowre, and full of fancies fraile
>   She woxe; yet wist she neither how, nor why,
>   She wist not, silly Mayd, what she did aile,
>   Yet wist, she was not well at ease perdy,
> Yet thought it was not love, but some melancholy. (2.27)

The first quatrain can only refer to the chivalric episodes that happened "earst" strictly in the order of storytelling; they have not yet happened in Britomart's career. Such a "mistake" may be dismissed as part of the loose and baggy conventions of romance narrative; but it does not have to be. To notice it is to regard with genial suspicion the motives of the narrator who takes advantage of those conventions in order to have his revenge on the upstart heroine. And as we know, the high comedy of the stanzas that follow derives from the parading of his "silly" victim's misconceptions and the often hilarious reactions of an "aged Nurse" who mixes epic rhetoric (2.32) and classical references with folk remedies and motherly hugs.

Before leaving this discussion, I want to explore a little further the function of a feature of the poem everyone has noticed since people stopped revering Spenser as a sage and serious and therefore permissibly boring poet. This feature can be expressed in one word: *The Faerie Queene*, more often than not, is funny. The comedy varies from understatement to slapstick, and readers who have appreciated it have until recently responded more often with pleasure than with analysis. Maureen Quilligan was one of the first critics to take the humor seriously, showing how Spenser uses it to contain or defuse the excessive or anomalous power granted females in positions of political and cultural authority, and both my substantial debt to her work and my superficial departures from it are registered in an account of the Gardens of Adonis I published several years ago.[35] What makes the poem funny for me

---

[35] Harry Berger Jr., "Actaeon at the Hinder Gate: The Stag Party in Spenser's Gardens of Adonis," in *Desire in the Renaissance: Psychoanalysis and Literature*, ed. Regina

is my continuous awareness of the altered "voice" of the textual impersonator saturating the voices it parodies. Thus even when the narrative is at its sagest and most serious, even when such diegetic motives as gynephobia are suggested through complex textual articulations, the discernible sense that some voice in the poem is not taking it as seriously as the story is — may indeed be having fun pretending to be serious — produces the effect of internal distantiation. I want to illustrate this by returning to the figure of Glauce.

The invention of an aged female figure whose name is Glauce and who is both nutrix and squire draws on but complicates a Hellenistic stereotype, a figure that is often the butt of ageist, classist, and sexist humor. This edition of the garrulous old nurse is condescendingly dismissed by Merlin (3.19), and though she is not identified when first introduced in crossdressed guise, the narrative is already on her case, describing her as "an aged Squire"

> That seem'd to couch under his shield three-square,
> As if that age bad him that burden spare,
> And yield it those, that stouter could it wield.... (1.4)

After this she disappears until 2.30, when she gets baptized. The etymological provenance of "Glauce" from *glaux*, the owl that signifies the male-identified wisdom of Athene, reinforces the idea that Britomart's nurse is to oppose the bad influence of her subtextual precursors in *Ciris* and *Metamorphoses* 10, and so also does the fact that she fills the position of squire previously occupied by the Palmer, most exemplary of ideological policemen. Subtextual interactions are nevertheless ambiguous and hard to control: the affiliation of Glauce's discourse with that of the nurses who accommodated the desires and "wicked art" (2.41) of Myrrha and Scylla sends residual tremors of old treacheries through her words. These are male tremors, and they are illuminated by Lanham's remark that in the case of Scylla, who "loves her father's enemy ... the pains of love are exacerbated by her awareness that they are treacherous. Spenser transfers this conflicting loyalty to Britomart's first stirrings of love for Arthur [sic], where it does not altogether fit" ("Literal Britomart," 435). It does not fit at all; it is a conspicuous misfit which, if it cannot be explained or justified by attributing the transfer to "Spenser," makes good sense as part of a pattern of fictive constructions that objectify

---

Schwartz and Valeria Finucci (Princeton: Princeton University Press, 1994), 91–119. See Quilligan, "The Comedy of Female Authority in *The Faerie Queene*."

the insecurity of a narrative unsure of its control of the heroine's behavior and desire.

Similar tremors may be sensed in the following descriptions of Glauce's attempts to comfort Britomart:

> Her aged Nurse, whose name was Glauce hight,
> Feeling her leape out of her loathed nest,
> Betwixt her feeble armes her quickly keight,
> And downe againe in her warme bed her dight .... (2.30)

> So having said, her twixt her armes twaine
> She straightly strayed, and colled tenderly,
> And every trembling joynt, and every vaine
> She softly felt, and rubbed busily,
> To doe the frosen cold away to fly;
> And her faire deawy eies with kisses deare
> She oft did bath, and oft againe did dry .... (2.34)
> With that upleaning on her elbow weake,
> Her alablaster brest she soft did kis .... (2.42)

The first passage is straightforward by itself but receives a comically erotic charge from the lines it clearly recalls, the moment in which Britomart, feeling Malecasta "close couched by her side, / ... lightly lept out of her filed bed" (1.62). In the second passage Spenser departs from his source (Carme "dulcia ... genis rorantibus oscula figens," "planting sweet kisses on Scylla's tear-bedewed cheeks"[36]) to produce an echo of Venus bathing the eyes of Myrrha's son "with ambrosiall kisses" (1.36). The third passage gets its charge from "alablaster," a term of art that indexically signifies the admiring gaze of the ardent Petrarchan connoisseur. In their slippage from maternal to erotic gestures these passages adumbrate a form of bonding that mirrors the potentially unstable and affectively potent bonding of fathers and sons, elders and juniors, pedagogues and pupils. The associations with Malecasta and Venus bring out the latent sexuality and extend it into the futile attempts of aggressive women to seduce and dominate men.

---

[36] *Ciris* 253, in *Virgil: Aeneid 7–12, The Minor Poems*, ed. and trans. H. R. Fairclough, 2nd ed., Loeb Classical Library (Cambridge, MA: Harvard University Press, 1934). I have slightly altered the translation.

These cross-connections throw a strange light on the nurse's relation to her "deare daughter" and "dearest dread" (2.30; "dread" is an object of reverence, but also a danger, an object of worry). For one thing, they highlight an implication present but minimized in the accounts of Scylla's and Myrrha's nurses: the complicity and influence of the older but socially inferior confidante in facilitating the crime against the father is linked here with the nurse's homoerotic attachment. For another thing, the fact that Britomart's passion is not at all criminal does not nullify the implication; it only displaces and generalizes it. What the homoerotic innuendo glances at is the specter of a female conspiracy against men in patriarchy. The strangeness, the apparent irrelevance and incoherence, of this tissue of cross-connections itself becomes relevant and coherent when we read it as a symptom of narrative anxiety. At the same time, whatever anxiety the narrative displays is not likely to infect a reader entertained by the image of Glauce consolingly cuddling the large well-built hysteric whose bed she shares. The textual prankster responsible for intensifying this droll effect by associating Glauce with Malecasta and Venus also, and with the same move, intensifies the latent scariness of the image.

Readers who think the image funny and the associations witty may apprehend the scary implications and laugh them away.[37] They may mark them as an interpretation, gratuitous with respect to the "facts" of the story of Britomart the narrative is constructing, therefore motivated by the gynephobic fantasy represented in Book 3 as a reaction inseparably linked to the profeminist sympathies of the legend of chastity. There is, however, an alternative reading of the situation I just described: the reader is offered an image shadowed by hints of transgressive desire, but the image is comical. The disordered passion evoked by the Malecastan associations is self-subverting and bound to fail; the danger is laughed away and the reader is soothed. This represents a strategy by which the ideological police try to keep the reader in line, whereas the other interpretation emphasizes the displacement of anxiety to the police. My point about this is that although the two readings of the situation are different they reinforce each other, for it is the possibly gratuitous anxiety of the police that moves them to manipulate the (male) reader

---

[37] This is Quilligan's thesis, modified to bring out my focus on the textual critique of the narrative. She argues that Spenser responds to the dangerous conferral of political and cultural authority on Britomart "by surrounding her with comedy" ("Comedy of Female Authority," 164). See also Wofford, *Choice*, 463 n. 44.

by throwing a scare into him and then neutralizing it with laughter. In the very process of imagining the episode, constructing it, filling in its details, and describing it, the narrative inscribes its worries, its "dearest dread," in its product and inoculates its readers against them.

Harry Berger Jr.
UNIVERSITY OF CALIFORNIA, SANTA CRUZ

INDEX

Abelard, xv, 89–107
Adelman, Janet, 145, 146n, 151n
Aers, David, 9
Alan of Lille, 171n, 175n, 183
All's Well That Ends Well, xv, 133–154
allegory, 2, 3, 67n, 68, 137n, 162–64, 168, 179, 183, 189, 215–18, 220–222, 227n, 236, 239
Amadis, 152
Amours, 31n, 32n, 33, 35, 37–38
Amtower, Laurel, xiiin
Anderson, Judith, xn
Andrew, Malcolm, 1n, 12n, 17, 20
androgyny (see also cross dressing), 49–50, 52–53, 60–61, 70, 210, 219
Antonio Rambaldo di Collalto, 122
Ariosto, Ludovico, xiv, 49–85, 152, 214, 227, 237, 243n
Aristotle, ix, 56n, 161, 165, 176, 186n
Ars dictaminis, 89n, 99–101, 162–64, 166
Asolani, 116n, 118n
Augustine, Saint, 110–12, 169n
Barkan, Leonard, xin, 65n
Barolini, Teodolinda, 67n, 112–13
Bembo, Pietro, 33n, 116–18, 235
Benson, Pamela, 49n, 51n–53n, 59n–60n, 68n, 71n, 75n, 229–30
Boccaccio, 4, 51n, 55n, 62n, 116
body, bodies, xiv–xv, 6n, 18, 28, 34–35, 50n, 56–59, 78–79, 82, 85n, 100, 104, 125, 127n, 171, 176–77, 191; and torture, 38–39, 43–46; and the monstrous, 55, 61, 78–79, 232; and chastity, 95–96, 209, 235–36, the body politic, 62, 65n, 160, 178–79, Christ's body, 73, 120–21, 122n
Boethius, 4, 21
Bonagiunta da Lucca, 66–67
The Book of the Courtier, 235
Britomart, xvi, 151, 207–49
Brownlee, Kevin, 63n, 163
Brunetto Latini, xvi, 157–89
Bullock, A., 68n, 118–20n
Burckhardt, Jacob, 110
Butler, Judith, 60n, 85n
Camargo, Martin, 100n, 101
Capellanus, Andreas, 158n
Catullus, xv, 31–32, 33n, 40–43, 47
Chaucer, x, 184n, 188n
childhood, children, xiii, xiv, 1–29, 55, 66, 199, 202, 204–5, 222, 231
Chrétien de Troyes, 198–99, 203
citizenship, xiii, xvi, 157, 162–63, 166–67, 173–74, 178, 179n 181–82, 187–88, 190
Classen, Albrecht, 100
Clerk's Tale, x
Colonna, Vittoria, xv, 63, 66–69, 74–77, 85, 109–10, 115–22, 129–30
Commedia (see also Dante), 57n, 64n, 66, 67n, 80n, 111, 116, 122n, 158–59, 162n, 163n, 166n, 171, 174, 179

Complaint of Nature (see also *De planctu*), 175
contrapasso, 76
Copeland, Rita, xi
Cressida, 134–35, 138–43, 150–54
Crossan, John Dominic, 26n, 27n
cross-dressing (see also transvestism), xvi, 61, 153, 191, 193n, 194–95, 204, 244–47; and androgyny, 49–50, 52–53, 60–61, 70, 210, 219
Dahmen, Lynne, 196
Daniel, Samuel, 136, 141
Dante (see also *Commedia*), 4, 21, 57n, 63, 64n, 66, 67n, 74, 80n, 111, 116, 122n, 158–59, 164–65, 166n, 171, 174, 176n, 179n, 185n, 187, 189
d'Aubigné, Theodore Agrippa, xiv, 31–47
De planctu (see also *Complaint of Nature*), 175
death / dying (see also shame),11–13, 15n, 71, 75–76, 137, 173, 153, 231; love as death, xiv, 31–32, 40, 71, 74, 127–28, 143–45, 147; death of infant and baptism, 1, 5, 17, 18, 20, 27–28; and melancholy or mourning, 6, 119, 122; and violence (see torture), 34, 39, 40, 70; and inheritance, 197, 202, 205–6
Délie, 37, 40
Delilah, 97
Desportes, Philippe, 33
Diana (see *All's Well*), 146–47, 151–52
Diana / Belphoebe, 232–33
Dragonetti, Roger, 181
Drayton, Michael, 141
Dronke, Peter, 101–2
Duby, Georges, 195n
Duino Elegies, 109
Elderton, William, 138

envy (see also *invidia*), xiv, 50–52, 56, 67–69, 74, 105–6, 230–31, 235, 238; sexual envy, 57–58, 60, 76–79, 83–85
epistolarity (see also *Ars Dictaminis*), xv, 51n, 91, 99–102, 106
Eve, 97
exile (see also journey), xvi, 63, 70, 90, 157–68, 172–73, 178, 181–83, 187–90
Faerie Queene, xvi, 151, 207–50
fantasy, xvi, 8, 14, 24, 79, 85, 195, 206–9, 211, 215, 217, 227–28, 230, 235–37, 249
Faustus, 142–43
Finucane, Ronald, 18–20
Fradenberg, L. O. Aranye, xii
Freccero, John, 80n, 113
Freud, Sigmund, x–xii, 7, 55n, 57–58, 79–81
Frye, Northrop, 194
Genesis, 173
Geoffrey of Vinsauf, ix, 173
Girard, René, 102–3, 105
Gordon, E. V., 8, 11, 12n
Greenblatt, Stephen, 110n, 233n
Guillaume de Lorris, 159, 167n, 181, 184, 186n
Guillory, John, 214–15
Guinizelli, Guido, 67
Hamilton, A. C., 212n, 217, 225, 241
Hamilton, Marie, 12
Hanawalt, Barbara, 9, 13n, 19n, 20
hawthorn / "The Hawthorne Tree," 137–40, 149
Hécatombe à Diane, 33, 35, 40, 45, 46
Heldris of Cornwall, xvi, 191–206
Helen of Troy, 134–35, 138–39, 141–42, 144, 146, 149–51, 154
Heloise (see also Abelard), xv, 89–107

Index

Historia Calamitatum, 103, 106
Hoffman, Stanton, 5, 13n, 24n
homosexuality (see also lesbianism), 41n, 235
homosociality, xvi, 52, 152n, 157, 183, 235
humanism, 50–51, 68, 113–15, 121, 229–30
Hunter, Robert Grams, 145
imitatio / imitation (see also translation), 31, 33–35, 44, 72n, 116–17, 141, 221n, 227
ingenium, 171n, 173–75, 181
invidia (see also envy), 50, 52, 57–59, 67, 82
Jaeger, Stephen, xi, xiin
Jameson, Fredric, 197–98
Jean de Meun, 159, 181n, 183–84, 186n
Jesus (and the children), 21–28
Job's wife, 97
John, 121
journey (see also exile), xiii, xvi, 115, 135, 157–58, 161, 167, 172, 183–84, 189, 238
Kamuf, Peggy, 90, 98
Kauffman, Linda, 90, 105
Kennedy, Duncan, xii, 164
Kennedy, William, 31n, 116n, 117
Kerrigan, John, 136
King Henry IV, 136
Laqueur, Thomas, 56n
Lamentations, 62
Lanham, Richard, 227, 242, 247
Latini, Brunetto, xvi, 157–179
law, 52, 60–64, 66, 69–78, 84, 90, 100, 134, 161n, 191–92, 195–200, 204–5, 230, 235
Le Printemps, 33, 35–36, 40, 46–47
Les Fleurs du Mal, 34
Les Tragiques, 33–34, 36

lesbianism (see also homosexuality), 41–42, 234–35, 245, 248–49
Luke, 22
Marc-Antoine de Muret, 32
Mark, 22
Matthew (see also Bible), 14, 22–25, 27, 173
Matthew of Vendôme, 173
McLeod, Glenda, 89n, 90n, 92
McLucas, John, 49n, 50n, 52n, 53n, 59n, 60n, 67–69, 70n, 79n
Metamorphoses, 55n, 79n, 80n, 83, 151n, 213, 247
Mews, Constant J., 89n, 90, 91n, 101n
Middleton, Thomas, 136
Milsom, S. F. C., 199n, 201n, 202n, 205n
misogyny (see also sexual envy), 52–53, 54n, 57n, 63–64, 66, 70–71, 74, 77, 85, 207, 230, 235
monstrosity, 56, 78
Montemayor, 152
Montrose, Louis, 231–33
Moorman, Charles, 4, 11n, 12n, 20n
Moulton, Frederick, 142
mourning (loss), 2–7, 9–11, 21, 26, 28, 40, 47, 65, 98, 126, 136, 139, 141, 148n, 161, 163, 187, 190, 197, 204–5
Murphy, Sarah, 244–45
narrative "I", 53, 167
Neely, Carol Thomas, 145, 146n, 151n
Neoplatonism, 121n, 129–30, 235
Nicomachean Ethics, ix
Ong, Walter, 137
Orlando furioso, xiv, 49–85, 152n, 243n
Ovid, xi, 57n, 80n, 79, 83, 136, 141, 157, 167n, 168–69, 179–81, 183, 186–89
patriarchy, 18, 52–53, 58–59, 64–66, 68, 71, 73–78, 82–84, 117n, 206–208, 213, 217n, 225, 228, 249

Patterson, Lee, xivn, 193n
Pearl, xiii, xiv, 1–29
Petrarch, xiii–xv, 31–34, 36–38, 40, 41n, 43–47, 80n, 110–18, 121–31, 144, 240, 248
Pico, Giovan Francesco, 116
Purgatorio, 57n, 66n, 67n, 80n, 111, 122n, 174, 179n
Queen Elizabeth I, 136, 210, 215, 222, 230–34, 237, 240
Quilligan, Maureen, 51n, 227n, 230n, 232n, 246, 249n
rape, 55, 81–82, 136, 186, 210, 217, 234
The Rape of Lucrece, 136
religious persecution, 31, 36, 46–47
Rerum vulgarium fragmenta, 113, 126
Revelation, 27
Richard III, 141, 143
Rilke, 109
Rime Amorose, 68n, 118–19, 121–22
Rime Sparse, 41n, 113n
Roman de la Rose, xvi, 157, 162n, 167n, 169n, 171n, 175
Roman de Silence, xvi, 191–206
romance genre, xv, xvi, 7–9, 135, 152, 191, 193–94, 196–98, 206, 216, 237, 246
Ronsard, Pierre de, 32, 35–39, 42, 47
sacrifice, xiin, 32–33, 39,
Scarry, Elaine, 43–44
Scève, 40
Schmitz, Götz, 136
Schofield, William Henry, 3–4
Scott, Bernard Brandon, 16
secrecy, xiv, 52–58, 71, 78–79, 81, 83–85, 111, 135, 141, 149, 186n, 210–12, 225–26, 235, 236–37, 240
shame (see also spectacle), 3n, 54–56, 61, 64, 75, 137, 140, 143–47, 149
Shakespeare, William, xi, xv, 80n, 110n, 134–54, 191

Shore, Jane, 140–44, 147n, 149, 153
Sidney, Sir Philip, 133, 138
Snyder, Susan, 135, 144, 146n, 148–49n
spectacle (see also shame), 54, 61, 134, 139, 149, 210–11
Spenser, Edmund, xvi, 50n, 151–52, 207–50
Spiegel, Gabrielle M., 193
Spitzer, Leo, 171
Stampa, Gaspara, xv, 109–31
Stanbury, Sarah, 5–6, 21n, 28n
Strohm, Paul, 167
Symposium, 235
Tesoretto, xvi, 157–90
Thiébaux, Marcelle, 89–90
torture, xiii, 35–36, 39, 43–45, 147n
transgressive desire, 40, 104, 142, 145, 153, 217, 244–45
translatio studii and *translatio imperii*, x
translation, ix–xvii, 31, 40, 52, 104–7, 176; and *imitatio*, 116–17, 163n, 186–88; poetic translation, 152n, 157–59, 241
transvestism (see also cross-dessing), 191, 217, 240
Trésor, 157, 159n, 162–63, 165, 176, 182
typology, 62, 64n, 74
Virgil, 62, 111, 174, 248n
Vulgate (Lancelot-Grail), 204
Waldron, Ronald, 1n, 12n, 17, 20
Wallace, David, xn, 20n, 89n
Wars of Religion, 33, 37, 39–40, 43, 46
Wellek, Rene, 2n, 5
Wheeler, Richard, 146
The Winter's Tale, 150
Wofford, Susanne, 215n, 216, 218–23, 226–27, 231, 239n, 240, 249n
Wyatt, Thomas, 144
Zumthor, Paul, 169n